The Politics of Place

A History of Zoning in Chicago

The Politics of Place

A History of Zoning in Chicago

By Joseph P. Schwieterman and Dana M. Caspall

Edited by Jane Heron

First Edition

LAKE CLAREMONT PRESS
www.lakeclaremont.com
Chicago

The Politics of Place: A History of Zoning in Chicago
Joseph P. Schwieterman and Dana M. Caspall

Published January, 2006, by:

LAKE CLAREMONT PRESS

4650 N. Rockwell Street
Chicago, IL 60625
773/583-7800
lcp@lakeclaremont.com
www.lakeclaremont.com

Copyright © 2006 by Joseph P. Schwieterman and Dana M. Caspall

Publisher's Cataloging-In-Publication Data
(Prepared by The Donohue Group, Inc.)

Schwieterman, Joseph P., 1959-
   The politics of place : a history of zoning in Chicago / by Joseph P. Schwieterman and Dana M. Caspall ; edited by Jane Heron.-- 1st ed.

   p. : ill. ; cm.
   Includes bibliographical references and index.
   ISBN: 1-893121-26-7

1. Zoning--Illinois--Chicago--History. 2. Zoning law--Illinois--Chicago--History. 3. City planning--Illinois--Chicago--History. I. Caspall, Dana M. II. Heron, Jane. III. Title.

HT169.73.C45 S39 2006
307/.0773/11   2003107616

        12 11 10 09 08 07 06   10 9 8 7 6 5 4 3 2 1

Printed in the United States of America by United Graphics, Inc., of Mattoon, Illinois.

To my father, Donald J. Schwieterman, and my uncle, David U. Schwieterman,
who cultivated in me an appreciation for America's great cities.
— J.P.S.

To Scott Caspall, who shares my enthusiasm for the Windy City,
and our daughter, Olivia.
— D.M.C.

Publisher's Credits: Cover design by Timothy Kocher and Ashley Huston. Interior design by Mainline Publications, Inc. Proof-reading by Sharon Woodhouse. Editing by Jane Heron and Renee Michaels.

Note: Readers of this volume will find a list of emendations on the Chaddick Institute for Metropolitan Development at DePaul University website, located at www.depaul.edu/~chaddick.

Cover Photo: An aerial view looking east toward the downtown area shows the prevalence of "zoning-law towers"—buildings with slender towers that conformed to the strict limits imposed by the city's first zoning ordinance—in the central business district, circa 1935. The industrial belt north and west of the Loop is also clearly evident in this photograph, as is the city's ubiquitous street grid. (Chicago Historical Society, no. IHCi-20961; image was altered from original.)

Contents

Appendices

Acknowledgments

A rewarding aspect of writing this history has been working with individuals who have devoted much of their lives to improving planning and zoning in Chicago.

We are especially indebted to Norman Elkin, Larry Lund, Wendy Plotkin, Joel Rast, Tom Smith, and Rick Wendy for their extensive technical assistance. We would also like to acknowledge the following individuals who provided interviews or shared information: Susan Aaron, William Banks, Alicia Mazur Berg, Miles Berger, Kirk Bishop, Fred Bosselman, Bernard Citron, Michael Davidson, Leon Despres, Max Dieber, Douglas Farr, Mary Fishman, Joe Fitzgerald, Joe Gattuso, Erik Glass, Jacques Gourguechon, Graham Grady, Jack Guthman, Albert Hanna, Jack Hartray, Reuben Hedlund, Elizabeth Hollander, Andrew King, Ruth Knack, Edward Kus, John Macsai, Dennis McClendon, Stuart Meck, Allen Mellis, Edwin Mills, John Murray, Mark Nora, Marty Oberman, Lawrence Okrent, Gary Papke, Dick Pavia, Donna Pugh, Marvin Salzenstein, John Schmidt, Jared Shlaes, Jack Siegal, Dick Simpson, William Singer, Peter Skosey, Christine Slattery, Frank So, Jack Swenson, Gary Wigoda, and David M. Young.

Many individuals at DePaul University also lent a hand, including Kadee Mullarkey, Professor Susanne Cannon, and Professor Gloria Simo as well as Kirsten Carlo, Douglas Ferguson, Joseph Kearney, Vanessa Quail, and Jennifer Slatkay, who, as students in the Public Services Graduate Program, prepared thesis or seminar papers to support our research. We also thank Renee Michaels, Bob Lange, Patty Moyer, and Laurie Marston for their editorial assistance.

Finally, we would be remiss if we did not recognize the Harry F. and Elaine M. Chaddick Foundation, and Robert J. Boylan in particular, for assistance and support. Mr. Boylan conceived the idea of this book, generously provided historical information, and waited patiently for its completion. His knowledge of and commitment to effective zoning in our city is an inspiration to us all.

The Prudential Building (at center) nears completion in 1955, ending a long drought in skyscraper construction and marking the beginning of an era dominated by towers on plazas. Although the Michigan Avenue "cliff" (or wall) has changed relatively little since then, the increased bulk of buildings in the Loop district—facilitated by the generous floor-area-ratio limits established in 1957—can be seen by comparing this photograph with the one on page 96. (Chicago Historical Society)

CHAPTER 1
Introduction

The history of zoning in Chicago is a saga of optimism and disappointment, lofty ideas and gritty reality, and continual reassessment. It is a story of bold visions trimmed by political reality, residents battling developers, and occasional misfires stirring up great controversy. As one Chicago journalist put it years ago, "zoning fights a tug of war between the dreams and goals of previous generations and the need to adjust to new technological advances or land use requirements."[1]

Our book begins with a look at the effects of the city's spectacular growth on its physical character and its efforts to resolve land-use conflicts prior to the advent of zoning. We then explore the adoption and evolution of Chicago's zoning ordinance and the many ways zoning has changed the appearance and ambience of this great city. Our historical narrative puts into perspective the interplay among development, planning, and zoning in the evolution of the famed Chicago skyline, the Gold Coast, and, much later, massive "Planned Developments" such as Marina City, Illinois Center, and Dearborn Park.

   In the early part of the twentieth century, when the idea of zoning began to be seriously discussed, it was a hard sell. In 1919, Charles M. Nichols of the Chicago Real Estate Board urged a group of professionals to open their minds to the benefits of citywide controls on the use of land, stating, "in the human body, each organ performs its function without interfering with any other organ ... So, if, likewise, Chicago adds an intelligent and scientific distribution of the activities of the entire city, in such a manner that the least friction shall exist between its various operations, we may expect her to become the most efficient as well as the most beautiful city in the world."[2] Not only did the push to bring the practice of zoning to Chicago succeed, the city eventually became a springboard for new zoning techniques.

This work is not intended to be an all-inclusive account of Chicago's experience with zoning. We make no attempt to summarize the city's architecture, planning initiatives, and civic leadership—books on these topics already line the shelves of libraries. Nor do we delve into the field of real-estate economics, which is beyond the scope of our work. Rather, we focus on the regulation of land use in the city, the landmark events that have broadened the scope of zoning, and the social contexts and technological advances that precipitated major changes to the city's regulation of land use.

As readers will recognize, zoning in Chicago is a tale of "fits and starts." There are bursts of initiative separated by periods of incremental change and political stalemate. The city has at certain times offered developers great incentives to tear down the old in favor of the new and, at other times, implemented policies intended to achieve quite the opposite effect.

At one time, building in the city was simple—one went to the alderman and got permission. Then the city adopted a building code and, much later, a zoning ordinance, which established regulations on the design, size, shape, and use of buildings. The first zoning ordinance was administered by the building commissioner; today, the city has a Department of Zoning and several zoning-related positions in the planning department. The ordinance has grown, too, from a simple handbook to a complex manual.

Although zoning has become more institutionalized and sophisticated, aldermen remain at the heart of the system, continuing to wield influence over the use of land in their wards. Some aldermen work closely with neighborhood representatives to pursue shared goals, while others act in more autonomous fashion. There are others who have failed to listen to their constituents and have been voted out of office; a few have misused their influence and been sent to jail.

Our descriptions of events leading up to the city's first comprehensive ordinance in 1923 and the revisions of 1942 are based primarily on historical documents not widely read, including government reports and journal and newspaper articles from years ago. To describe more recent initiatives, we have had the benefit of more diverse sources of information, including interviews with many individuals willing to offer insights and recollections. To our surprise, many of these individuals had not been asked before to draw upon their experience to help form a historical perspective. We are pleased to be able to share this never-before-published information.

The story we present rekindles the legacy of some of Chicago's best known citizen advocates, business leaders, and government officials. Each chapter explores a different dimension of the city's zoning experience. Along the way, we try to dispel the notion that zoning is too mundane or technical a topic to be of more than passing interest to readers of general history.

CHAPTER 2
Before Zoning:
Early Land-Use Control in Chicago

Many parts of Chicago were a hodgepodge of apartments, businesses, factories, homes, and railroad lines at the end of the nineteenth century. Although the city had reaped the benefits of spectacular growth before and after the Great Fire of 1871, in some areas blight stretched as far as the eye could see. Chicago did not have the capacity to engage in large-scale planning; it even lacked a complete sewer system. Congestion, smoke from burning coal, and animal waste made many streets notoriously unpleasant and unsanitary places.

Nonetheless, Chicago had tremendous energy. This energy found an outlet in the first quarter of the twentieth century, when major public works projects and the now-famous *Plan of Chicago* pushed the city in new directions. Various forms of neighborhood-based land-use concepts blossomed, and the city made a concerted effort to adopt "districting"—or zoning.[1]

EARLY LAND-USE CONTROLS

Since colonial times, municipal governments in the United States have tried to ensure the safety of residents amid the prospect of competing interests within close quarters.[2] A notable early example is the Council of the Dutch Colony, which in the mid-seventeenth century established controls over the types and location of houses in New Amsterdam. The Commonwealth of Massachusetts in 1692 authorized "market towns" to assign locations for slaughterhouses and other objectionable uses.[3] One of its largest towns, Cambridge, required that houses stand six feet from the street. Such controls, of course, were primitive by modern standards, but they planted the seed of the idea that the potentially injurious consequences of private land-use decisions warranted a regulatory response.

There were no restrictions of this sort in Fort Dearborn, the outpost founded on the frontier in 1817 that later became Chicago. The inhabitants of this settlement had no local government as they struggled to overcome disease, harsh winters, and hostilities with native tribes.

The completion of the Erie Canal in 1825 brought new opportunities for the lakeside enclave. Connecting the Hudson River to Lake Ontario, the canal became part of a vital shipping route between New York City and the Great Lakes, improving the accessibility of the American heartland. As commerce expanded, Fort Dearborn evolved into a bustling port caught up in plans for a waterway connecting Lake Michigan to the Mississippi River— one that would provide a continuous shipping route to New Orleans.[4]

Map of Chicago, circa 1833. (Chaddick collection)

A newly formed canal commission platted Chicago (its name meaning "wild onion" in the Algonquin tongue) at the site of Fort Dearborn in 1830, and by the time Chicago incorporated as a village in 1833, it had established its reputation as a major transfer point between vessels on the

Great Lakes and overland trading routes. Investors throughout the country took an interest in this fledgling settlement on the lake. Charles Butler, a noted real-estate investor from New York and brother-in-law of William B. Ogden, who later became the city's first mayor, noted in his diary in 1833: "There is no reason why [Chicago] should not become a very large city. It is at the head of navigation—it enjoys commercial advantages equal to Buffalo, [and] in addition to this it has the finest back country in the world. It will be on the great western thoroughfare to St. Louis on the Mississippi."[5]

Butler's intuition was correct. By 1835, the city had started a long-term project to adapt the Chicago River as a harbor and had grown in population to more than 3,000. Sawmills and warehouses lined the North Branch of the river and emerged as major sources of jobs and investment.[6] As tens of thousands of Americans headed west, capitalists invested in new industrial and shipping facilities along the city's waterfronts.

Along with expansion came severe sanitation problems.[7] Smoke billowed from steam-powered industries and sawmills while livestock and dogs wandered through streets sometimes strewn with animal carcasses, garbage, and manure.[8] In 1837, the municipal government took its first notable steps to alleviate these problems by adopting a city charter, which established the municipal government's power "to abate and remove nuisances." The city also enacted a municipal code that prohibited any landowner or tenant from maintaining certain nuisances on their property, especially those affecting public health, such as dead animals, dung, and "putrid meat or fish entrails."[9] These regulatory mechanisms had their roots in sixteenth-century English Common Law.[10]

The pace of industrial development quickened after completion of the Illinois and Michigan Canal in 1848. Connecting the Chicago River to the Des Plaines River (a tributary of the Illinois River), the canal created the long-desired direct water route to the Mississippi, making Chicago the principal port in the country's heartland and the logical choice to become a terminus for railroads.[11] The first boats made their way through the newly completed canal the same year Chicago's first steam railroad—the Galena & Chicago Union, with the irrepressible Ogden as its president—initiated service west into the heartland.[12]

A more favorable script for the city's development could hardly have been written. Chicago grew to nearly 30,000 residents by the middle of the nineteenth century. The expansion of industry and the synergy between water and railroad transportation pushed its incorporated boundaries outward into the prairie. The promise of plentiful jobs and fair wages spurred the arrival of tens of thousands of European immigrants and their descendants, setting in motion a period of robust industrial expansion that, within 20 years, would make Chicago one of the nation's largest cities.

The city became the nation's leader in the grain trade and the lumber industry.[13] By the mid-1850s, distillers, tanners, livery stables, food processing concerns, railroads, and other industries crowded along the riverbanks. For all practical purposes, the primary factor controlling industrial development was the availability of space along the river. "No city of size and wealth was ever built in such a helter-skelter manner," noted the *Chicago Tribune*, looking back on the city before the fire.[14]

In the five years prior to 1853, the city overcame a devastating cholera epidemic, built a waterworks system, and doubled its population to 60,000. Local leaders put in place a complex system of special assessments that provided tax revenue for local public-works projects and improved life in many of the neighborhoods.[15] In the 1850s, work began on a sewer system that required some streets to be raised by more than ten feet while the city's woefully unsanitary cemetery was relocated away from Lincoln Park.

The city also gradually broadened its definition of "undesirable uses"— that is, activities harmful to nearby land uses. Its charter of 1851 further established the city's right to control certain land uses by allowing the local government "to abate and remove nuisances, and punish the authors thereof, . . . and to define and declare what shall be deemed nuisances."[16]

The nuisance ordinances of the early 1850s were remarkably explicit, containing language devoted to almost every conceivable annoyance that might be caused by livestock, improper sanitation, and industrial production. "Any tanner, skinner, or other persons who shall bring to or keep for a period of twenty-four hours in any part of the city, except where the same are to be manufactured, any undressed or uncured hides, skins or leather, or blubber, shall be subject to a penalty of five dollars for each offense," noted Section 7. Fines also awaited any person who permitted "any cellar, vault, private drain, pool, privy, sewer or grounds upon any premises . . . to become nauseous, foul, offensive or injurious to the public health." In 1862, the city adopted an ordinance to reduce the notoriously unsanitary practices of the meatpacking industry.[17]

Such measures, while important, were an ineffective way to deal with some of the problems stemming from the city's jumble of land uses. Voters authorized funding for major parks around the established neighborhoods on the South, West, and near Northwest sides in 1869, but relief from crowding and congestion in many neighborhoods was still years away. Shacks and debris even cluttered the downtown lakefront, which the Illinois and Michigan Canal Commission had declared to be "public ground . . . forever open, clear and free."

AFTER THE GREAT FIRE

With Chicago growing larger and more economically diverse—its population rose tenfold between 1850 and 1870—it would take a disaster of almost unimaginable proportions to interrupt its expansion. That disaster came on October 8, 1871, when the Great Fire decimated vast parts of this city of 300,000.

Starting on the West Side, the legendary fire spread across the river and consumed nearly everything in its path, destroying more than two-thirds of the city and virtually all of Chicago's industrial and commercial core before being halted by the lake.[18] The devastation was almost beyond comprehension. Nearly 18,000 buildings burned, reducing entire neighborhoods to smoldering rubble.

Businesses and residents quickly acted upon their desire to rebuild the city. The layout of the "new" Chicago was not significantly different from its pre-fire configuration, with businesses still concentrated near its center. State Street emerged as the city's primary retail-oriented thoroughfare but industry tended to decentralize as many firms moved to locations along the Calumet River and railroad lines. One notable difference in the new city, however, was the size and height of buildings in the central business district. New construction methods, such as the use of steel framing, allowed for taller and larger structures.[19]

In 1872, the state enacted the Cities and Village Act, granting local governments greater powers to regulate activities affecting health, safety, and the general welfare of their residents.[20] Although this legislation gave the city new options, there was not a workable consensus on how to exercise them. Leaders, for example, hotly debated the need for new "fire limits," areas where regulations required structures to be built of fire-resistant material and placed limits on the storage of flammable materials.[21] Although the merits of fireproofing were widely understood, the scope of fire limits in the city remained a contentious issue. Fire limits had been adopted for the Central Area in 1850, but their coverage was not expanded as the downtown grew.

Business and civic leaders argued that the entire city should be within the limits, but people of modest means, many of whom had lost their homes and businesses to the fire, felt this was unfair. Although an ordinance governing the whole city was adopted, it was soon nullified, culminating in several years of political maneuvering. When fire limits were finally adopted citywide in 1874, it was in response to a threat by insurance companies to embargo Chicago. However, by that time, much of the city had been rebuilt and much of it in wood frame, as builders rushed to avoid the new requirements.

Chicago was also slow to adopt a building code with more general regulations governing materials and methods of construction. Not until 1875—25 years after New York adopted the country's first comprehensive building code—did the city finally codify such regulations.[22] Nevertheless, by creating a building department to enforce this code, Chicago emerged as a pioneer in the development of this municipal function, a full 17 years ahead of New York.

The building code inaugurated the era of fine brick buildings with steel frames that became a widely known part of the city's architectural heritage. By the mid-1880s, attractive downtown skyscrapers, including the acclaimed Home Insurance, Monadnock, and Manhattan buildings, as well as improvements to harbors, railroads, and canals, heralded Chicago's return to the forefront of the national economy. New sanitary and water facilities as well as a spectacular rise in manufacturing laid the groundwork for another development boom. In 1889, the city annexed more than 125 square miles in a single day, nearly quadrupling its size and giving it jurisdiction over Hyde Park, Kenwood, and Pullman. The following year, the U.S. Census reported that Chicago's population had exceeded one million for the first time.

Despite the economic success the city enjoyed, congestion, noise, and air pollution remained deplorable problems in many neighborhoods. Among the most serious sources of pollution was the clatter, smoke, and soot emanating from the steam locomotives operating over the city's railroads and elevated transit routes.[23] In response, affluent city dwellers increasingly migrated to suburbs located on commuter railroad lines, such as Evanston, Hinsdale, Park Ridge, and Riverside. The arrival of tens of thousands of newcomers, many from overseas, filled the void, fostering such rapid develop-ment that it eventually overwhelmed the city's water and sanitation facilities, allowing water-borne diseases to spread.

As the years passed and the governance of cities in Illinois grew more complex, the state's courts recog-nized the necessity of providing local govern-ments more authority to place reasonable limits on land use. Although the courts had long acknowl-edged the need to protect property own-ers from trespassing and other types of direct invasion, it had not been customary for them to require that compensation be pro-vided to those affected by odor, noise, and other nuisances. The courts had a change of heart, how-ever, as the urban economy grew and unprecedented numbers of residents filed nuisance lawsuits related to incompatible land uses.[24]

Several types of nuisance lawsuits, consequently, proliferated in the late nineteenth century. *Private-nuisance litigation* involved disputes between pri-vate parties, such as neighbors, that were adjudicated by the courts with-out the involvement of the municipal govern-ment. *Public-nuisance lit-igation* involved legal action at the behest of the local government to protect the health and safety of its resi-dents. Using the doc-trine of police power established in Com-mon Law, municipal governments used the latter technique to the extent possible to pro-tect the public welfare.

Both methods of dispute resolution, however, had notable limitations. Outcomes tended to be unpre-dictable and subject to the peculiarities of dif-ferent judges and courts. In Illinois, courts often ignored the content of local ordinances and instead viewed nuisances as a judicial matter to be decided on a case-by-case basis. The court often evaluated the merits of the plain-tiff's and defendant's positions and came to a judgment that it considered

This sketch depicts an Illinois Central train traversing the bustling waterfront along the Chicago River, near the foot of Madison Street and Michigan Avenue, in 1860. Public nuisance lawsuits were the prin-cipal means of mitigating conflicts created by the multiplicity of land uses evident in this scene; the building code, zoning ordinance, and movement to reclaim the lakefront for public use were still years away. (Association of American Railroads)

Much of Chicago's Lake Michigan shoreline, including the area shown here, circa 1892, at the foot of 23rd Street, was marred by debris, rubbish, and industrial facilities—a fact distressingly evident to many of the visitors to the World's Columbian Exposition the following year. (Chicago Historical Society)

fair and reasonable without considering the specific language of the relevant city regulation.[25]

Although private-nuisance lawsuits may have been able to provide remedies for individual property owners, they were wholly incapable of addressing general concerns about problems affecting thousands of property owners simultaneously. Public-nuisance lawsuits, on the other hand, had the potential to resolve such problems, but courts still had a tendency to define the concept of a public nuisance narrowly. Many judges favored businesses over residential concerns and dismissed complaints motivated solely by a desire to improve neighborhood aesthetics or relieve residents' psychological distress.

By the early 1890s, the belief was widespread that the court system was no longer the appropriate venue to resolve many land-use problems. The sheer number of lawsuits—and the breadth of the cases—put a strain on the system. Land-use conflicts increasingly affected large areas of the city rather than only the nearest residents. The Chicago Stockyards, where several thousand head of livestock were slaughtered daily, for example, generated noxious fumes that could sometimes be smelled for miles. The scale of these conflicts rendered them difficult to resolve through litigation alone.

THE RISE OF THE CITY BEAUTIFUL MOVEMENT

Despite the risk that their efforts would be struck down by the courts, municipal officials began to push for public-nuisance laws that could be consistently applied and enforced across an entire spectrum of situations.[26] Rather than focusing on past nuisances, officials sought to use the nuisance concept to limit the prospective activities of builders, thus safeguarding the public from foreseeable future risks. In doing so, they contemplated regulations that would separate residential and industrial activity—an idea that years later became known as "districting" or zoning.

Daniel H. Burnham.

After adopting a series of regulations in the early 1890s to eliminate some of the problems associated with railroad and streetcar operations, the city turned its attention to other forms of urban development.[27] In 1893, the city imposed a height limit of 130 feet on downtown buildings, largely to protect the public from the risk of fire and falling debris, but also to mitigate the evolving "canyon effect" created by rows of tall buildings along downtown streets. These height restrictions (see discussion in Chapter 9), drawing protests from the real-estate community, were part of the building code and sanctioned by the courts; their creation reflected a more liberal interpretation of the police power held by the city.[28] Later, the city strengthened the building code to regulate such issues as side-yard setbacks and the height of multi-family buildings.

These controls were manifestations of Chicago's blossoming civic leadership, which was triumphantly put on display during the World's Columbian Exposition—an event held during 1893 commemorating the quadricentennial of Columbus's arrival in the New World. Under the leadership of Daniel H. Burnham, the country's foremost planners, architects, landscapers, and sculptors created exhibit grounds in Jackson Park, showcasing the era's recent advances in civic design and architecture. Hundreds of thousands arrived to visit the event's attractions, including the famed Midway Plaisance. The public's response to the fair was evident in a report to the *Chicago Tribune:* "We are greatly impressed by the mind that conceived this splendid city of the lagoon, that made it so harmonious, that decorated it with statuary, and adorned it with native and exotic plants, [but] the administrative detail excites fully as much wonder," noted writer Charles Warner.[29]

More than 700 acres of Jackson Park underwent a dramatic transformation amid preparations for the Columbian Exposition of 1893. The palatial grounds of the exposition, including the Midway Plaisance (above), showcased recent advances in civic design and architecture. The enthusiasm generated by this world's fair was a catalyst for comprehensive urban planning both in Chicago and the nation as a whole. (Chicago Public Library, Special Collections and Preservation Division)

Edward Bennett.

The exposition was truly awe-inspiring, encompassing almost 700 acres of land roughly bounded by Cottage Grove Avenue, Lake Michigan, 56th Street, and 67th Street.[30] The great neoclassic city built for the fair, however, had an unexpected legacy. Although the exposition's buildings and grounds were meant to highlight Chicago's progress in planning and design, many visitors had difficulty coming to terms with the blight in the neighborhoods adjacent to the fair and downtown. Railroad yards, freight facilities, and the unseemly Levee district, which was notorious for its taverns and brothels, blemished the downtown lakefront and riverfront. In fact, in 1890 Montgomery Ward sued the city to compel it to "clear the lakefront of unsightly structures … and refuse."[31]

To many Chicagoans, the unsightliness of these blighted areas was a municipal embarrassment that could no longer be tolerated. Observers began to question why the city could not transform all of its neighborhoods into attractive and orderly places resembling the gleaming "White City" created for the fair. In some areas, sewage flowed into the lake during heavy rains, contaminating the city's drinking water and dramatically increasing death rates from typhoid and other water-borne diseases.[32] Many streets were notoriously overcrowded, lined with dingy buildings and unseemly businesses. Some lots were cluttered with multiple buildings while rain made some streets into quagmires of mud and nearly impassible.

The enthusiasm generated by the fair was a catalyst for comprehensive urban planning both in Chicago and the nation as a whole.[33] Inspired by the event, Burnham, a Chicagoan deeply committed to better urban design, helped launch the City Beautiful Movement. Burnham and other proponents, drawing upon the ideals of progressivism, called for planners to place emphasis on creating cities that delight and inspire. Going beyond past efforts to improve the quality of life, which tended to focus on improving housing and sanitary conditions, the City Beautiful Movement sought to build cities that would promote civic virtue.

Sensing the time to be right for action, municipal officials drafted plans for major public works initiatives. The city completely reengineered the Chicago River and, in 1900, reversed its flow so that its waters flowed from east to west—one of the most significant municipal projects of its time. Prominent business and civic leaders encouraged the city to think boldly about ways to improve living standards and create governmental institutions responsive to both the material and social needs of its residents. In 1906, the Merchants Club, later renamed the Commercial Club, created several committees to evaluate Chicago's physical condition and commission a plan for the city.

Spearheaded by Burnham and Edward Bennett, the now-famous *Plan of Chicago* was completed in 1909 and constituted a milestone in the city's history.[34] This heavily illustrated manuscript was not only the first plan conceived and developed by private individuals, it was also the first comprehensive plan for any U.S. city outside of Washington, D.C. The document spurred the creation of the Chicago Plan Commission, with the hardworking Charles Wacker as chairman, and stimulated citizen interest and support for the planning process. To ensure that residents understood the plan's essential components and its profound implications for the city, an educational booklet was delivered to all property owners in the city and any citizen who paid monthly rent of $25 or more.[35]

Charles J. Wacker.

A panoramic view of State Street, circa 1900, shows the intensity of development in this busy retail corridor. In the distance, the Masonic Temple rises more than 300 feet. All new buildings, however, were subject to a 130-foot height limit at the time. (Chicago Public Library, Special Collections and Preservation Division)

By making a persuasive and eloquent case for new infrastructure and aesthetic improvement, the document created a framework for aggressive public investment.[36] Its most noteworthy features included a regional highway system, a well-organized system of streets, improvements to rail and waterway transportation, a civic center, forest preserves surrounding the city, and the creation of lakefront beaches and parks.[37] Although there was controversy, Mayor Fred Busse accepted the plan in 1910.

The *Plan of Chicago* lent support to the idea that the city needed to exert greater control over its cultural and economic identity. At the time, extensions to streetcar lines and the elevated-railroad system were greatly improving mobility and allowing residents to live greater distances from their workplaces than before. Motor vehicles were becoming affordable to small businesses, and even wage earners could now afford to move to newly annexed areas near the edge of Chicago or in outlying communities. The tree-lined streets of the suburbs, buffered by parks and nature areas, offered a welcome respite from the congestion and clamor of city life.

Those unable or unwilling to move away from crowded city neighborhoods often bore the brunt of rising population densities. Primarily members of the middle and lower classes, these residents remained exposed to the growing intensity of commercial activity in their neighborhoods, noise created by elevated trains and streetcars, and worsening traffic congestion. The accelerating tempo of urban life, bolstered by advancements in technology and transportation, encouraged leaders to think about ways of separating various types of land uses.

RESTRICTIVE COVENANTS AND FRONTAGE CONSENTS

The early twentieth century brought not only a great surge in public investment, but also the rise of several neighborhood-based techniques to deal with land-use conflicts. Restrictive covenants—written agreements between property owners whereby the property owners agree to certain conditions or restrictions concerning the future use, maintenance, or sale of land—were widely used in newer residential areas near the edge of town.[38] Landowners often established these covenants when subdividing property for the creation of residential subdivisions. Enforceable in court, restrictive covenants could protect the interests of all property owners in a neighborhood.

Although restrictive covenants were often quite effective, they could only be used to resolve certain issues and had limited potential in the oldest and most densely populated parts of town, where the ownership of land was divided among hundreds of residents. Such covenants also had an ominous underside as they were sometimes employed to exclude certain minority groups, particularly African-Americans, from neighborhoods—leading the courts many years later to rule the practice unconstitutional (see discussion, Chapter 4).[39]

Frontage-consent ordinances, on the other hand, had a more dynamic quality. These ordinances, which date back to 1887 in the city, were based on nuisance doctrines and required that the majority of residential owners on a block provide consent before certain land uses would be permitted.[40] The ordinances were applicable only along blocks with two-thirds of the property in residential use. Although initially created to protect landowners whose property bordered proposed streetcar routes, frontage consents soon grew to encompass the threat posed by saloons, livery stables, elevated railways, and other undesirable uses.[41]

The justification for frontage consents lay in the belief that regulation was the only way to prevent a single property owner from violating the uniformity of land uses in a neighborhood. Livery stables, which provided quarters for horses, wagons, and related items, for example, commonly established themselves in residential neighborhoods to the detriment of those living nearby. Despite the odor, noise, and nighttime light they generated, livery stables were difficult to prevent through conventional nuisance lawsuits. The courts generally would not declare livery stables a nuisance until they could determine unambiguously that such land uses had negative effects on the surrounding neighborhoods, which meant waiting until after the stables had already been built.

Property owners, in some instances, became so desperate to keep livery stables out of their neighborhoods that they purchased vacant lots as a preemptive move. It has been reported, however, that unscrupulous individuals sometimes bought vacant lots in neighborhoods, threatened to build a livery stable, and then forced neighboring property owners to pay a premium for the land.[42]

Relief came in the form of a livery-stable ordinance drafted and submitted to the city by the Chicago Real Estate Board, which prohibited these establishments adjacent to or within 75 feet of a residential area, unless the owner had the written consent of every property owner within 600 feet. The ordinance, approved by the city in 1887, was upheld by the Illinois Supreme Court.[43] By requiring that consent be obtained before the issuance of a building permit, the livery-stable ordinance became a prototype for more general frontage-consent ordinances applying to a broader range of land uses.[44]

Despite the enthusiasm for frontage consents—a phenomenon that reached its peak around 1910—this approach had obvious problems. Frontage consents were cumbersome and ineffective in a variety of situations. Businesses seeking approval would often hire "canvassers" to gather petitions from residents—an arrangement that tended to foster corruption. Questions arose about whether renters should be given a vote, whether votes could be purchased, and whether votes cast by those in close proximity to a proposed new business should be given more weight than those farther away. Landowners also occasionally bribed neighbors, in effect buying their votes—another form of corruption.[45] Moreover, frontage-consent ordinances were adopted on a ward-by-ward basis and, as such, offered only a piecemeal approach to land-use control. Like nuisance lawsuits or restrictive covenants, they were too limited in scope to resolve many of the more pressing problems facing the city.[46]

When frontage consents were initially developed, the city established a list of specific nuisances that would require residential consent. With the support of their aldermen, however, neighborhood groups petitioned the city to gradually expand the classifications of nuisances, creating new categories of activities that were thought to be objectionable.[47] Citizen groups increasingly turned to these ordinances to resolve issues related to aesthetics and other matters not historically viewed by the courts as essential to the public's welfare.

After neighborhood groups demanded that the city expand the list of nuisances requiring consent to include retail stores, the stage was set for a legal battle and, indeed, the retail-consent ordinance was challenged in the Illinois Supreme Court in 1912. While the case was pending, the U.S. Supreme Court declared a frontage-consent ordinance in Richmond, Virginia, invalid. The following year, the Illinois Supreme Court ruled Chicago's retail-consent ordinance similarly invalid, concluding that the city did not have a sound legal basis for controlling the location of businesses that were not nuisances and did not threaten the public welfare.[48]

The limitations on frontage-consent ordinances gave municipalities another reason to push for authority to establish more far-reaching methods of land-use regulation. With the courts already suffering from heavy caseloads, many cities felt they had little choice but to experiment with districting (or zoning). In 1909, Los Angeles took the notable step of establishing districts with prohibitions on noxious and heavy industry. In 1913, Boston, Indianapolis, Milwaukee, and Washington, D.C., combined height control with some form of districting. In 1916, New York City adopted the nation's first comprehensive zoning ordinance. Chicago's business, real-estate, and political leaders watched closely as the zoning movement began to spread across the country.[49]

Districting—or zoning—was a direct extension of the concept of police power, which, when narrowly defined, included the right to protect the public through the regulation of health and safety.[50] More broadly defined, it encompassed aesthetic concerns, such as the desire to improve the livability of a community, protect cultural norms, and promote a distinctive town character.[51]

This portion of Sheridan Road near Pine Grove Avenue, circa 1912, is lined with apartment buildings. City residents of this era used nuisance lawsuits, restrictive covenants, and frontage-consent ordinances to discourage development that would interrupt the continuity of land uses. Frontage consents were also a way to keep out streetcar lines (note the trolley on Broadway in the distance) before being ruled illegal by the court. This area was later zoned for apartments and made an R6 district in 1957. (Photo by Charles R. Childs, Chicago Historical Society)

Zoning's purpose was to minimize the risk of land-use conflicts by dividing land into districts or zones comprising compatible uses. Residential land was generally at the top of the pyramid of land uses, while industrial land was almost universally at the bottom. While it might be permissible for a property owner to construct a residence in an industrial district, it was generally not permissible for an industrial entity to move into a residential area.

Despite the adoption of zoning ordinances in other cities, there were formidable legal and political obstacles to the creation of one in Chicago—a fact obvious to all after the demise of the Residential District Bill, which the city drafted in 1911 to protect homeowners from the encroachment of commerce and industry. Although the measure passed the state assembly that year, it was vetoed by the governor after the attorney general deemed it unconstitutional.[52]

A GREAT CITY TAKES SHAPE

The push to bring zoning to Chicago gained traction during the wartime industrial boom. As the nation's economy mobilized to support the World War I effort, manufacturers retooled their factories for armament production, and the pace of residential and commercial construction decreased substantially.

Following the armistice ending the war in 1918, resources that had been tied up for military use suddenly became available for construction.[53] The Loop saw the creation of dozens of new buildings, many built to the maximum height allowable. Along the shoreline, the city made recreational facilities available and turned to the newly completed Municipal Pier (later called Navy Pier) to handle enormous commodity shipments and passenger traffic. Railroads and streetcar lines expanded their facilities to manage the growing traffic among city neighborhoods and between the city and suburbs. Motor buses appeared as inexpensive alternatives to extending streetcar lines.

The completion of a two-level bridge spanning the Chicago River

The intersection of Dearborn Street and Randolph Street, looking southward, 1909. Severe congestion in the central business district, as evident above, encouraged City Hall to consider new methods of controlling development, but the effort to draft a zoning ordinance was still several years away. (Photo by Frank M. Hallenbeck, Chicago Historical Society)

The Railway Exchange Building, shown here circa 1902, rose to nearly the maximum height permitted by city law at the time and towered above its South Michigan Avenue neighbors. Typical of quarter-block office buildings constructed during this period, this landmark (designed by Daniel H. Burnham & Company) was laid out in the "O-plan" with a large interior court. (Chicago Public Library, Special Collections and Preservation Division)

along Michigan Avenue in 1920 stimulated development north of the river. That same year, the city relaxed its restrictions on the height of downtown buildings, allowing ornamental towers atop buildings to rise up to 400 feet, a provision made manifest in such notable edifices as the Chicago Temple, the Tribune Tower, and the Wrigley Building (see discussion in Chapter 9).

Across the country, municipal governments wrestled with the problems associated with rapid and high-density development and the ever-rising numbers of cars and trucks. Many planners looked to New York City for insights about the relative benefits and costs of zoning.[54] Without state legislation authorizing municipalities to use zoning, business and real-estate leaders had legitimate concerns that court rulings would preclude Chicago from following Gotham's example.[55]

The proponents of zoning, consequently, had to bide their time.

Chapter 3
Zoning the Great City

Championing the creation of Chicago's first zoning ordinance in the late 1910s, Charles Nichols described the city as an anatomical body. "The business district may be likened to the great pulsating heart of the living body, and the traffic streets to the arteries carrying nourishment to every part. The administrative center may be compared to the brain, and the telephone and telegraph wire to the nerves."[1] As progress in medicine and natural sciences accelerated, optimism about the potential achievements of scientific study soared. Zoning thus was advocated as a tool that could be used with surgical precision to alleviate problems that had plagued cities for decades.[2]

Despite the zeal of its early supporters like Nichols, the effort to bring zoning to Chicago was lengthy and complex—hampered by formidable legal and legislative barriers. One of these supporters, Alderman Charles Merriam, a political science professor at The University of Chicago, had been pushing for zoning since 1914 when he wrote a report calling attention to the apparent necessity, efficiency, and legality of this technique.[3] His work highlighted the weaknesses of alternative methods of land-use control, including frontage consents and restrictive covenants.[4]

Merriam's report laid the groundwork for a bill he introduced to the Illinois General Assembly in February, 1917, granting cities and villages the power to establish residential, business, and industrial districts—legislation of special interest to the Chicago Real Estate Board.[5] The board voiced concern about unregulated industrial and commercial land use, arguing that it lowered property values and was a source of anxiety among prospective buyers of land.[6] In 1917, Mayor William Thompson appointed a Zoning Commission consisting of various city officials to delve further into the possibility of establishing state laws to facilitate the regulation of land use in Illinois cities.

Charles Merriam, alderman and
University of Chicago professor.
(University of Chicago Library)

Initially, the Chicago Zoning Commission's work did not go smoothly. Despite extensive lobbying, the state legislature failed to pass the Merriam bill.[7] Dispirited supporters of zoning heeded the advice of State Senator Edward Glackin, who warned that the legislature would be reluctant to enact any measure giving municipalities absolute power in establishing zoning districts. Senator Glackin instead recommended an amended bill that included selected aspects of the frontage-consent system and revolved around a requirement that municipalities present their district plans to neighborhood property owners. If at least 40 percent of the owners disapproved of the zoning plan, the district would remain exempt from zoning. If the owners endorsed the plan, the municipality could formulate a zoning ordinance appropriate for the neighborhood.[8]

Senator Glackin introduced his controversial ideas to the state assembly in 1919 as part of a zoning enabling bill that would authorize municipalities in certain situations to use this emerging regulatory tool. Following a concerted lobbying effort by some of Chicago's most influential commercial and professional associations, the legislature passed this measure, christened the Glackin Law, in June, 1919.[9]

THE DRAFTING PROCESS BEGINS

The Glackin Law was far from perfect—it did not afford cities in Illinois the same powers held by cities in other states—but it did provide the impetus for Chicago to embark on the laborious process of drafting an ordinance. Within months, the city sent officials and members of influential associations, including the Chicago Real Estate Board, to Montreal, New York, Philadelphia, St. Louis, and other cities, to study the dynamics of zoning in cities with densities and streetscapes comparable to those in Chicago.[10]

Certain members of the Chicago Real Estate Board, however, were dubious about the power that would be held by a newly created zoning commission, an entity that would be given the task of both creating and implementing a zoning ordinance. Among many business owners, zoning raised the specter of excessive government intervention in the marketplace. Nichols, now chairman of the Real Estate Board's zoning committee, tried to assuage this concern and rallied members around the idea that it would allow the owners of buildings "to feel more secure against depreciation," promising that "citizens then will dwell together in comfort and contentment."[11]

The Chicago Real Estate Board urged the city to seek guidance about this matter from other cities and move ahead with due caution.[12] This led to a historic conference in December, 1919, at Chicago's Morrison Hotel, where authorities from New York and other distant cities gathered to share their experiences and offer legal advice about zoning.[13]

Few events in Chicago history were as significant to the evolution of the city's land-use policies as the conversations that transpired inside this well-known downtown hotel.[14] Local

Illinois State Senator Edward
Glackin. (Courtesy of the Illinois
State Historical Society)

businesses, civic organizations, and city officials used the gathering to develop a conceptual blueprint for a zoning ordinance. Among the featured speakers was Edward M. Bassett—the principal architect of New York's ordinance and the country's leading authority on zoning. The event's banquet attracted 400 participants, many of whom took part in the two days of discussion exploring the value of both comprehensive zoning initiatives (that is, those broadly administered across the city) and piecemeal zoning initiatives (that is, those of a more ad hoc nature, such as measures targeted at particular neighborhoods or land uses).[15] Experts from other cities, however, warned of the limitations of a piecemeal approach to zoning, claiming that it would set different standards for various sections of the city and undermine efforts to demonstrate in court that zoning was nondiscriminatory and essential to public health and safety.

In February, 1920, the city created a 22-member Zoning Commission to prepare the zoning ordinance and maps. The commission consisted of eight aldermen, five cabinet members, Charles Wacker (chairman of the Chicago Plan Commission), and eight private citizens. Charles Bostrom, Chicago's building commissioner, was appointed committee chairman, and architect Edward Bennett, known for his pioneering work with Daniel Burnham on the *Plan of Chicago*, was named an advisor. The commission hired Bassett as a legal consultant (see Appendix D for a discussion of Bassett's role).

The commission turned to the Chicago Real Estate Board for help drafting the ordinance; the board, in turn, created a new committee for that purpose. Over the next 18 months, the commission supervised four field teams, each with an automobile at its disposal, who traveled

The Real Estate Board building (above circa 1907) at 151–179 N. Dearborn Street. The trade group's offices and meeting rooms were on the upper floors, with shops on ground level. (Chicago Historical Society)

Charles Bostrom.

At an exposition held in the summer of 1922, H.T. Frost, chief of staff of the Chicago Zoning Commission, describes one of the city's tentative zoning maps. The Chicago Real Estate Board's Eva L. Nelson, secretary, and Charles M. Nichols, head of the zoning committee, are also standing in front of the map. (Chaddick collection)

In order to adopt a comprehensive zoning ordinance similar to that of New York, Chicago still needed to persuade state legislators to amend sections of the Glackin Law, especially the language requiring the municipal government to obtain neighborhood consent before putting land-use controls into place.[17] Glackin himself pushed hard for such changes. The breakthrough came in June, 1921, when the state repealed the older law and replaced it with a new state zoning enabling act drafted by the zoning committee of the Chicago Real Estate Board.

The new law allowed for a more centralized approach to land-use control than the old Glackin Law, thus providing the legal foundation many believed necessary for the zoning initiative to succeed.[18] Although citizens lost their power to block changes through a majority voting system, this legislation gave them some residual power by stipulating that if 20 percent of landowners affected by a zoning change protested the change in writing, a two-thirds vote by the City Council was necessary for a zoning law to take effect.[19]

Although zoning advocates had scored a great victory, other legal and political issues still needed to be resolved. No law could be expected to fit every land-use situation, so arrangements would be needed to provide relief in the case of hardship. Relying on the courts to serve this role, however, would be unpredictable, time-consuming, and costly. As a result, the Real Estate Board urged the city to create a Zoning Board of Appeals (ZBA) or, as this type of institution was sometimes called, a board of zoning adjustments.

Regardless of how the city handled this issue, it was destined to be controversial. Without a ZBA to provide relief in extenuating circumstances, the courts might rule the ordinance unconstitutional.[20] Nevertheless, the creation of such a board would meet strong opposition in the City Council and risked delaying passage of the law. The compromise solution was to omit the provision for a ZBA from the original ordinance and to create it later through an amendment.

The debate over the role of the ZBA was inextricably linked to the problem of nonconforming uses (such as businesses on blocks zoned for

throughout the city to check the use, height, setback, area, age, and extent of depreciation of all property in the city. This field work was critical to the efforts of the Plan Commission staff to create and code land-use maps for the new ordinance.[16]

residences). Officials exhaustively debated whether protecting noncon-forming businesses would give these establishments an unacceptable monopoly. Requiring these businesses to immediately close or relocate was not seen as a feasible option—the courts in most states had con-cluded that mandating the termination of these businesses, even after lengthy transitional periods, would result in undue hardship. This could become a "taking without compensation" and deprive owners and work-ers of their livelihood.

Businesses wanted assurances that they would not be shut down, but simply "grandfathering" nonconforming uses was not considered to be legally advisable. The committee's response was to develop rules to restrict the expansion of such businesses or improvements to such properties and to terminate these businesses upon a change of ownership, anticipating that these rules would cause the problem to gradually wither away (see discussion in Appendix E). Neverthe-less, as some had feared, the Illinois Supreme Court ruled in 1922 that any pro-tection of existing business-es constituted an unfair monopoly.[21] Although city officials were troubled by this decision, some felt that subsequent Illinois court rulings would more closely follow the example of courts in other states.

Despite the city's inability to resolve all of the out-standing issues, the effort to draft the new ordinance moved forward on an expeditious timetable with generous municipal financial support. According to the *Chicago Tribune*, this effort cost the city approximately $200,000, an appreciable sum for a planning project at the time.[22] The framers of the ordinance relied heavily on the newly com-pleted land-use survey, which showed that the city had 20,000 industrial buildings, 133,000 single-family homes, 96,000 two-flat apartment buildings, and 37,000 multi-unit apartment buildings; its manufacturing areas encompassed more than 26 square miles.[23] The survey provided the basis for the city's first set of zoning maps, which established an ideal dis-tribution of land uses to be achieved over time.

To build public support for its initiative, the Chicago Zoning Com-mission published a booklet in April, 1922, entitled *Zoning Chicago*.[24] This easy-to-follow manuscript explained the purpose of zoning, its legality, and the process that would be used to allow for amendments to the ordi-nance. To shape public opinion, it emphasized the idea that giving municipal governments more control over privately owned land would make neighborhoods more orderly and attractive.[25]

Civic interest in the commission's work greatly escalated when its pre-liminary report was presented at public hearings between January and March of 1923 in the Chicago City Council chamber.[26] These hearings were the impetus for numerous changes to the draft ordinance, which the commission unanimously approved on March 12, 1923. The newly com-pleted comprehensive ordinance was submitted to the City Council two days later.

Chicago Daily News headline, April 6, 1923.

Inside the 1923 Ordinance

Unlike most modern zoning ordinances, which have several dozen different use districts, the 1923 ordinance contained just four classes of use districts—residential, apartment, commercial, and manufacturing. In the residential districts, the ordinance permitted single-family homes, churches, schools, parks, and neighborhood businesses. In the apartment district, it established regulations governing the permissible types of multi-unit dwellings. The ordinance established three types of commercial and manufacturing districts, each with restrictions of varying intensity covering such diverse issues as the hours of operation and the proximity of industrial concerns to residential and apartment districts.

In addition to being in one of the four classes of *use* districts, each parcel of land was assigned to one of five *volume* districts. For each district, restrictions governed height, the percentage of lot coverage allowed, and the cubical area of the building in proportion to the lot size.[27] In the highest intensity zone (Volume District 5), the city allowed buildings to rise 264 feet from the street (an increase of just four feet over the previous limit) but also allowed towers of greater heights containing rentable floor space to be constructed on up to 25 percent of

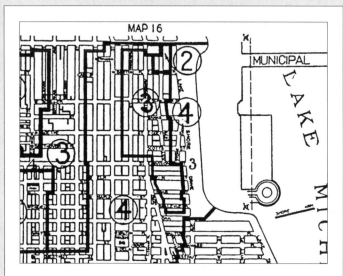

This volume district map from the 1923 ordinance shows that 3rd and 4th volume districts were dominant in the Gold Coast neighborhood at the time. (City of Chicago)

the lot, creating an entirely new architectural style in the Central Area (see Chapter 9).

The city maintained separate maps depicting use and volume districts, each divided into areas of one square mile. The first, second, and third volume districts tended to be a considerable distance from the lake. Volume District 4 was predominately along the lakefront, where the demand for high-density development outside of the downtown was the strongest. Most of the Volume District 5 was confined to the Central Area.

Thousands of nonconforming properties were grandfathered by the municipal government and hence became "legal nonconformities"—a policy that, for reasons previously described, soon would be challenged in court. The ordinance, however, did put restrictions on the expansion of these uses.

The administration and implementation of the ordinance came under the purview of the building commissioner. Once established, the Zoning Board of Appeals (ZBA) could consider amendments or variations ("variances") in cases of "particular hardship" but was required to hold public hearings on these petitions. All recommendations had to be approved by the City Council. If the ZBA denied a request for an amendment, an appeal could be made to the City Council; with a two-thirds vote, it could overturn the decision. As previously described, if 20 percent of the landowners in close proximity protested a proposed amendment, a change required a two-thirds vote by the City Council.[28]

This pioneering ordinance was relatively concise, having just 20 pages of text—less than a third of the length of the text portion of the ordinance adopted 54 years later.

The Jewelers Building (later the Pure Oil Building) is a classic 1920s skyscraper that emerged at 35 E. Wacker Drive shortly after the advent of zoning. When completed in 1926, the Jewelers was among Chicago's tallest buildings, boasting a 17-story tower that was within the volume limit set by the city's zoning law. (Photo by Raymond Trowbridge, Chicago Historical Society)

The Morrison Hotel, located at 15–29 S. Clark, was the site of the
Chicago Zone Plan conference in 1919. The massive tower (shown
above enclosed by scaffolding) was added to its large rectangular base
in 1926, allowing it to claim the title of the tallest hotel in the world.
Soon after this photograph was taken in 1965, the 526-foot building
was demolished to create One First National Plaza, giving the befallen
landmark the dubious distinction of being the tallest building ever
demolished up to that time. (Chicago Historical Society)

CHICAGO'S FIRST ORDINANCE: THE CITY COUNCIL'S "BIGGEST WORK"

With considerable fanfare, the Chicago City Council adopted the zoning
ordinance by a unanimous vote on April 5, 1923. The next day, the *Chicago Tribune* published news about this seminal event in a front-page story.
Charles Bostrom, the building commissioner, referred to the ordinance as
"the biggest work done by any City Council." Alderman Guy Guernsey
was even more enthusiastic, calling it "the greatest thing in the way of
progress which Chicago has done in fifty years."[29] The landmark measure
took effect on May 12. As planned, the city soon turned its attention to
an amendment establishing the Zoning Board of Appeals, and this measure became law in July of the same year.

According to the *Chicago Tribune*, aldermen proposed many other
amendments to the ordinance that year. One official wanted to eliminate
the newly created Board of Appeals, claiming that its power to alleviate
cases of hardship was too liberally defined. Alderman William O'Toole,
vice chairman of the committee creating the ordinance, reportedly
protested that he did not want to see the ordinance "shot full of ill-considered amendments on the council floor" and that he would rather see
the ordinance sent back to the committee than burdened with a multitude
of amendments.[30]

"IMMEASURABLE" BENEFITS TO THE CITY

Zoning was not only a tool to reduce land-use conflicts, it was seen as an
integral part of the effort to rid Chicago of its image as a crowded, dirty,
and corrupt city. Amid growing optimism during the 1920s about the
city's place in the nation's industrial and commercial affairs, investment
flowed to rapid-transit lines, parks, and streets. Apartment towers sprouted up along the lakefront and new office towers pierced the sky, creating
an aura of great prosperity.[31]

Under the astute leadership of chairman Wacker, the Plan Commission made notable strides in implementing many of the proposals outlined in Burnham and Bennett's *Plan of Chicago*. In the eyes of some historians, the Roaring Twenties was the "Golden Age" of comprehensively planned improvement in the city.[32] Wacker later wrote: "We knew our plan was right, that it was basically sound and that its adoption and completion would benefit every citizen of our city immeasurably."[33] Yet city planning was still in its infancy, often more concerned with civic spaces and monuments than with the technical detail that dominates many planning decisions today.

Several court decisions also supported the work of city planners. In 1926, the U.S. Supreme Court issued its landmark decision, *Village of Euclid v. Ambler Realty Company*. The Ambler Realty Company had sued the village of Euclid, Ohio, arguing that the comprehensive zoning plan that the city had developed interfered unconstitutionally with the company's plan to develop a tract of land for industrial use. The company contended that the restrictions substantially diminished the land's value, but the Supreme Court ruled in favor of the village, upholding the right to use zoning.[34] The *Euclid* decision and the reversal of a state court decision about the grandfathering of nonconforming uses swept away much of the ambiguity about the city's ability to enforce the ordinance.[35]

As the zoning movement gained steam across the country, Secretary of Commerce Herbert Hoover assembled a panel of experts, including Edward Bassett and Alfred Bettman, who exhorted local governments to use this planning tool. Hoover offered the following analogy to state the case: "Someone has asked, 'Does your city keep its gas range in the parlor and its piano in the kitchen?' That is what many an American city permits households to do."[36] In 1927, the committee's work bore fruit in the form of the Standard City Planning Act, which established a framework for local governments across the country to use zoning to support the implementation of long-range "development plans."

Business and real estate professionals believed that Chicago's zoning ordinance would accelerate the process of modernization and increase land values by upwards of $1 billion—the equivalent of more than $1,000 per household in the city.[37] As Chicago soon learned, however, the struggle to resolve long entrenched land-use problems had only begun.

Unlike the preponderance of the city's housing stock, which antedates zoning, most of the homes that surround Municipal (Midway) Airport (shown here circa 1936) were built subsequent to the adoption of the zoning ordinance. Built on narrow lots, many of these homes were bungalows ranging in size from 1,200 to 1,500 square feet. The "Bungalow Belt" stretched from the South Side to the city's western boundary and north to Rogers Park. (Chicago Historical Society)

CHAPTER 4

Zoning Comes of Age

Optimism about zoning in the city began to wane by the end of the 1920s. The rhetoric about "immeasurable benefits" gave way to a more sobering assessment, which centered on the belief that the ordinance was largely reinforcing land-use patterns already in place and failed to deliver on the promise of fostering significant improvements in property values.[1] Out of the disappointment, however, came an enhanced municipal commitment to planning and a heightened level of technical sophistication.

The 1923 ordinance never became the national showpiece of zoning excellence its early proponents had desired. As in other cities, the zoning ordinance could not fix problems that had their roots in past practices. Nor could it reasonably be expected to anticipate emerging trends in communication, technology, and transportation. Social and economic changes made the scope of early zoning ordinances too limited to create the harmonious living environments some people envisioned.

At a time when the expectations of city dwellers were on the rise, the problems of congestion, noise, and inadequate parking seemed destined to grow worse. The age of automation and mass production was also underway, aided by advances in manufacturing. Urban residents with extra spending money and leisure time became more attentive to neighborhood aesthetics.

Residents began to push their aldermen and the Zoning Board of Appeals for zoning changes that would benefit them. Amendments to the zoning ordinance became more frequent than the framers of the ordinance had apparently anticipated. From its original "scientific" approach to guiding development, the zoning ordinance was becoming increasingly complex and its administration all too human.[2]

Adding to the city's woes, the amendment that had created the ZBA proved to be legally problematic. In 1931, an Illinois Supreme Court decision ruled that the original language establishing the Board was inadequate to guide its discretionary power. The city amended the ordinance in 1934 to address this objection, but questions continued to be voiced about the ZBA.[3]

Meanwhile, the city continued to grow, as did its African-American population. Transportation improvements and rising incomes stimulated development of more new communities around the city, eroding the vitality of many inner-city neighborhoods. Eighty-nine new suburbs—nearly all enforcing a strict separation of land uses—were incorporated over the course of the decade, giving those working in the city more residential choices than ever before.[4] The expansion of Berwyn, Elmhurst, Maywood, Oak Park, and other suburban boomtowns gradually changed the inner city's demographic and socioeconomic composition. Taking the place of many of the departing white residents of European ancestry were African-Americans arriving from the Deep South in search of better-paying jobs.

ZONING AND RACE

While the new zoning ordinance brought disappointment to those who had believed its adoption would radically affect the city's land-use patterns, others found the ordinance a useful tool for exercising less idealistic kinds of control. By determining what could be built or maintained in a given area, this ordinance became a tool used to limit housing opportunities for low-income residents, particularly African-Americans. The various strategies that emerged to enforce patterns of racial segregation were a sad departure from the early and lofty goals of zoning.

The practice of racial zoning was neither new nor unique to Chicago. Laws discouraging certain racial groups from occupying particular districts were among the earliest forms of municipal zoning.[5] The practice had informal roots in the late nineteenth century when San Francisco ordinances banned laundries from certain areas of the city. Although such zoning ostensibly was intended to prohibit "nuisance" uses, historians and legal scholars generally agree that the motive was to prevent the Chinese, who dominated the laundry business, from living in these districts.

After the turn of the century, more formal attempts to adopt racial zon-ing took root in the South. As tens of thousands of African-Americans migrated from Southern farms to urban areas between 1910 and 1913, many Dixie cities—including Baltimore, Maryland; Richmond, Norfolk, Ashland, Roanoke, and Portsmouth, Virginia; Winston-Salem, North Carolina; and Atlanta, Georgia—created racially based zoning districts. This practice gradually spread westward to include Louisville, Kentucky; St. Louis, Missouri; New Orleans, Louisiana; and Oklahoma City, Oklahoma.[6]

When African-Americans headed northward, attracted by the rising wartime demand for labor, Chicago and other cities showed interest in adopting this Southern tool. In 1917, the Chicago Real Estate Board, led by realtors from the Hyde Park, Kenwood, and Oakland neighborhoods, urged the city to consider adopting a racial zoning ordinance similar to that of St. Louis. The realtors argued that the dispersion of African-Americans throughout the city could lead to more than $250 million in property-value depreciation. The board's effort to promote segregation, however, was at odds with *Buchanan v. Warley*, a November, 1917, U.S. Supreme Court ruling that found racial zoning unconstitutional. Although challenged in Southern cities up through the 1960s, the *Buchanan* decision constituted a major barrier to racial zoning in Chicago—even in the heated period following a 1919 race riot that culminated in renewed calls for the City Council to enact a racial zoning ordinance.[7]

Rather than enact an ordinance that would be invalidated, Chicagoans led the nation in fashioning a new form of "private" zoning through the use of racial deed restrictions and restrictive covenants.[8] Both racial deed restrictions and restrictive covenants were attached to new subdivisions in the city and its suburbs as early as the 1910s, and their use spread as subdivision activity rose to a peak in the 1920s. These deed restrictions prohibited the future sale or lease of all property in the subdivision to African-Americans and (outside of Chicago) to Jews and/or Asians.

Such exclusionary practices flourished as white residents looked for ways to protect the "quality" of their neighborhoods in the mid-1920s. Many turned to the Chicago Real Estate Board for technical assistance, which obliged by fashioning a model "racial restrictive covenant" that could legally bind property owners to sell or lease their residential properties only to non-African-Americans. These covenants took effect after being signed by 75 percent of those living in a clearly defined areas.

Methods of this sort reached their zenith in Chicago from the late 1920s through the 1940s. By one estimate, racial restrictive covenants applied to at least a quarter of all the residential property on the South Side—a level apparently unmatched in other urban areas in the country.[9] The clustering of these exclusionary devices had the effect of forming de facto racial zones. The courts, however, took a dim view of such "private" zoning tools, which lost their potency in May, 1948, when the U.S. Supreme Court ruled in *Shelley v. Kraemer* that their enforcement in court was unconstitutional.[10]

African-Americans were also attuned to the risk that racial motives would pervade the efforts to create the city's first zoning ordinance. During the early 1920s, the Chicago Urban League warned that negative stereotypes expressed by zoning advocates about African-Americans were laying the groundwork for zoning measures that would indirectly lead to racial segregation.[11]

Charles S. Duke, a prominent African-American developer who worked with the NAACP, had particular concerns about this issue. As a member of the Zoning Commission, Duke closely observed the writing of Chicago's first zoning ordinance to ensure that it would not compromise the city's Black Belt. Some historians credit Duke's presence on the commission for the removal of two objectionable parts of the zoning ordinance, one of which would have "extend[ed] the commercial district throughout Grand Boulevard where most of the better colored homes are situated."[12]

Not all attitudes about zoning expressed on behalf of the African-American community were negative. Madge Headley, a white Women's City Club member who was active in the Urban League, penned an article during 1923 in the first issue of *Opportunity*, the league's national publication, making the case that zoning would bring the same benefits to African-Americans as to whites. In the limited coverage it gave to the 1923 zoning ordinance, the *Chicago Defender* seemed to agree.[13]

Although once-ubiquitous clotheslines have fallen out of favor, narrow lots with detached garages and porches on multiple levels remain a hallmark in Chicago neighborhoods. This photograph (date unknown) shows the rear views of apartments typical of buildings that were later part of R4 zoning districts. The crowded conditions evident in this photograph were endemic to many of the city's African-American neighborhoods. (Chicago Historical Society)

However, in subsequent years, the *Defender* remained a watchdog, warning its readers about the potential misuses of zoning and devoting a great deal of coverage to the efforts of cities (such as Birmingham) to enact racial zoning ordinances in defiance of the U.S. Supreme Court ruling.[14]

Once zoning took effect, white neighborhood organizations routinely screened requests for zoning amendments to preserve racial segregation.

Charles S. Duke, Zoning
Commission member.

The Woodlawn Property Owners Association, for example, organized to prevent the passage of those amendments that would promote "Negro encroachment." The Oakland-Kenwood Property Owners Association rallied to block amendments that would allow apartments in the area on the grounds that this would encourage the entry of African-Americans, who could not afford single-family homes.[15]

African-Americans in the late 1920s also bore the brunt of lax enforcement of zoning as well as amendments that threatened to change the mix of land uses in their neighborhoods.[16] The Chicago Urban League formed various African-American block- and neighborhood-improvement associations to monitor the city's zoning activities. Such oversight was especially important in neighborhoods that bordered industrial areas, where there was fear that new or expanded factories would generate pollution and other nuisances.

Despite the diligence of these groups during the Great Depression, the City Council approved many requests for zoning changes submitted by businesses wanting to operate in low-income residential neighborhoods.[17] Although the extent of this phenomenon has not been quantified, there is evidence to suggest that African-Americans felt the effects of incompatible land uses more severely than their white counterparts.[18]

CHANGING TIMES

Nearly all Chicagoans experienced a drop in living standards during the Great Depression, but the changes were particularly severe in crowded neighborhoods beset with an aging housing stock. Much of this housing deteriorated as landlords subdivided homes and apartments, first to provide low-cost tenements and later to house wartime workers.

The Chicago Plan Commission recognized the inadequacy of the city's supply of housing: "A century of haphazard building has left Chicago with a heritage of thousands of obsolete and physically decayed structures arranged in monotonous rows in badly planned neighborhoods,"[19] it wrote. Complaints that the 1923 ordinance had allocated too much land for apartments and not enough for single family homes and duplexes escalated, as did criticism that the allowable densities were too high.[20] As planner Homer Hoyt claimed, "If all the land in Chicago were built to the limit allowed by the zoning law, the entire population of the United States could be housed in the city."[21]

Another prominent official, Hugh E. Young, the Chicago Plan Commission's chief engineer, had raised similar issues as early as 1937. Young recognized the pioneering goals of zoning's early proponents; in his view, they deserved credit for trying to "rezone men's minds as well as the physical structure of cities."[22] Nevertheless, he also recognized that implementation fell short of the ideal and criticized the growing number of variations and the thousands of nonconforming uses that were allowed to continue. Young saw the need to encourage such practices as "step-down" buffering to protect prime residential areas from heavy manufacturing as well as new policies to combat the blight surrounding the downtown.[23]

Young called for a citywide land-use survey and a new zoning plan, saying: "The survey … will be of tremendous value to the entire city, to every owner of property, to everyone engaged in business or industry, and to those who live and work here."[24] Many other people were of the same mind, believing that the problems could not be resolved merely through incremental changes to the zoning ordinance.

The city heeded Young's call after reorganizing the Chicago Plan Commission in 1939. Although the commission was trimmed in size from its original 328 citizen members to a mere 28 (a dozen public appointees and 16 city officials), it emerged as a more active and professional agency with its own full-time staff. The commission joined the Works Progress Administration (WPA) to produce the survey,

The impressive street wall along South Michigan Avenue across from the Art Institute of Chicago, circa 1940, reflects the designs fostered by different phases of city regulation. Most of the buildings opposite the museum have the flat-topped shape encouraged by height restrictions in place prior to the advent of zoning. In the distance, the Wrigley Building (center) and Tribune Tower (far right) boast ornamental towers allowed by the city in 1920, while the 333 N. Michigan Avenue building (behind the Chevrolet billboard) and the Carbide and Carbon Building (the slender building to the left of the Wrigley) have towers permitted by the 1923 zoning law. (Chaddick collection)

A view of the Douglas Park neighborhood, circa 1940, shows the vastness of the building stock in this part of the West Side (note Sacramento Boulevard at upper right). Little except Douglas Boulevard (a corridor lined with trees extending across the bottom of the photograph) and the B&O Railroad tracks (upper center) interrupt the street grid. The comprehensive inventory of land uses undertaken during World War II revealed the deteriorating condition of this and many other neighborhoods. (Chicago Historical Society)

successfully completing the task in 1940. Illustrating in vivid detail the prevailing use of land, the survey drew attention to the fact that that much of the city—especially poorer residential neighborhoods—was severely congested and desperately in need of renovation.

The survey lent a sense of urgency to the City Council's decision that year to embark on the first major revision of the zoning ordinance. As one would expect in a time of war, this initiative, led by Alderman William A. Rowan, chairman of the City Council's Committee on Zoning and Buildings, was completed without much fanfare. After public hearings in each of the 50 wards, the City Council adopted a set of comprehensive amendments in December, 1942, which, as described in the sidebar on page 34, reduced the allowable density of development in much of the city and zoned more land for heavy industry but less land for apartments and businesses. These changes, designed to help the city deal with the enormous burdens created by World War II, apparently generated little controversy or civic debate.

Although a surge in production reinvigorated Chicago's manufacturing

This view of the area surrounding the Edgewater Beach Hotel, circa 1925, illustrates the uniformity of development along some parts of the Chicago lakefront as zoning was taking effect. The photograph shows the "ratcheting down" of density as one moves from the lake. In 1923, the blocks closest to the lake were designed as Volume District 3, which permitted apartment towers similar to those visible on Sheridan Road at the bottom left. The storied hotel is no more; the landmark was razed just prior to the construction of Lake Shore Drive through the area. (Chicago Historical Society)

sector and infused new life into its long-struggling downtown district, wartime considerations drew attention away from civic affairs and resulted in a deferral of both basic maintenance and capital investment in infrastructure. As the end of the conflict neared, the city recognized that it was at a crossroads: to re-create the atmosphere of prosperity that had characterized the 1920s, it would need to think broadly about ways to improve streets, eradicate slums, and provide new housing.

The city's Master Plan of Residential Land Use, completed in 1943, sternly warned of the need for new highways, parks, and commercial areas as well as reversing the plight of deteriorating neighborhoods.[25] This plan called for another series of zoning changes to prepare the city for the dramatic changes that lay ahead: "When victory comes, there will be frantic haste in shifting millions of men and women from war to peace production. Unless blueprints for rebuilding our cities on a new and better plan are ready for immediate use, our buildings will copy the out-worn patterns of the past...."[26]

Inside the 1942 Ordinance

The 1942 zoning code was a forerunner to an era of great innovation, introducing a variety of new concepts, including a new method to regulate the bulk of buildings. The amendment, however, perpetuated the "two map" system, with one map restricting land use and another restricting volume.

The vast majority of the changes made to the zoning text had the effect of limiting the intensity of development. Allowable building heights and bulk fell sharply and off-street parking requirements for apartment buildings were put into place. The highest volume district, Volume District 5, was eliminated, giving the fourth volume district the highest density cap. In this district, the old height limit was replaced with a new regulation capping bulk at 144 feet times the size of the lot, which was the equivalent of a floor area ratio (FAR) of about 12. (A building could be 288 feet if it only covered half the lot.) This regulation reduced maximum bulk of buildings in much of the downtown area by as much as 50 percent but also provided developers a higher degree of flexibility.

There was also a major reorganization of the use districts. Three different types of districts were now devoted to residences: one limited to homes, one allowing homes and townhomes, and a third allowing homes, townhomes, and small group homes. The

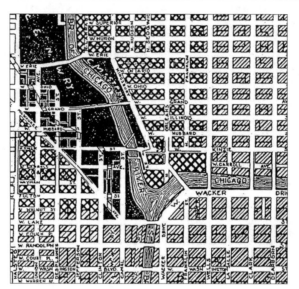

This "use map" from the 1942 ordinance depicts the area around Wolf Point. Parallel lines denote commercial districts; crossed lines denote manufacturing districts. A separate map governed the volume of buildings. (City of Chicago)

ordinance still had just one type of apartment district, but there were two newly created business districts intended to serve nearby residents: one for specialty shops and another for general business. The ordinance retained the commercial and manufacturing districts but added a new industrial classification. These changes made the ordinance easier to understand and to administer.

As part of the amendment, the City Council took the weighty step of approving the concept of amortizing nonconforming uses, a policy that, if fully enforced, would allow for the gradual elimination of these properties. Under amortization, property owners had a specified number of years to phase out the use of property that failed to conform to the conditions set forth in the zoning ordinance. Failure to do so could lead to eventual condemnation by the city.

Other changes were driven by the state of scarcity endemic to wars. The Board of Appeals could recommend variations to subdivide apartments, which added to the supply of low-cost housing but (as history would show) opened the door to blight. Applications for special uses now had to be given public hearings, and some limits were placed on suitable locations for these uses.

The amendments also rezoned land to meet wartime needs. On the Southwest Side, a farm was zoned for industrial use, despite being adjacent to a residential neighborhood, thus allowing the Ford Motor Company to create an airplane-engine plant on the site that later became the Ford City mall. The amendment greatly shortened the length of the text portion of the ordinance, reducing it to a mere eight pages—less than half the length of the ordinance that had previously been in effect.

CHAPTER 5

Renewing the City

New architectural styles, advanced building techniques, and innovative planning concepts pushed real-estate development in new directions after World War II. These changes carried with them enormous potential for urban renewal. Yet, if the city hoped to capitalize on these opportunities, the zoning ordinance had to change. Developers needed modern and flexible zoning techniques. Thus began a period of great innovation and experimentation that made Chicago's zoning ordinance a prototype for cities nationwide.

Several major projects launched during the Great Depression served as precursors to development patterns that would change the face of postwar Chicago. The Jane Addams Houses (1938) on the Near West Side and the Ida B. Wells Homes (1941) on the Near South Side were the first redevelopments in the city requiring large-scale slum clearance. Both projects, created by teams of local architects with WPA financing, featured site plans with ample open space and a creative arrangement of buildings.

As the postwar era dawned, plans were afoot to dramatically expand the scale of the city's redevelopment activity. There was a great push to rejuvenate the downtown and the inner-city neighborhoods as well as to provide new housing that could compete with suburban development. Achieving these objectives, however, would require the creation of new institutions and the restructuring of existing ones. Newly elected Mayor Martin Kennelly was committed to taking the necessary steps, and in 1947 he established the Chicago Land Clearance Commission (CLCC) with a mandate to redevelop areas of the city where "the old block pattern can be wiped out and a new one conforming to modern planning standards can be substituted."[1]

The city launched its urban renewal program in 1948 by acquiring property near Michael Reese Hospital on the Near South Side for slum clearance and the creation of Lake Meadows. This massive mixed-use complex would

Prairie Shores at 2801–3001 S. Martin Luther King Drive, shown above on May 5, 1992, encompassing more than 2,000 apartments, helped meet the housing needs of Michael Reese Hospital (right center). The complex showcases postwar design innovations that fueled the push for more flexible zoning techniques. Many acres of slum housing were cleared to create this mixed-use redevelopment. (Photo by Lawrence Okrent)

eventually consist of nine tall buildings with 2,033 residential units sep-arated by parking and open space. Using federal funds for slum clearance under the Housing Act of 1949, the city worked to prepare the site while Ferd Kramer, a real-estate developer serving as chairman of the Michael Reese board, arranged the sale of the property to New York Life Insur-ance Company for development.

In 1951, as the construction of Lake Meadows was set to begin, dem-olition work got underway for neighboring Prairie Shores. Embracing a similarly creative design, this community had five high-rise apartment buildings with a slightly southeast orientation for maximizing sunlight. With its structures covering only nine percent of its 55-acre site, Prairie Shores represented a radical departure from prewar development patterns.

Zoning was not a factor in either development: the use of federal funds exempted them from local zoning laws. Their size and complexity, however, stimulated interest in large-scale development. Recognizing that enormous changes were on the horizon, the city reorganized the Chicago Plan Commission once again, further expanding its levels of technical sophistication. In 1952, under the direction of Frederick T. Aschman, the commission established a professional planning staff and appointed architect John Cordwell as director. Under Cordwell's leadership, the staff prepared the city's first set of small-section base maps, showing buildings and infrastructure block-by-block for each community.[2]

Integral to the city's postwar development plan was attracting a more urbane, higher-income population. The success of new high-rise apart-ments in the modern style of Ludwig Mies van der Rohe, developed by Herbert Greenwald at 900–910 Lake Shore Drive between 1949 and 1951, showed it could be done. Furthermore, groundbreaking for the Prudential Building at 130 E. Randolph Street in 1952 ended a long drought in office-building construction. Upon its completion in 1955, the Prudential was Chicago's second tallest building and a business address of considerable prestige.

Despite the importance of these sleek new buildings to the city, their developers had to overcome zoning obstacles. Each pair of Greenwald's

Chicago saw the completion of only one tall office building—the Pru-dential Building—while the 1942 zoning amendments were in effect. This 41-story skyscraper conformed to the requirement that the bulk of buildings could not exceed 144 feet times the size of the lot area (the equivalent of a FAR of about 13) by virtue of its large lot, which con-sisted largely of air rights over Illinois Central Railroad tracks. The building's completion in 1955 stimulated further office-tower construc-tion and added to civic interest in bolstering the city's level of planning sophistication. (Chicago Public Library, Special Collections and Preser-vation Division)

buildings required connecting covered walkways in order to make them one unit. Prudential, due to the constraints of the city's bulk limits, had to acquire extensive air rights from the Illinois Central Railroad to assemble a site that could accommodate a building of its proposed size (see the discussion in Chapter 9).

Recognizing that developers were eager to depart from the conventional grid and needed to understand the limits of what they were allowed to do, the Plan Commission urged the city to adopt a more flexible approach to zoning. There was a need for a new instrument to facilitate innovative development and emerging building styles. As we will see, that instrument would ultimately be Planned Development.

By the early 1950s, the city's zoning ordinance had been amended so many times that some of the maps were akin to patchwork quilts. The sheer number of amendments and variations undermined the ordinance's role as a template guiding development. Between 1942 and 1952, the City Council received more than 4,000 applications for zoning map amendments. In the same period, the Zoning Board of Appeals received more than 3,000 applications for variations.[3]

Another problem hampering the administration of zoning was the legacy of land-use issues that predated zoning. As officials had feared, businesses in residential zoning districts that had been grandfathered at the advent of zoning still generated complaints for having an unfair advantage in retail trade.[4] Angered by the ineffectiveness of the city's effort to eliminate nonconforming uses, some property owners brought their land-use disputes directly to the Illinois courts.[5] Land-use attorney Richard Babcock (see his biography in Appendix C) later chastised Chicago and other cities in the state for "avoid[ing] the legal and political risks of telling a property owner that after a given period he must cease using his property for the purpose to which it is now devoted."[6]

By early 1952, the movement to overhaul zoning had garnered a full head of steam and the unequivocal support of Mayor Kennelly.[7] That April, Alderman P.J. Cullerton, the chairman of the Committee on Buildings and Zoning, announced that a new committee would begin a comprehensive rezoning effort. H. Evert Kincaid, former Plan Commission director turned private consultant, was appointed head of the committee.[8] The city was divided into three parts (north, central, and south), with each part supported by an aldermanic committee given the task of reviewing land-use problems.[9]

Frederick T. Aschman, advisor to the city.

The effort to modernize zoning took a step backward that August, however, when Kincaid announced that he was not up to serving as committee chair. Mayor Kennelly then turned to his colleague in the trucking industry, Harry F. Chaddick, to help find a new director. Chaddick was no stranger to zoning; he had been responsible for conducting the Motor Freight Terminal study in 1950 that led to the creation of a new type of district, the Motor Freight Terminal District.[10]

Chaddick asked Ted Aschman, then a respected planning consultant, to chair the committee. Aschman suggested that Chaddick himself accept the post, and the mayor agreed. Chaddick accepted the assignment and immediately began work by combing the Plan Commission and the Corporation Counsel's office to put together a staff that had the requisite professional and technical qualifications.[11] He knew this would be a multi-year project of huge proportions.

The first task—preparing a new set of land-use maps for the city—drew upon the Plan Commission's new base maps and required surveying 643,000 parcels of land within the municipal boundaries, an area encompassing more than 213 square miles.[12] Chaddick had a dozen people to help with this task but had such a deep commitment to it that he often spent Sundays driving the city's streets with his wife, Elaine, exploring the panorama of land uses in various neighborhoods.

An illustration from the pamphlet *Zoning and You* explains the concept of a special use permit, a mechanism used to regulate the placement of certain land uses—in this case a church—in various zoning districts. (City of Chicago)

Chaddick eventually took so many of these weekend excursions in his white Cadillac that he claimed to have traveled the entire length of every street and alley. Along the way, he took more than 1,000 photographs of unusual buildings and land uses. "I could see from the beginning," he later wrote, "that dividing the city into zoned areas termed simply residential, apartments, business, commercial, and industrial was in no way sufficient to cope with the multiplicity of land uses in an urban giant like Chicago."[13]

THE MONUMENTAL TASK BEGINS

As Chaddick's team worked to overhaul the ordinance, rulings by the Illinois courts emboldened cities to regulate land use more aggressively.

Before 1950, the courts tended to rule piecemeal in favor of those parties who could make a reasonable case for relief from zoning. In the early 1950s, however, the courts increasingly recognized that zoning classifications had a compelling public purpose and exercised greater restraint when hearing appeals. With increased regularity, rulings affirmed the right of local government to make zoning decisions without judicial interference. This encouraged municipalities to experiment with new zoning techniques.[14]

Although Chaddick knew that it would take several years to draft a truly modern ordinance, the rise in population anticipated by the city added to the urgency of his assignment. A forecast by the Plan Commission anticipated a city of 3.8 million people—an increase of about 300,000—by 1965. Such projections, together with a new vision of urban living and the expanding scope of the urban renewal programs, supported the notion that the ordinance needed to be more permissive toward large-scale and high-density development in certain parts of the city.

Among the first sections of the zoning ordinance evaluated by Chaddick's team was the section devoted to the residential districts. The proposal drafted in early 1953 placed primary emphasis on population density and the bulk of buildings rather than on building type.[15] This proposal called for a minimum square footage of lot area per dwelling unit, ranging from 6,250 square feet for homes to 115 square feet for tall apartment buildings, depending on the zoning district.[16]

Another bold departure from the past was a method of assuring the "economic compatibility" of businesses within each zoning district.

Harry F. Chaddick.

Alderman P.J. Cullerton and H. Evert Kincaid. (DePaul Special Collections and Archives)

Chaddick's team developed a classification system that took into account the frequency with which various types of businesses were patronized by nearby residents.[17] The more regularly that citizens who lived nearby used a particular type of business, the more compelling was the case for allowing it to exist in close proximity to residential areas. The team also considered the size of the area from which the business attracted its clientele as well as the extent to which each type of business competed with other businesses in the same area. It felt that businesses selling products that attracted customers from a broad geographic area posed a greater risk of neighborhood congestion, noise, and parking shortages and should be suitably located.[18]

Due to compatibility issues, for example, the team assigned auto showrooms to the newly defined CI commercial zoning district but not the BI neighborhood business district. "Gone was the old zoning practice of allowing any business to come into a business district as long as it did not smell worse nor make more noise than the other permitted uses," observed Chaddick in his memoirs.[19]

Quantitative analysis also made possible the creation of new standards to address the city's notorious parking problems.[20] Not only had earlier zoning amendments failed to anticipate the scope of these problems, they were also on shaky legal ground. The Circuit Court of Cook County ruled in 1954 that the amendment requiring apartment houses to provide off-street parking was discriminatory due to the absence of a similar standard for other land uses.[21]

To evaluate the options, the city hired Evert Kincaid to survey the experiences of other cities and apartment houses throughout Chicago with respect to off-street parking. Kincaid showed that the typical apartment development generated significantly more automobiles than it had allotted parking spaces. His finding helped the city document the disparity between available spaces and resident needs, providing a legally sound basis for increasing off-street parking requirements.[22]

Owing to their urgency, the parking requirements were adopted in the summer of 1953 and took effect immediately. The rules required apartment buildings to have 0.75 parking spaces for each dwelling unit with one or more bedrooms and 0.50 parking spaces for each dwelling unit without a separate bedroom.[23] Businesses and office buildings needed one parking spot for every 100 square feet of space. Larger retail stores needed one spot for every 200 square feet, but businesses in the downtown area were excluded. The standards also applied to places of assembly (sports arenas and theaters) and retail and industrial sites, and dealt with placement and design of loading areas, parking garages, and surface lots.[24]

Chaddick took considerable pride in the fact that these standards were later introduced in many other communities. As he recalled in his biography, "These parking reforms seem mild but they were strong medicine at the time and subsequently were imitated in cities all over the country."[25]

Few of the city's innovations, however, were as significant to the practice of zoning as the newly drafted industrial performance standards (explicit limits related to nuisances that a particular use or process may not exceed).

Walter C. McCrone, noted chemist.

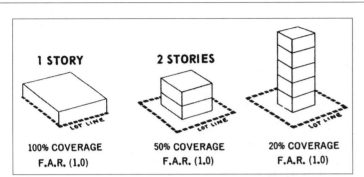

1 STORY

2 STORIES

100% COVERAGE
F.A.R. (1.0)

50% COVERAGE
F.A.R. (1.0)

20% COVERAGE
F.A.R. (1.0)

An illustration of the floor-area-ratio concept appearing in the *Zoning and You* pamphlet. (City of Chicago)

With the assistance of Walter C. McCrone, Ph.D., a respected local chemist with his own consulting firm, the city classified manufacturing uses into districts with measurable and clearly defined standards pertaining to noise, vibration, smoke, and particulate matter; toxic or noxious matter; odorous matter; fire and explosive hazards; and glare or heat.[26] In May, 1953, engineers and chemists endorsed the committee's plan to apply performance standards to the city's industrial zoning districts.[27]

"This will provide the manufacturer with a greater incentive to 'clean house' so as to be afforded a wider choice of select locations within the city," noted the rezoning team.[28] The approach differed from earlier zoning measures that had simply named the types of industries allowed in each district; over the next 20 years, many other cities—with McCrone's assistance—used it as a basis for their own industrial zoning policies.

Chaddick's team also expanded the use of a planning tool known as floor area ratio (FAR). This technique, first used in New York, limited a building's bulk and total usable space based on the size of the lot and the applicable zoning. The FAR approach, which replaced traditional height and volume restrictions and setback standards, afforded developers more flexibility. A developer providing a setback greater than the minimum required could construct a taller building, as long as it was within the allowable FAR for the district (see illustration at left).[29] Other cities had adopted the FAR concept in commercial areas, but the use of this concept to regulate development in all types of zoning districts, including residential areas, was novel.

Notable changes to the city's government did little to slow the team's progress. In August, 1953, Alderman Emil Pacini replaced P.J. Cullerton as chairman of the Committee on Buildings and Zoning. The following year, Chaddick hired George H. Kranenberg, Jr., a veteran planner, to serve as the technical director of the zoning initiative, a full-time position with the city. In April, 1955, Richard J. Daley, who was determined to modernize Chicago, succeeded Mayor Kennelly. In 1956, Daley created the Department of City Planning, with Ira J. Bach as commissioner (see history in Appendix H). "The difference between Kennelly and Daley was the difference between night and day," observed planning director Cordwell.[30]

The zoning team quickly acclimated itself to the new mayor, who brimmed with self-confidence and earned broad public support due to his willingness to take decisive action.[31] After spending much of 1954 and the early part of 1955 preparing the zoning maps, in August, 1955, the team unveiled a more comprehensive and clearly articulated amortization schedule for the termination of nonconforming uses than was provided by the 1942 amendments.[32] Babcock believed that the details of the earlier measure "were so geologic that no alderman or enforcement official had to worry that he would be taken seriously."[33] Chaddick also did not mince words about the necessity of the new schedule, writing "As far as my staff and I were concerned ...

George H. Kranenberg, Jr., zoning director.

Richard J. Daley and Harry F. Chaddick. (DePaul Special Collections and Archives)

A billboard for Calvert whiskey, mounted on a large metal frame and illuminated with neon—which would violate the zoning law today—dominates the view of motorists using Lake Shore Drive, circa 1955. (Charles Stade photo, Chicago Historical Society)

allowing a nonconforming use to remain had served as a comfortable excuse for the intrusion of other nonconforming uses which, in turn, led to a breakdown of an entire zoning program."[34]

The new timetable took into account a structure's purpose, construction type, and value. Smaller structures with only modest values would be amortized over a relatively short period, generally eight years or less. Larger and more valuable structures, such as commercial buildings, would be typically amortized over a longer interval.

The zoning team then did battle with the visual clutter created by the proliferation of signs and billboards. In September, 1955, it submitted for review a package of new controls restricting not only the proximity of signs and billboards to major streets and public parks, but also their size, height, and projection from buildings. In addition to these changes, the statute included an amortization schedule for nonconforming signs and billboards, which had not been part of the 1942 amendments. This latter change met strong opposition from the sign industry.[35]

To afford developers of large-scale projects greater flexibility, the team introduced two concepts. The first was Planned Development (PD),

Inside the 1957 Zoning Ordinance

An overarching goal of the Chaddick team was to develop policies that would be easy to understand, easy to use, and easy to administer. The team sought to achieve this by organizing the regulations in a more thorough and less cumbersome way than the existing code, which contained many lists of specific types of uses allowed in each district and a long list of permitted special uses. They also wanted to eliminate the need to consult both use and volume regulations, which involved two sets of maps.

Each major classification was divided into districts with particular specifications. There were four commercial zoning districts: C1, Restricted; C2, General (which allowed auto showrooms, small factories, and other uses that generated traffic from points outside a neighborhood); C3, Manufacturing (which allowed larger factories); and C4, Motor Freight Terminals only.

There were seven business districts, ranging from neighborhood retail to service districts (such as State Street) and central business districts for downtown office buildings. There were eight different residential districts, R1 through R8, each with different FAR, different minimum-lot area requirements per dwelling unit, and different yard requirements.

The 1957 code used the theory of economic compatibility to determine permitted uses in commercial districts. It was the first in the country to apply performance standards to manufacturing districts—standards that provided criteria to limit air pollution, noise, emissions, odors, vibration, dust, dirt, glare,

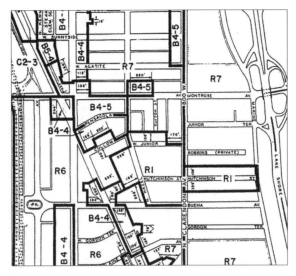

A zoning map of the Lake View neighborhood shows the "single map" system adopted by the city in 1957. Note how the high-density R7 districts are in close proximity to the low-density R1 districts in this neighborhood. (City of Chicago)

traffic impact, and other problems. New policies also tackled the regulation of signs and billboards, and a more comprehensive phase-out schedule for nonconforming uses.

As we discuss in later chapters, the code also established a policy for planned unit development (called Planned Development, or PD) and a system of FAR premiums (informally called bonuses) that allowed an increase in the FAR for commercial and residential developments that met certain criteria. PDs gave developers considerable latitude while still allowing the city to achieve its planning goals, a

process that we will consider separately in Chapter 6. Bonuses had been offered in the 1923 ordinance, but the new code defined the conditions in which these incentives applied and spelled out the increases that a developer could obtain (see our discussion of this in Chapter 9).

Major changes were also made to streamline the work of the Zoning Board of Appeals (ZBA). The list of allowable variations was completely rewritten, with the focus now on providing the kind of relief sought by both builders seeking support for new construction and the owners of older buildings interested in remodeling. Among the most common variations the ZBA could grant were reductions in the dimensions of yards and off-street parking requirements as well as limited increases in FAR. There was also a more objective standard for hardship, ending the practice of interpreting this term subjectively (see discussion in Appendix H).

The number of permissible special uses was reduced and codified by district, in contrast to the 1923 code, which listed special uses allowed in any zoning district. Special uses now had to be reviewed by the planning department and heard by the ZBA at a public hearing. Previously, the building commissioner had granted special-use permits.

The ordinance that emerged was a thick, well-indexed book that bore little resemblance, either in size or content, to the zoning code previously in place.

sometimes known as "Planned Unit Development"—a technique that was particularly well-suited for sites with multiple buildings and a mix of land uses, or other innovative ideas. The second technique, FAR premiums (more commonly called "bonuses"), rewarded developers whose projects met certain criteria with an increase in allowable floor area, often yielding several more stories in downtown office buildings.

The duration of the rezoning effort, however, was not without consequences. As the team conducted its work, economic and technological forces affected city life in unanticipated ways. Some of the assumptions that seemed reasonable when work begin in the early 1950s, especially those relating to the rate of population growth and vehicle ownership, were gradually proven false. Parts of the ordinance, consequently, were in need of revision as soon as they took effect (see discussion in Chapter 7).

MAKING ZONING MORE UNDERSTANDABLE

The rezoning staff and Committee on Buildings and Zoning introduced the complete package to the City Council in October, 1955.[36] Between March and May, 1956, the city held 17 public hearings and at least 50 community meetings to discuss both the text and maps.[37] The vigorous debate surrounding the content of the ordinance inspired Richard Babcock to write: "The disputes, charges, countercharges, and the headlines and editorial comment by the metropolitan press are a foretaste of the changes this document will bring to control over land use in the city."[38]

Chaddick's team reportedly considered 3,500 revisions suggested by attendees of public hearings and other stakeholders. In December, 1956,

after many modifications and refinements to the ordinance, the rezoning staff and the Committee on Buildings and Zoning submitted the revised document to the City Council for further consideration.[39] On May 29, 1957, by a unanimous vote, the City Council adopted the comprehensive zoning ordinance.[40]

Officials throughout the city trumpeted the significance of the occasion. In the *Chicago Tribune*,

PROPOSED COMPREHENSIVE AMENDMENT
TO THE
CHICAGO ZONING ORDINANCE

GENERAL REVIEW
JANUARY, 1954

City of Chicago
CITY COUNCIL COMMITTEE ON BUILDINGS AND ZONING
Emil V. Pacini, Chairman

Alderman Emil Pacini proudly described the new ordinance as "the most modern and practical zoning ordinance in the United States." He boasted that the new code would encourage development and control the conversion of large apartments into smaller units—something that had become a major problem. He went so far as to call the ordinance "the greatest weapon the city can use to stop the flight to the suburbs."[41] Mayor Richard J. Daley addressed concerns that the city would be lax in enforcement. "I want to assure you that the executive arm of government will carry out the policies and programs laid out in the ordinance. I'm confident we'll win any legal battles that ensue," he told the *Tribune*.[42]

CHAPTER 6
PDs:
The Rise of Planned Development

The advent of Planned Development in 1957 was a milestone in the evolution of zoning for Chicago. No longer did the developer or the city just check the existing zoning map. Instead, the two parties sat down to negotiate over height, density, parking, setbacks, and other features. For developers, Planned Development offered greater flexibility and opened the door to more innovative site plans, while the city gained mandatory review by the Department of Planning for all large-scale projects.

By the late 1950s, new forms of architecture and the push for urban renewal were rapidly transforming the look and feel of cities. Architects working in the International Style (often called the Modernist Movement) emphasized unadorned geometric forms, open interiors, and glass, steel, and reinforced concrete. Originating at the Bauhaus in Germany, the style eventually spread worldwide, enjoying great prominence in Chicago due to the work of Ludwig Mies van der Rohe, who came to Chicago to join the New Bauhaus in 1938.

The Modernist vision foresaw the creation of new, comprehensively planned communities. French architect LeCorbusier championed the use of this design concept to rebuild Europe after the devastation of the war, while in New York, the completion of Peter Cooper Village/Stuyvesant Town in 1947 demonstrated that new residential high rises arranged in campus-like environments could revitalize decaying neighborhoods in American cities. The latter communities, located on Manhattan's east side, were enormous in scale, boasting 35 twelve-story buildings and providing housing for some 24,000 people.

These planning paradigms helped gradually change the face of postwar Chicago. A series of massive projects with a mix of land uses began to appear; the first was Lake Meadows, a 70-acre development on the Near South Side that exemplified the emerging vision of urban living. This lakeside complex at 31st Street has super blocks of high-rise

John Cordwell, former planning director for the Chicago Plan Commission, discussing the proposed Sandburg Village redevelopment. This 16-acre Planned Development, approved in 1962, was instrumental to the city's strategy for the revitalization of the Near North Side. (Solomon Cordwell Buenz & Associates)

buildings surrounded by open space, with extensive parking, a medical center, a private club with pool and tennis courts, parks and playgrounds, and the first postwar shopping mall built in the inner city.

Three miles south, the Hyde Park urban renewal project altered the postwar landscape in similarly dramatic fashion. Acres of townhomes with off-street parking, many on streets previously lined with businesses, brought modern housing to a neighborhood that had fallen on hard times. A stretch of 55th Street was vacated and re-routed to accommodate University Apartments, a pair of ten-story buildings in what had been the middle of the street. Clearly, the look of the city was changing, and design concepts rarely seen before the end of the war were becoming established tools of the trade.

The authors of the city's 1957 ordinance saw Planned Development (PD) as a vehicle to accommodate these exciting new designs and afford developers greater flexibility. Projects backed by federal urban renewal funds, such as Lake Meadows and Prairie Shores, were exempt from local zoning, but similar opportunities were needed for privately financed projects. The PD track provided relief from the limits of lot-line zoning to developers who wanted to experiment with unconventional designs or build complexes with several buildings. As planning commissioner Lewis W. Hill noted in 1973, "planned developments employ ... a unified rather than lot-by-lot approach to desirable zoning controls, help to ensure an economic and efficient land use, a higher level of amenities and a pleasing variety of construction."[1] The city managed PDs through a process in which a developer first submitted a project proposal to the city and then participated in an interactive process with officials in order to reach a final plan that satisfied both parties.

PLANNED DEVELOPMENT IN PRACTICE

Initially, a general planned development had to be at least four acres in size. The minimum size was two acres for institutional PDs and ten acres for manufacturing. A PD application had to be submitted to the planning

department for review and, once approved, would become a proposed ordinance ready for adoption by the City Council as a zoning amendment.

The PD approach gave developers great latitude in developing proposed plans, stipulating only "that the uses permitted are not of such a nature ... as to exercise a detrimental influence on the

This drawing was used by the city to illustrate the process of Planned Development. (City of Chicago)

surrounding neighborhood." In 1962, however, the city strengthened its language with a new ordinance, stipulating that PDs "shall be in general conformity with the scope and overall use and bulk provisions" of the zoning district. This passage affirmed the idea that PDs should adhere to floor-area-ratio (FAR) and density limits imposed by the underlying zoning. Nevertheless, the city could make exceptions if the proposed development were deemed necessary or desirable to achieving its goals.

The 1962 ordinance also made the process more formal, requiring that proposals for PDs be first introduced to the City Council's Buildings and Zoning Committee, which gave the general public notice. Once approved by the planning department, PDs were subject to review by the Plan Commission, which held a public hearing where questions could be asked and protests could be voiced.

Such requirements did little to dampen enthusiasm for the PD approach. The number of PDs approved by the city rose sharply during the late 1960s. In the Central Area, Marina City, the Gateway Center, the IBM Building, and other PDs approved showcased the kinds of development that could bring great prestige to the city. In outlying areas, a variety of PDs reshaped large swaths of land.

By the early 1970s, however, some stalwarts of traditional zoning were skeptical of the city's growing dependence on planned development.

Demolition of auxiliary buildings and boarding platforms at Dearborn Station is underway, circa 1975. Zoned for commercial and manufacturing use, this property on the Near South Side was transformed into Dearborn Park, a pair of Planned Developments that eventually housed more than 10,000 people. (Courtesy of the American Planning Association)

Harry Chaddick warned that the city government—specifically Hill—was "whittling away at the zoning ordinance with PDs."[2] Chaddick and others emphasized that conventional zoning had the advantage of allowing both developers and land owners to clearly understand what was permissible and what was not on any given piece of property. Traditional zoning provided a framework, Chaddick believed, that protected communities from developers who were blind to local considerations, while helping ensure that municipal policies would not become subjective and overly politicized. Land-use attorney Richard Babcock echoed these sentiments and once wrote, "Conventional regulations may be either over-strict or over-permissive but this is a lesser evil than the vagueness inherent in the repudiation of use districts."[3]

Nevertheless, Planned Development was here to stay as the city considered it essential to bringing in new business and new population groups. Reviewing proposals and negotiating with developers was now an accepted part of Chicago's economic-development landscape. Without the PD strategy, Chicago would not have many of its most successful recent developments nor the nearby properties they spawned. By thinking big, Chicago hoped it could distance itself from its "second city" status and achieve its goal of becoming a world-class city.

In the spring of 1973, Mayor Daley proposed more changes to the zoning ordinance that would expand the definition of PDs. The mayor set forth a plan to extend the PD provisions to any site larger than one acre and any building of more than 100 feet in height or with more than 100 apartments. Under Daley's plan, the PD ordinance would apply to any building whose height would be twice the average of buildings within a 330 foot radius.[4] It would also require developments near Lake Michigan to be governed by the PD process.

The mayor's primary motive appears to have been to help the city exert greater control over density in residential areas along the north lakefront. Paul Gapp, the *Chicago Tribune*'s highly respected urban-affairs editor, supported this idea, noting that "tough application of these [PD] criteria might halt or at least slow such trends as the destruction of fine old homes and attractive

From this vantage point above Streeterville on June 19, 2000, one sees the full extent of the Randolph Terminal (Illinois Center) Planned Development, which has been dubbed the largest mixed-use development in the world. The 24-acre development includes a labyrinthine shopping concourse, several hotels, numerous residential towers, and a three-level street system. An agreement gave the developer the discretion to exchange a designated number of residential units for commercial space, or vice versa, as the project moved forward—an option exercised on several occasions. (Photo by Lawrence Okrent)

Three Pioneering Planned Developments

Illinois Institute of Technology: Chicago's First Planned Development. At the end of World War II, the future of IIT was a burning question with enormous implications for the Near South Side. This educational institution's image suffered as a result of its proximity to run-down communities, with much of the nearby housing cut up into rooming units. Like its neighbors, Mercy Hospital, Michael Reese Hospital, and The University of Chicago, IIT faced the difficult choice of whether to stay or move to a safer and more affluent area. Each elected to stay, due to the efforts of the coalitions of stakeholders in their areas, including the South Side Planning Board and the South East Chicago Commission.

During the early 1950s, IIT hired the famed architect Ludwig Mies van der Rohe, director of the Institute's School of Architecture, to design a new campus at State Street and 33rd Street. Consisting of 20 buildings, his master plan had great synergy with the redevelopment effort underway around Michael Reese, less than two miles away. To support a series of urban renewal initiatives that included new hospital buildings as well as the Lake Meadows and Prairie Shores complexes, the city set about acquiring property, relocating people and clear-

Mies van der Rohe's Crown Hall on the Illinois Institute of Technology campus exemplifies the Modernist style that gained great prominence in the city after World War II. IIT became the city's first Planned Development in 1959. (Chicago Historical Society)

ing land. The hospital hired its own planning director and designed a master plan for its campus.

The cooperation between the city, IIT, and Michael Reese provided valuable experience that was instrumental to the creation of the city's PD ordinance in 1957. Negotiations between these parties made possible a variety of public improvements to the sites, and the City Council formally designated IIT Chicago's first PD on June 24, 1959. Completed in the early 1960s, the IIT and Michael Reese redevelopment

efforts helped stabilize their neighborhoods and encouraged other institutions to join the coalition working to rejuvenate these areas.

The legacy of this PD can still be felt. During America's bicentennial year, the American Institute of Architects recognized the IIT campus—the largest and most significant collection of Mies buildings in the world—as one of the country's 200 most significant works of architecture.[5]

Illinois Center: The "World's Largest Mixed-Use Development." The Randolph Terminal Redevelopment, now known as Illinois Center, encompasses 24 acres of land roughly bounded by North Michigan Avenue, E. Randolph Street, Lake Shore Drive, and the Chicago River. This redevelopment project began soon after the courts ruled in 1966 that the Illlinois Central Railroad could sell air rights over much of its underutilized downtown property. The ruling set the stage for a PD agreement calling for an intensive mix of land uses in the area but affording the developer, Bernard Weissbourd, great flexibility. Weissbourd was given the discretion to exchange a designated number of residential units for a designated number of square feet of commercial space, or vice versa, as the project moved forward.[6]

Weissbourd was adept in using this flexibility: Over the next 20 years, the Illinois Center complex grew to encompass 15 high-rise buildings, including several major hotels, residential towers, and corporate offices, making it the largest mixed-use development in North America. The development has a system of above-ground streets and two levels of underground streets as well as a labyrinthine shopping concourse connecting its various buildings. The 1973 completion of the Standard Oil Building (now Aon Center)—briefly the city's tallest building—brought considerable visibility to this PD.

An undeveloped portion of the PD near Lake Shore Drive was eventually transformed into a golf course and then sold to other developers for new residential high-rises. The success of Illinois Center paved the way for Cityfront Center, a 41-acre PD on the opposite side of the Chicago River.

Dearborn Park: From Railroads to Residences.

During the early 1970s, much of the inner ring around Chicago's Loop, especially to the south and west, was marred by aging manufacturing plants, warehouses, and abandoned rail lines. This underutilized land offered opportunities to build multi-family housing complexes with indoor parking and abundant

Contemporary view of Dearborn Park. (Chaddick collection)

open space—features that later became commonplace in upscale urban developments.

Out of such opportunities grew Dearborn Park, one of the first major residential projects south of downtown. This massive undertaking gradually transformed the venerable Dearborn Station, a masonry building built in 1885, and its adjacent 51 acres of railroad yards into a modern residential area.

The movement to reclaim this land drew its strength from the sponsorship and financial support of

28 Chicago business leaders and their firms, including Ferdinand Kramer (Draper & Kramer), Thomas G. Ayers (Commonwealth Edison), and Philip Klutznick (Urban Investment & Development Co.). The mix of building types that emerged attracted people of all ages. Phase I of the project, which encompassed some 900 units, included The Oaks (subsidized housing for seniors), along with townhomes and a mix of mid-rise and high-rise apartment buildings.

The old terminal building was attractively restored and used for restaurants, shops, professional offices, and community organizations. A derelict rail yard behind the station was converted into a park. The street system, through the use of cul-de-sacs with an internal grid, created a pedestrian-friendly and safe environment. Some likened this development to a "suburb in the city."

Ten years after it opened in the late 1970s, the demographic composition of Dearborn Park and its surrounding buildings was 54% Caucasian and 40% African-American, making it a prototype for a city that had struggled greatly with racial segregation. By the early 1990s, the completed first phase of Dearborn Park and the expanding Dearborn Park II development to its south were home to 10,000 residents. Dearborn Park is today an anchor to the city's booming South Loop district.

With guidance from Thomas G. Ayers, president of Commonwealth Edison Company and chairman of the board of Dearborn Park Corporation, Mayor Jane Byrne inserts the American flag into the last bucket of concrete to be hoisted atop a 27-story building. This topping-out ceremony in 1979 symbolized the completion of the first phase of the $150 million Dearborn Park development. (Bernard E. Ury Associates)

neighborhoods on the North Side, where huge, high-density apartment buildings are multiplying." Gapp believed that the city could draw upon the experiences of New York, which had recently revised its zoning law to discourage the construction of high-rise housing in low-rise neighborhoods.[7]

Yet the changes Daley envisioned generated a firestorm of criticism. Chaddick warned that the proposed ordinance would make "zoning czars out of the City planning commissioner and the Chicago Plan Commission."[8] Jared Shlaes made known his vehement opposition to any requirement that, by lowering the minimum size thresholds, would force a great number of developments to become PDs. "I scarcely need to remind you of the horrors which result when, through carelessness, indifference, or perfidy, excessive power is entrusted to individuals and groups unworthy ... of trust," he testified before the Plan Commission.[9] Metropolitan Housing & Planning Council vice president John R. Womer was similarly skeptical, commenting to a *Chicago Daily News* reporter that "planned development will supercede the zoning process."[10] Planning commissioner Hill responded to skeptics with the reminder that developers would still need to observe density regulations established in the zoning ordinance.[11]

These concerns notwithstanding, Daley's proposal garnered the support of many members of the City Council, who wanted new tools to manage development in their wards, as well as the backing of certain developers who, wanting more flexibility, hoped that the city would give them the option of using the PD approach even for projects involving less than two acres of land. Neighborhood groups also voiced their support of the measure.[12] After six months of study and compromise, a significantly modified PD ordinance passed the City Council in February, 1974. The final version *required* developers to follow PD guidelines for the following types of developments:

1. Single-family housing covering seven or more acres;
2. Multi-family or mixed-use developments in *low-density areas* covering two or more acres or exceeding 100 feet in height or containing 100 or more dwelling units;
3. Multi-family or mixed-use developments in *high-density areas* covering

two or more acres, exceeding a height of 120 feet, or containing 150 or more dwelling units;

4. In the densest business and commercial districts, any building surpassing 600 feet in height.

A new provision gave high-rise developers the *option* of using Planned Development on sites as small as one acre. All PDs—regardless of their size—had to be completed within 20 years.

These rules, while less stringent than those initially proposed, achieved the apparent goal of bringing more development under the purview of the planning department. In the five years before the adoption of the guidelines in 1974, the city approved 57 planned developments; over the next five years, the number rose to 84. As would be expected, the average size of PDs also fell markedly, dropping from 12.3 acres to 8.9 acres during the same period.[13] The new policy, coupled with the City Council's adoption of the Lakefront Protection Ordinance in 1973 (discussed in Chapter 10), greatly enhanced the city's control over large-scale construction projects initiated by private developers.

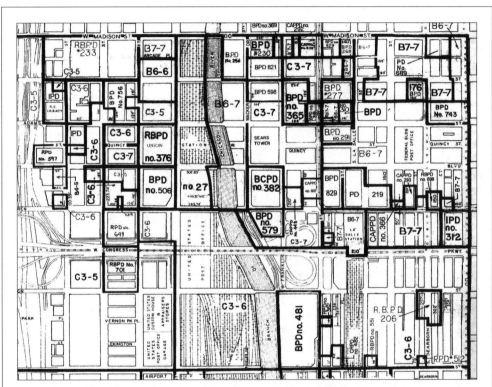

This zoning map published in 2002 shows a preponderance of PDs near the western edge of the Loop business district. The prefixes before the letters "PD" refer to the type of land uses in that development, with B, C, and R referring to business, commercial, and residential, respectively. (City of Chicago)

Both developers and the city used PDs to their maximum advantage. Developers not only devised creative site plans with a mix of land uses but also negotiated with the city for added density to maximize the return on their investment. The city, on the other hand, used the flexibility afforded by PDs to encourage developers to support its planning goals. By the end of the 1980s, the list of PDs had grown to include such prominent mixed-use projects as Dearborn Park, Illinois Center, Presidential Towers, and River City.

A resource for both developers and the city, Planned Development made possible many developments that might not otherwise have occurred. Thomas Rosenberg used PDs, for example, to build several mixed-density, low-income developments in the early 1980s, when the real-estate market was in a slump. Former mayor Jane Byrne recently observed: "interest rates were 22½ percent almost my whole term. To get any kind of construction going and people working ... it was like a gift."[14]

Developer John Buck used PD to build a 40-story office tower at 190

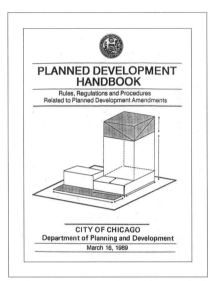

S. LaSalle Street at a time when downtown development was virtually at a standstill. Although Buck received FAR bonuses for upper-story setbacks, underground parking, and an arcade, which the city waived (see Chapter 9 for discussion of the waiver technique), he needed an additional increase in FAR to meet the commitments made to an anchor tenant and render the project financially viable.[15] Former planning commissioner Ira Bach, serving as Mayor Washington's development advisor, helped orchestrate a deal, persuading City Hall to increase the maximum allowable FAR by six on the premise that this world-class building (which was designed by famed architects Philip Johnson and John Burgee) would enhance LaSalle Street and bring distinction to Chicago.

PDs remained a heavily used strategic tool after Richard M. Daley was elected mayor in 1989. Daley encouraged the Department of Planning to actively manage development, especially large-scale projects, and appointed David Mosena as his planning commissioner. Mosena and his deputy commissioner, Richard Wendy, brought new talent to City Hall and established more rigorous requirements for PD approval, including compliance with detailed site plans and building elevations. The city also began to impose deadlines for starting construction.

These policies did not daunt development: the office-building development boom of the late 1980s and the subsequent downtown residential boom added greatly to the number of PDs awaiting city approval and put a burden on staff. Between 1989 and 1993, the city approved more than 100 PDs. Nevertheless, some developers found the PD timeline and demands onerous and voiced complaints that PD approval often required costly changes to the site plan. Developers holding this view often preferred to find sites where they could build "as of right"—that is, by adhering to the existing zoning.[16] The rising cost of land, the desire to maximize the rate-of-return, and the complexity of building design, however, often necessitated following the PD approach.

Daley's staff aggressively negotiated the fine points of site plans and reached agreements concerning an assortment of issues related to design, density, landscaping, and traffic generation.[17] City Hall also used the PD approach to gain greater control over the types of amenities that would be eligible for FAR bonuses (see Chapter 9). Under as-of-right zoning, developers automatically received bonuses for providing amenities like setbacks and plazas, even when they were poorly designed. With PDs, the city could work with the developer to assure that these and other amenities would benefit the surrounding neighborhood.

Due to the strength of the real-estate market during the early and middle 1990s, developers were often willing to agree to the demands placed on them by the city in order to keep projects moving. The city, in turn, used its leverage to gradually become more forceful in its demands. This leverage expanded when the city adopted the text of its new zoning ordinance in 2004, making the PD approach mandatory for an even wider range of projects than in the past (see discussion in Chapter 13).

It is probably not an exaggeration to say that the rise of Planned Development is the most significant change in Chicago's zoning policy since the 1923 ordinance. In 1973, the *Chicago Daily News* printed an article probing the question of whether the city's policies toward PDs were fundamentally changing its urban character. Today, most observers would argue, the answer is "yes."[18]

CHAPTER 7
Protecting the Neighborhood:
Downzoning and Density Controls

Within a decade, some of the optimism that had surrounded the zoning amendments of 1957 had been replaced with dismay. Along the north lakefront, tensions escalated as the construction of new high-density, residential developments—apartment towers and the so-called "four-plus-ones"—began to alter the character of many neighborhoods. Citizen groups opposed these developments and fought aggressively to protect their communities. The resulting push for more restrictive zoning ushered in an era of extensive community involvement in neighborhood planning and zoning.

With hindsight, it is easy to question why the 1957 zoning ordinance was so permissive, seeming to invite high-density development in certain residential areas without regard to the surroundings. A fair critique, however, requires examining the forces that were driving the decisions about urban policy at the time—namely the expectation of an imminent surge in population and the widespread belief in the value of modernization. For many, the prevailing belief was that modern living meant high-rise living. Charles Swibel, a backer of Marina City, stated the case: "Virtually all new construction in the city is high-rise ... [A]ll large centers of population must plan for accommodating an ever increasing number of people within a prescribed land area."[1]

Population forecasts in the mid-1950s predicted dramatic growth, something the city took to heart. Planners saw an opportunity to establish Chicago as a world-class city and sought to promote high-density office and residential development. As a result, a zoning ordinance rooted in the idea of rising population density was forged. The assumption that

Residential towers between Division Street and North Avenue create an almost continuous wall along North Lake Shore Drive, as shown above on May 21, 1997. During the 1960s and early 1970s, several dozen high-rises sprouted up in this neighborhood, dwarfing older buildings and obstructing views of the lake. Despite eventual downzoning of much of the Gold Coast, most of the property along Lake Shore Drive shown here retained R8 zoning through 2004. (Photo by Lawrence Okrent)

the city's population would grow, however, proved false—instead, the city suffered massive losses in population during the 1960s and 1970s. Much as the 1923 ordinance had zoned too much land for apartments in general, the 1957 code had allocated too much land for high-rise apartments. Long stretches of the north lakefront were zoned to encourage high-density housing.

Despite the decline in population, demand for high-rise housing along the lakefront grew stronger, especially on the North Side, ending a long drought in large-scale residential construction. During the 1940s, less than a half-dozen tall apartment buildings (12 stories or higher) were added to the city's neighborhoods. In the decades that followed, the number skyrocketed, surpassing 170 in the 1950s and 180 during the 1960s.[2] Dozens of apartment towers sprouted up along North Lake Shore Drive

while many more were built in the residential blocks nearby, dwarfing existing structures and bringing burdensome traffic congestion to once homey streets.

The market for older homes was strong in the same neighborhoods that were in the throes of new high-rise construction. Buying and renovating older buildings became fashionable, as did living in older apartment buildings near the lakefront. Fueling these trends were not only rising incomes and growing awareness of historic preservation, but also the conservation programs with low-interest loans launched by the city as part of urban renewal in Hyde Park and Lincoln Park. By the mid-1970s, banks were on board, making rehabilitation loans across large parts of the city.

Many residents who lived in those homes and small apartment buildings felt threatened by the surge in high-density construction and rallied

Outlooks of Optimism

Population forecasts were exceedingly optimistic during the 1950s. Harry Chaddick's team conducted its work at a time when the Chicago Plan Commission predicted that the city's population would rise by more than 300,000 by 1965.[3]

Even when projections were lowered to account for greater movement from the city to the suburbs (the number of residents peaked at about 3.7 million in the early 1950s), forecasters didn't anticipate the impending drop in population. The 1959 population forecast predicted that the population would rise to about 4.2 million by 1980.[4] Although the 1960 census confirmed that the city was in the midst of a precipitous drop in population, the 1964 forecast nonetheless anticipated that the city would add hundreds of thousands of new residents over the following 15 years.

The reality was quite different. Between 1950 and 1990, the city lost more than 600,000 residents. By 1990, Chicago's population was only 2.8 million, about one-third less than the number anticipated a quarter-century before. Yet the zoning ordinance continued to encourage high-rise, high-density development.

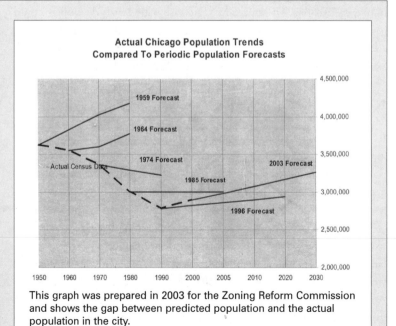

This graph was prepared in 2003 for the Zoning Reform Commission and shows the gap between predicted population and the actual population in the city.

to preserve their neighborhoods. With much of the densest development confined to a few select areas, there was an alarming rise in noise and traffic congestion on some streets. During the 1960s, lakefront neighborhoods reportedly enjoyed a net gain of about 21,000 housing units, while the rest of the city suffered a net loss of 40,000 units.[5] Lake Shore Drive had become a wall of apartment towers, and Sheridan Road was taking on the same character. By the early 1970s, aldermen along the north lakefront were responding to community pressure for more protective zoning.

Concerned citizens formed organizations around local quality-of-life issues with the goal of curbing the construction of high-rise buildings. These groups took aim at the zoning maps created in 1957, which had classified many blocks on the basis of the largest existing buildings, opening the door to high-rises on streets with single-family homes and three-flats. On some streets, tall buildings were built mid-block, with homes or two-flats on both sides. The ease with which developers could get amendments to "upzone" land adjoining such higher-density parcels added to the perception that the zoning ordinance was not doing its job. Some neighborhoods witnessed a virtual "domino effect."

NEIGHBORHOOD DOWNZONING

In the early 1970s, Lake View and Lincoln Park organizations were exerting pressure on planning commissioner Lewis Hill to curb development poised to dramatically change the densities and land-use patterns in their neighborhoods.[6] The push to ban high-rise construction was a particularly strong issue in Lake View, home to Wrigley Field, where the Campaign to Control High Rises alleged that developers were playing "monopoly" with Chicago neighborhoods. This organization and others were particularly eager to rid their neighborhoods of R7 and R8 zoning districts, which allowed for buildings far taller than most existing structures.[7] In April, 1974, Hill told an audience in this neighborhood: "The mayor has told me we should aggressively pursue with you what can be done [to curb excessive increases in density and undesirable development]."[8]

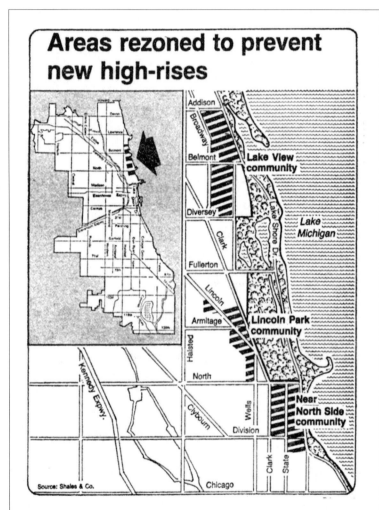

This map, created in 1979, shows the first neighborhoods to be downzoned on the north lakefront. (Chaddick collection)

The downzoning of Lake View moved forward on an ambitious timetable, with Daley himself agreeing to sponsor the necessary amendments.[9] By early 1975, eight amendments had been introduced in City Council to downzone portions of the 24-block area bounded by Diversey, Addison, Broadway, and the lakefront. Before the end of the year, the amendments had been approved. The amendment changed much of the zoning from R7 to the more restrictive R6 and R5 categories, which constituted 37 percent and 69 percent drops, respectively, in the maximum floor area ratio.

By the end of 1975, 48th Ward Alderman Dennis Block was pushing to downzone the area along Sheridan Road between Granville and Hollywood avenues, with the goal of restricting further high-rise development.[10] The Organization of the Northeast (ONE) led a public outcry over the loss of three-flats and six-flats, making the case that apartment towers brought congestion, traffic, and noise and fostered the deterioration of the housing stock. As a *Chicago Tribune* reporter noted, "If landlords know they eventually can sell off the land beneath low-rise housing for high-rise development, they will let existing structures deteriorate."[11] After the City Council approved Block's amendment, the downzoning phenomenon spread through the Uptown and Edgewater neighborhoods, affecting large swaths of land in the area bounded by Irving Park, Devon, Broadway, and the lake.

By this time, even Harry Chaddick, now Chairman of the Zoning Board of Appeals, considered the north lakefront to be "tremendously overzoned."[12] He worried that high-density residential buildings were chipping away at neighborhood character, overloading local services, and increasing traffic and parking congestion. Noting that 90 percent of the units built in the city in recent years had been built within a mile of the lake, Chaddick called in the mid-1970s for extensive downzoning of this area as well as other policies to encourage residential development to shift to other parts of the city.[13]

Yet the building boom continued, setting the stage for the rezoning of

A row of high-rises in the Edgewater neighborhood offers a striking backdrop to vehicular traffic at the northern end of Lake Shore Drive. Seven apartment towers, including the nearly identical Hollywood Towers (left), appeared on the 5700 block of Sheridan between 1961 and 1965. A zoning amendment eventually banned such high-rise construction in the area. (Courtesy of the American Planning Association)

This scene near the intersection of Division and LaSalle, circa 1972, shows the Old Town neighborhood at a time when high-rise apartment towers were rapidly replacing older, lower-rise buildings. Opponents of these towers charged that generous zoning fostered land speculation and reduced the incentive for owners of older buildings to maintain their property. (Note the boarded-up building on Division.) The City Council downzoned the area around this intersection in 1979. Today, the vacant parcel in the foreground is a Walgreens pharmacy. (Courtesy of the American Planning Association)

Martin Oberman, 43rd Ward alderman.

prestigious areas of Lincoln Park and Old Town in the 43rd Ward. By the late 1970s, Lincoln Park had a skyline rivaling that of smaller cities, boasting six residential buildings rising at least 20 stories and one—the massive Lincoln Park West—towering 39 floors.[14] Alderman Marty Oberman, who had been elected in 1975 with a mandate to halt the alarming rise in density in neighborhoods closest to the lake, attended dozens of community meetings while formulating a plan to curb high-rise development. During the summer of 1979, he proposed an amendment to downzone the east end of Lincoln Park between North and Armitage avenues and continuing north along Lincoln Avenue. The purpose of the downzoning, Oberman argued, was to maintain the best of "what is here now" and to protect residents from excessive congestion.[15]

The amendment, developed in cooperation with the Lincoln Park Conservation Association, the Mid-North Association, and the Old-Town Triangle Association, sailed through the City Council in October, 1979. Large areas along the lakefront were transformed from R7 and R8 to the more restrictive R5 and R6 categories. Due to the apparent success of these initiatives, still more leaders in lakefront neighborhoods turned to their aldermen with hopes of pushing similar zoning changes through the City Council.

The battle over density along the lakefront did more than affect the zoning maps. It empowered community organizations, broadened grassroots support for new controls on development, and raised awareness of the role of aldermen in the zoning process. The Lake View Citizens Council, the Park West Community Association, the Mid-North Association, Sheffield Neighbors, and the Wrightwood Neighbors Association (WNA) all became stronger and more visible amid the push to rezone more of the North Side.

The Wrightwood group, under the leadership of Allan Mellis, a resident planner nicknamed "the mayor of Lincoln Park," had particular success after preparing one of the first neighborhood plans of its kind for the city, giving the group considerable credibility with officials and developers.[16] Among WNA's most notable achievements was pioneering the practice of

Allan Mellis, Wrightwood Neighbors Association.

negotiating formal contracts with developers independently of City Hall. Such "development agreements" gave developers willing to commit to site plans that were consistent with neighborhood goals the benefit of WNA's support. This form of collective action proved highly effective and was eventually emulated in other parts of the city.

Alderman Edwin Eisendrath, who succeeded Oberman, carried on his predecessor's practice of confronting powerful developers in defense of neighborhood goals. Eisendrath was amenable to the construction of new townhomes and other lower-density housing in his neighborhood but minced no words about his stance on residential towers, telling a reporter in 1987 that "I want to make sure no new high-rises get built."[17]

THE BATTLE OVER FOUR-PLUS-ONES

High-rises were not the only source of controversy in the lakefront neighborhoods. There was also a backlash against so-called four-plus-one apartment buildings.

Citizens came out in droves to protest the construction of these boxy buildings, which exploded on the scene in the mid-to-late 1960s. Shoehorned into many residential blocks, four-plus-ones were built from lot

Several hundred "four-plus-ones" (a type of residential building with four floors of apartments atop a parking garage) were shoehorned into areas zoned R5 and higher during the early 1970s. These boxy and crowded buildings, which had a high proportion of efficiency units and generally the minimum required parking, triggered a great outcry in many neighborhoods on the north lakefront. The city amended the zoning ordinance in 1973 to discourage their construction. (Courtesy of the American Planning Association)

line to lot line and consisted of four floors of efficiency or one-bedroom apartments elevated on pylons or columns to allow parking at or below grade.[18] With the parking level (which was exempt from FAR calculations), these buildings stood five stories tall (hence their name, "four-plus-ones").

The on-street parking problem created by four-plus-ones was a lightning-rod issue. Far more of the tenants of apartment buildings owned cars than had been expected when the city drafted its parking regulations in the mid-1950s—a problem made worse by the high proportion of efficiency units in most four-plus-ones. Developers had to provide parking spaces for only 40 percent to 50 percent of such units, adding greatly to the competition for on-street parking.

Developers of four-plus-ones generally did not need zoning changes; these buildings were permitted in areas designated R5 and higher. Watchdog groups were aghast that these structures—dozens of units squeezed in where only a few had existed before—were becoming common in areas zoned R5 to R7. "The community is up in arms about this type of building," noted H. Patrick Feely of the Lincoln Park Conservation Association.[19] Indeed, the increase in density in some instances was astounding. In the late 1960s, a 126-unit four-plus-one built in the 400 block of West Barry, for example, replaced a building with 15 large family-style apartments. A 44-unit four-plus-one in the 600 block of West Arlington replaced two buildings containing just a handful of units.[20]

Mayor Richard J. Daley exercised little restraint in condemning these stark and uninviting buildings. "The immediate answer is rezoning the concerned areas," he announced during the summer of 1968.[21] Although Daley's recommendation was quickly dismissed as being impractical (the area that would need to be downzoned would be large, and there would be many nonconforming buildings as a result), the mayor continued to voice his concerns, as did influential neighborhood community leaders.[22]

Frustration over the city's lack of action on this front had escalated by 1969, when the South East Lake View Neighbors publicized an estimate that 48 four-plus-ones (37 already built and 11 under construction) would soon be scattered throughout the area bounded by Diversey, Irving Park, Broadway, and Sheridan. Dan Crowe, the organization's leader, called the buildings a "blighting time bomb" and complained that "we're trying to get rid of [urban slums] but are building new problems" by the construction of four-plus-ones.[23] In the early 1970s, the *Chicago Tribune* estimated that no fewer than 300 four-plus-ones had been built in the city, with the heaviest concentration in the Lake View and Edgewater neighborhoods.[24]

Neighborhood groups and concerned citizens gradually ratcheted up their pressure on City Hall, convincing many aldermen that four-plus-ones were bringing in transient populations and displacing families living in homes, two-flats, and three-flats. The Park West Community Association was particularly vocal about four-plus-ones and urged the city to enact a zoning law that would prevent increases in density on a block exceeding 25 percent. The association proposed that the city limit efficiencies to 25 percent of the units in a building and that it require one parking space for each unit.[25]

With both the mayor and neighborhood groups pushing for action, the City Council passed a sweeping measure on March 10, 1971, affecting districts zoned R4 and higher. In general, the ordinance mandated that developers provide one parking spot per dwelling unit, with no exceptions for efficiencies. (In large buildings in R6 through R8 districts, there was a one-to-one parking ratio up to a certain number of units; beyond this number, spaces were required for only 50 percent to 60 percent of the units.) The new measure also limited the percentage of efficiencies in a building, depending on the district, to between 20 percent and 50 percent of all units. Another change required that side yards be a designated percentage of the lot's width. Previously, districts zoned R5 and up had no such yard requirements.[26]

These requirements were strong medicine for the neighborhoods, effectively banning the construction of new four-plus-ones, but they were themselves controversial. Albert C. Hanna, vice-president of a major mortgage company, considered them unreasonable and arbitrary. There was "no rational support" for the heightened parking require-

Four-plus-one on East Briar Street. (Chaddick collection)

ments, Hanna noted in the *Chicago Tribune*, adding that the new rules were akin to "using a cannon to kill a fly."[27] He had a measure to repeal the new restrictions introduced in City Council in May, 1971, but it was sent to the Rules Committee and never came to the floor. A lawsuit by Hanna to force repeal was of no avail.[28]

John Buenz, an architect and planner, expressed technical concerns about the newly approved side-yard requirements, calling them "well intended" but "overkill."[29] Buenz believed that the requirements impeded not only four-plus-ones but also well-designed buildings on small parcels.[30] David Dubin, chairman of the Chicago chapter of the American Institute of Architects (AIA), argued that the parking requirements would force developers to "go underground" to get the extra space (greatly increasing costs). Although the AIA supported the effort to restrict four-plus-ones, it felt that the resulting regulation would have the unintended effect of hampering the construction of moderate- to high-rise buildings.[31]

This image of a three-flat was published by the city in 2002 to illustrate the problem of out-of-scale development. (City of Chicago)

Developers exerted intense pressure on the City Council to roll back some of its new regulations—a move that Alderman William S. Singer staunchly opposed. "They want to return to the old standards of build, build, build, and the public be damned," Singer told the *Chicago Daily News*.[32] The alderman accused four-plus-one developers of using "every square inch to build cubbyholes without regard to the problem of parking or other concerns."[33] Despite the objections, the City Council eventually struck a compromise and relaxed the new rules in accordance with amendments proposed by the mayor. Passed in July, 1971, these changes modestly reduced parking requirements (depending on the zoning district) and allowed up to 40 percent (rather than 30 percent) of all

units to be efficiencies in the R7 zoning districts. They also reduced the side-yard requirement. By this time, however, the construction of four-plus-ones had largely run its course, ending a period of great controversy in the lakefront neighborhoods.[34]

SPECIAL DISTRICTS: A NEW APPROACH TO NEIGHBORHOOD ZONING

The battles waged over density from the late 1960s to the late 1980s made apparent the need for new methods of dealing with developments that changed the character of neighborhoods. Dick Starr of Real Estate Research Corporation observed that the city needed an agreement between developers and residents on how to develop the "10 to 15 percent of the city" that was under pressure to develop.[35] Developer Thomas Rosenberg lamented that the system in place made "confrontation inevitable."[36]

The city studied the matter and issued a report whose vision differed radically from that prevalent in 1957. In *High-Rise High-Density, 1987,* the Mayor's Task Force on Neighborhood Land Use defended the downzoning trend. The report described the potential benefits of more restrictive zoning for River North, Streeterville, the neighborhoods near O'Hare Airport, and other areas in the midst of population growth. It echoed the sentiments of many neighborhood groups in its descriptions of the travails of traffic congestion, inappropriate mixing of land uses, the obstruction of views, and the overuse of public facilities.[37]

Appreciation also grew for the proposals offered by residents and grass-roots organizations to protect their neighborhoods from unwanted development. Recognizing that downzoning was a broad-brush approach that tended to be insensitive to qualities that made each neighborhood unique, the city looked for more contextual approaches to zoning and placed greater emphasis on negotiation, often serving as a mediator between the developer and the community.

By the late 1980s, the city had accumulated a great deal of experience in using negotiation to arrive at "site-specific" solutions to neighborhood problems and encouraging developers to create housing that would blend into the existing streetscape. Nevertheless, all recognized that there were limits to this approach. Due to the generous nature of the zoning ordinance, the city often had little leverage in negotiations. In addition, new issues arose as developers increasingly turned to sites along commercial streets and thoroughfares adjoining prestigious residential neighborhoods. Many neighborhoods witnessed the creation of new townhome enclaves and low-rise condominiums on properties vacated by retail businesses and industrial enterprises.

Pressure for residential development also shifted to areas of lower density, including neighborhoods far from the lake, dominated by a mix of two- or three-flats and single-family homes. Some observers applauded these trends for bringing more modern housing to parts of the city that had not seen significant investment in a half-century; others complained that the new buildings were intrusive and out of character with the surroundings. The concerns of some groups extended to new issues related to architecture, aesthetics, and the "feel" of particular streets. Their desire was to preserve the neighborhood without stifling new investment.

The city responded by creating a large number of special districts with rules tailored to the ambience of the area. These districts were typically used to impose restrictions on matters related to building height, the placement of doorways, the placement of patios, and the dimensions of yards. Almost all of the special districts created in the R4 zoning districts of Lincoln Park and Lake View limited buildings to 3½ stories and 38 feet.

Chicago's first two residential special districts, adopted on October 5, 1994, involved parts of Norwood Park, a community on the far Northwest Side. Developers there were demolishing ranch homes and replacing them with two newly built homes on the same lot. A third special district was designated on March 9, 1995, in a portion of Lake View (see adjacent map), where many old residential buildings were being razed to make room for taller and bulkier buildings. By the end of the decade, there were 23 special districts in the city.

In creating special districts, Chicago borrowed a page from the zoning

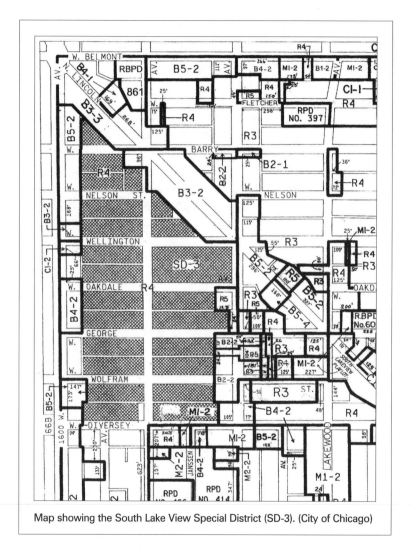

Map showing the South Lake View Special District (SD-3). (City of Chicago)

glossary of New York, which had long relied on this approach, largely to preserve certain historic areas. New York pioneered the use of the technique by creating an overlay for its Theater District in 1967, followed by special districts designed to protect Fifth Avenue and Lincoln Center. In contrast, Chicago tended to use special districts to protect lower-density neighborhoods with distinct types of character.

As the city gained experience with special districts, the limitations of this strategy became more widely apparent. This strategy added to the complexity of the city's zoning maps, generated staunch opposition from developers, and was only a piecemeal solution to a much larger problem. Although large swaths of the north lakefront and the Gold Coast (see discussion in Chapter 8) had either been downzoned or made part of a special district, most of the city was still governed by zoning maps and rules that had changed little since 1957. Recognizing that the zoning ordinance (with its heavy reliance on floor area ratios to control bulk) was still insensitive to the contextual qualities of many neighborhoods, the city looked to rewrite the entire document. In 2000, it took the important interim step of establishing height limits in certain residential zoning districts, thus curbing some of the emerging building styles that many neighborhoods found objectionable.

As the push to overhaul the zoning ordinance gathered momentum, Mayor Richard M. Daley reaffirmed his belief that "Chicago must continue to work to preserve, protect, and strengthen the rich character and diversity of our neighborhoods."[38] In 2004, the city adopted a comprehensive set of zoning changes that rendered most special districts superfluous and greatly shifted the parameters of the debate about high-density development. As we will see in Chapter 13, this move earned the applause of neighborhood leaders who had awaited such changes since the senior Daley was in power more than 30 years before.

CHAPTER 8

Zoning and
In-Town Living

By the early 1960s, high-rise downtown living was no longer a promise of the future; it was a reality. Promoted by the city and facilitated by the generous designations of the zoning map, sleek apartment towers sprouted up, in some instances towering hundreds of feet over the commercial buildings beside them. The rising demand for residential units within or near the central business district created problems not foreseen in 1957. Civic groups warned that these towers threatened to create a congested "skyscraper jungle" that would interfere with commerce. In response, the city enacted zoning changes that were assumed to be temporary; instead they remained on the books for more than 40 years.

High-rise residential construction in the downtown area was not on the agenda of the architects of the 1957 code. Most of the Central Area had been bereft of any significant residential population since the Great Fire. Throughout the first half of the twentieth century, the number of people living in prime business and commercial zones in or near the central business district totaled, at most, a few thousand.[1] Some hotels had permanent residents, but there were no large residential buildings within the "iron-bound" Loop created by the elevated transit lines.

To be sure, there were large apartment buildings in the Gold Coast, near the North Michigan Avenue commercial district. In 1912, famed architect Benjamin Marshall built the curving 999 N. Lake Shore Drive, followed in 1915 by "The Breakers," an elegant residential building at 199 E. Lake Shore Drive. These were not typical rental buildings with high turnover. Rather, they were exclusive co-ops with apartments owned by elite individuals and families.

The close proximity of tall residential and commercial structures north of the Chicago River, while an admired feature of the area today, raised fears about the creation of a "skyscraper jungle" in the 1960s. There were no parking requirements and density limits on apartment towers appearing in high-intensity nonresidential zoning districts at the time. This photograph, taken on July 5, 2001, shows the density of development between the Hancock Center and the Aon Center (at far right). (Photo by Lawrence Okrent)

In the 1920s, the new two-tier bridge across the river at Michigan Avenue eased access to the area and stimulated the construction of more apartment towers. Among the most notable of these were Marshall's 209 E. Lake Shore Drive building (1926) and the neighboring Drake Tower Apartments (1929) near the foot of Michigan Avenue, which created a striking "wall" of buildings that is today the East Lake Shore Drive Historic District.[2] At 900 N. Michigan Avenue, a unique, elegant apartment building designed by Jarvis Hunt opened in 1926. Many remember this graceful edifice for the fashionable Jacques restaurant housed in its interior courtyard.

Taller apartment buildings also began to appear along portions of Walton and Chestnut streets. Although these buildings were precursors to Streeterville's transformation into a high-rise community, new residential development was slow to spread south of Chicago Avenue. The land use survey of 1943 showed that only about one percent of the area bounded by Chicago Avenue, Halsted Street, Roosevelt Road, and Lake Michigan was devoted to residential use.[3]

In 1947, developer Arthur Rubloff displayed his unbridled optimism about the future of North Michigan Avenue and the areas surrounding it. Promising to make the avenue the "last word" in offices, stores, and apartment living, Rubloff invested heavily along the entire corridor, which he famously called "the Magnificent Mile." His plan included major residential development on underutilized land zoned for commercial and manufacturing uses east of Michigan Avenue. Along the north bank of the Chicago River, Rubloff envisioned a massive, mixed-use project called Fort Dearborn.

Although Fort Dearborn never came to fruition, much of Rubloff's vision for the area was gradually realized. By the mid-1950s, fine shops, office buildings, and restaurants lined the Magnificent Mile, making it indeed worthy of its name. With the area's rising prestige came more apartments catering to affluent individuals. In 1951, the area to the east was distinguished by the appearance of two 26-story, steel-frame apartment towers designed by Ludwig Mies van der Rohe at 860–880 N. Lake Shore

Completed in 1964 on land that had been zoned for commercial use, Marina City (at left) brought modern residential development ever closer to the heart of the central business district. Marina City's extensive parking spaces and boat docks (both visible in this photo) made it attractive to downtown professionals. The developer of the Executive House (far right) also had an interest in providing rental apartments but opted to make the building a hotel instead. (Chicago Historical Society)

Two Pioneering Residential Developments in the Central Area

Outer Drive East. (Photo by J. Kearney)

Outer Drive East: Living on the Lake. Developer Jerrold Wexler encountered legal difficulties in acquiring a lakefront site off the Outer Drive zoned for commercial use for a proposed residential development in 1957. Eager to see the project move forward, Mayor Richard J. Daley instructed the planning department to do "everything possible" to make the development work.[4] After the city secured state legislation resolving shoreline ownership disputes between it and the Illinois Central Railroad and extended Randolph Street eastward, this innovative development was set to proceed.

When completed in 1962, the 40-story Outer Drive East (400 E. Randolph) was one of the largest apart-

ment buildings in the world, boasting more than 900 units and incorporating shopping, recreation facilities and an up-scale restaurant. Its proximity to the lake and Grant Park, the Prudential Building, and the Loop made it appealing to downtown professionals. After standing alone for decades, it is today adjacent to a cluster of high-rises known as Lake Shore East.

Marina City: The "City within a City." Circular building forms were a trademark of architect Bertrand Goldberg, whose work includes Marina City, River City, and the Raymond Hilliard Homes public housing complex at 30 W. Cermak. In 1959, Goldberg created a design for the two "corncob towers" of Marina City on land zoned C3 (commercial manufacturing). The proposal incorporated more than 800 apartments, offices, movie theaters, boat slips, restaurants, a health club, and other amenities.

The project sparked a vigorous debate about the area's ability to handle high-rise residential development, culminating in the so-called "July 13 Amendments" of 1962 (which we discuss later in this chapter). Completed in 1964, Marina City's 58-story towers were the tallest apartment buildings in the world and also the tallest reinforced-concrete buildings.[5]

Goldberg hoped the towers would provide the impetus for further residential construction downtown and spark a renaissance along the river.

Marina City. (Chaddick collection)

Although such a renaissance did not immediately occur, the development of Marina City would indeed prove to be a watershed in Chicago planning history. Attracting many young professionals and empty nesters, it showcased the cosmopolitan lifestyle available to those living in the greater Loop. Its presence stimulated major efforts to revitalize the riverfront and paved the way for the later residential development in the area.

Drive. Two more of the architect's famed "glass houses" followed at 900–910 N. Lake Shore, showcasing the splendors of downtown living.

Despite this rising tide of residential development, little public attention was given to policies that would either provide for or prevent apartment buildings in areas zoned for high-intensity business and commercial use. The city published a plan for the Central Area in 1958 that proposed the "creation of new residential communities ... with special emphasis on the needs of [those] who wish to live ... close to the heart of the city." This plan envisioned high-rises with efficiency apartments on the Near North Side and recommended that the city support the effort to build Fort Dearborn. However, being a concept plan rather than an officially adopted working plan, this publication did not prompt the city to revisit the newly revised zoning ordinance.[6]

The consequences of such inaction were abundantly clear during the early 1960s. Although most of the apartment towers built in earlier periods were some distance away from prime commercial areas, residential towers now began appearing in bustling business and commercial districts. The 38-story building at 777 N. Michigan and the 33-story Michigan Terrace at 535 N. Michigan showcased the opportunities for residential development on the Magnificent Mile, while near the river, the creation of Marina City and Outer Drive East were further signs of the changing times. The *Chicago Sun-Times* reported in 1962 that apartment towers built near downtown had "caught the city by surprise."[7]

CALLS FOR ACTION AT CITY HALL

In the midst of the construction boom, civic leaders began to fear that tall residential towers would create congestion and, ultimately, "Manhattanize" the Central Area. Many considered the absence of minimum parking requirements or density limits for apartment buildings in high-intensity business and commercial districts to be a serious loophole. Thomas Nicholson, attorney for the Metropolitan Housing and Planning Council, called the absence of residential density standards in the

Ban On 'Skyscraper Jungle' OKd

A *Chicago Sun-Times* headline from June 22, 1962.

downtown area an "oversight" and went so far as to suggest it was tantamount to anarchy.[8] Clashes over noise, parking, traffic, and other issues, some feared, would stifle commerce in the Central Area.

The potential for conflict between users of commercial and residential space was an issue that many believed demanded City Hall action.[9] Not only would residential structures make less land available for commercial uses, they would also attract a permanent population that would likely demand more extensive services and more restrictive zoning. Such a residential population could pressure the city to provide schools, parks, grocery stores, and other amenities in an area that had traditionally been oriented to serve the needs of business.[10]

Marina City was a case in point. Just a block from the Loop, the cylindrical towers (still under construction at the time) were right across the river from prime office space. The complex was designed for both upper and middle-income tenants, including families with young children. Its riverfront site and boat docks seemed to suggest the possibility that the industrial waterway was becoming a recreational attraction. Marina City stood out from its surroundings; never before had the city seen residential development of this scale so close to the heart of the city.

Downzoning was not a solution to these apparent problems. Nor did the city want to prohibit close-in residential living; increasing urbanity was part of its overall growth plan. Amid escalating public concern, the City Council took the more practical step of amending the zoning regulations governing high-intensity commercial areas to set minimum standards on residential construction. On July 13, 1962, new rules took effect that applied to these zoning districts the density controls and parking requirements already in place for the highest-density residential zoning district (R8).[11] City officials considered these measures, termed the "July 13

Nelson Forrest, president of the Greater North Michigan Avenue Association.

amendments," precautionary steps until a formal investigation of residential high-rises in the downtown area could be conducted.[12]

The new regulations applied to most of the area between Division Street and Roosevelt Road, including the area east of Michigan Avenue occupied by the Illinois Central tracks. A minimum of 115 square feet of lot area was required for each dwelling unit, regardless of its size. Parking was required for 40 percent of all dwelling units, regardless of their size. This was slightly less burdensome than R8 zoning, which required parking for 60 percent of all dwelling units except for efficiencies, where the requirement was 40 percent.

The reaction from the development community was intense, especially with regard to the parking regulations. Many felt these regulations would stand in the way of much-needed investment in the Central Area and accelerate the loss of retail and corporate jobs.[13] Nelson Forrest, spokesman for the Greater North Michigan Avenue Association, claimed that this would stifle development of new residential units.[14] The organization warned that the limits on density would reduce the number of units in new apartment buildings by 30 to 40 percent.

These concerns added urgency to the study released by Jack Meltzer Associates in 1963. Meltzer, the principal of the firm who later directed the Center for Urban Studies at the University of Chicago, assembled a team of experts to study the future of downtown residential land uses, supervised by Norman Elkin, an urban development specialist and former city staffer.

Meltzer's study, sponsored by eight local business and civic associations, provided a blueprint for residential development within or near the central business district.[15] The study urged the city to adopt new planning tools, including "daylight performance standards" for all development and "vertical zoning controls" for air-rights development. At the same time, it recommended an outright prohibition on residential development within the "iron-bound" Loop to prevent "a dispersion of primary CBD functions" such as office and retail land uses. In effect, the study legitimized the view that residential development in the greater Loop area needed to be part of the city's long-range plan.

The authors supported the parking regulations imposed in 1962 but considered the new limits on density "an unnecessary deterrent to the policy of encouraging residential development in the Central Area." Their view was that "Density controls discourage residential development on economic grounds; if such development is to be discouraged, it should be on environmental grounds." At the same time, the study warned that "FAR alone does not constitute sufficient assurance of achieving desired environmental objectives." The authors encouraged the city to move away from simple density controls and develop more comprehensive approaches that took into account the effects of proposed high-rises on light, air, views, privacy, and open space.[16]

Despite these well-articulated conclusions, the City Council reportedly voted down a proposal to remove any of the July, 1962, amendments in 1963. City officials regarded Meltzer's recommendation calling for the adoption of a daylight performance standard as being too complicated and beyond the level of technical competence of city staff. As the years passed, however, conflict between the occupants of existing high-rises and the developers of new residential towers over the issue of the loss of views, shadows, and privacy became commonplace. Today, these issues are serious concerns to city planners.

Jack Meltzer, principal, Jack Meltzer Associates.

As time passed, it was clear Nelson Forrest's dire predictions about the future of residential development were unfounded and criticism of the amendments gradually dissipated. More residential towers appeared in Streeterville and in the Gold Coast, while the completion of the John Hancock Center in 1969 added hundreds more luxury units to the Magnificent Mile.

By the early 1970s, promoting residential development in high-intensity business and commercial districts in the Central Area had become a high-profile city goal. In its *Chicago 21* plan, the city anticipated massive residential development south of the Loop, which was gradually fulfilled by Dearborn Park and other mixed-use projects built on commercially zoned land that had fallen into disuse. North of the river, the opening of McClurg Court Center in 1971 added hundreds of units to an area zoned predominately for commercial uses, while the completion of Water Tower Place in 1976 insured that mixed-use development on the Magnificent Mile was here to stay. Like the adjacent Hancock Center, Water Tower Place provided luxury apartments, high-end shopping, and offices under the same roof and was a catalyst for additional residential developments on land previously envisioned for business and commercial use. In 1977, an apartment tower opened in the shadow of the Wrigley Building at 405 N. Wabash, and three years later, Chicago's famous Furniture Mart at 680 N. Lake Shore Drive was converted into elegant condominiums.

Developers used a variety of strategies to meet the demand for housing units in large-scale developments. Some chose the Planned Development route, which required that they negotiate with the city on bulk, density, parking, and other issues. Others pushed for amendments to the zoning map or looked for sites already suitably zoned.

GOLD COAST LIVING

Much development in this era gravitated toward the Gold Coast, where most of the land was already zoned for high-density residential use. By

This portion of North Michigan Avenue (circa 1993) was one of two corridors in the Central Area that witnessed extensive residential development during the early 1960s. This area was zoned for high-intensity business use until 2004, when the city introduced its new "DX" category to encourage mixed-use development. (Photo by Dennis McClendon, Courtesy of the American Planning Association)

the mid-1960s, grand apartments in turn-of-the-century buildings were being swept away for huge towers containing 200 studio and one-bedroom apartments. An apartment hotel with a lively night spot was built on sedate Astor Street, and another was proposed nearby (see inset box).

The changing character of the Gold Coast was a flashpoint for controversy and became the impetus for significant downzoning proposals that sent shock waves through the development community. Jared Shlaes, a consultant representing developers, was a spirited foe of downzoning

Apartment Hotels: An Illustrative Tale

The saga of Chicago's apartment hotels underscores how changing lifestyles and attitudes toward various types of land use can create unanticipated zoning problems. Once catering to people of all incomes, apartment hotels gradually lost their luster and became a loophole for savvy developers.

Apartment hotels have a rich history in Chicago. Dating from the 1920s, these buildings differed from traditional apartments by providing maid service, a concierge, and usually shops, restaurants, and other amenities for their residents. Offering efficiencies and often one- and two-bedroom suites, many of these buildings were home to well-heeled families, single persons, and empty nesters.

Motorists driving along the lakefront years ago found apartment hotels in many prominent and prestigious locations. The Webster and the Belden-Stratford apartment hotels faced Lincoln Park, the Windermere faced Jackson Park, and the Belmont Hotel looked out over Belmont Harbor. These institutions, anchors of their neighborhoods, all boasted popular restaurants and ground-floor shops.

Not all apartment hotels were so grand. Many were of a smaller scale and housed people of modest

The Belden-Stratford, an apartment hotel. (Chaddick collection)

means. Some were akin to the single-room-occupancy accommodations (SROs) of today. Few apartment hotels provided on-site parking.

Through the mid-1950s, all apartment hotels were treated in the same way as commercial hotels in the

zoning ordinance. Nevertheless, there was recognition that apartment hotels were less threatening to the ambience of residential areas than their commercial counterparts. In 1957, a zoning change made a formal distinction between the two and permitted apartment hotels (but not commercial hotels) in areas zoned R4 and higher. A property would be designated an apartment hotel only if at least half of all residents were permanent.

Increasing car ownership and shortages of on-street parking eventually created problems in many neighborhoods served by apartment hotels. As the construction of new high-rise apartment towers overwhelmed the supply of available garage space and on-street parking, shoppers as well as people out to enjoy the nightlife had no place to park. To help alleviate these problems, the city in 1959 took a notable step toward limiting the density of new residential buildings, passing an amendment limiting efficiency units to 50 percent of the units in areas zoned R4 to R8. Nevertheless, the amendment made an exception for apartment hotels and did nothing to address the nuisance issues associated with ground-floor shops and services in these hotels.

and believed that the limits on development being proposed were "far more drastic than good planning would allow," claiming that they "chopped away at the development potential of precisely those lakefront areas on the North Side where we have the best chance of getting much

needed new rental and condominium housing."[17]

The City Council apparently disagreed and approved a Gold Coast downzoning amendment on August 16, 1979. The measure effectively banned further construction of high-rises in the area bounded by Division

As the value of land rose, it was only a matter of time before developers grew interested in constructing more apartment hotels. A 1961 amendment redefined apartment hotels to require their having at least 90 percent permanent residents in order to avoid problems of transients in residential areas. With other issues still unresolved, however, the construction of new apartment hotels proved controversial. In the Gold Coast, the Astor Tower Hotel was the source of particular neighborhood concern when it opened in 1963. This 25-story building, designed by noted architect Bertrand Goldberg, dwarfed neighboring properties. On its lower level, a chic restaurant called Maxim's eventually became a popular disco, shattering the tranquility of Astor Street.

More controversy erupted in 1968, when a developer announced a plan for a 24-story apartment hotel at the corner of State and Scott, a prime location in the heart of the Gold Coast on the edge of the Rush Street nightlife district. Nearby business owners were incensed. "By using the phony apartment hotel classification, the builder gets around the limitation on efficiencies. He gets more units in the building, too … The cash register rings twice extra," complained Nelson Forrest.[18]

In 1969, the city again amended the zoning ordi-

The Astor Tower, formerly an apartment hotel. (Chaddick collection)

nance to minimize the number of efficiencies in new apartment buildings, limiting them to 50 percent of

the units in buildings located in the R6 through R8 districts. This time, no exceptions were made for apartment hotels. Although developers of efficiency units had previously enjoyed the benefits of substantially lower ratios of required parking spots to dwelling units, the city eliminated or scaled back these benefits, requiring spaces for 100 percent of efficiency units in R4 and R5 zoning districts, 50 percent in R6, and 40 percent in R7 and R8 districts.

Despite these measures, the concern over apartment hotels did not fully abate. In 1976, Zoning Administrator Harry L. Manley pointed to the apartment hotel as a persistent problem, noting that its definition was not based on a distinct type of land use but rather on contractual relationships between tenants and businesses. Aware of the difficulty of making a distinction between permanent and transient residents, property owners exploited the ambiguity by renaming both rental and condominium buildings as apartment hotels in order to provide shopping, restaurants, and other services on the ground floor.

Today, this loophole is gone: the city abolished its land-use category for apartment hotels with the comprehensive zoning revisions of 2004. Some apartment hotels today still offer rental housing; others have been converted to condominiums or become SROs.

Jared Shlaes, opponent of downzoning.

Street, North Avenue, Lake Shore Drive, and Clark Street, an area that had seen construction of more than 50 buildings exceeding 12 stories over the previous 20 years.[19] Generating fierce opposition from the development community, this amendment and others affecting the Near North neighborhoods set off an avalanche of criticism about the city's approach to dealing with concerns about density.

As the debate over density controls in the Gold Coast swirled, developers warned that further downzoning would choke off new housing construction and depress property values, as well as threaten the growth of the city's tax base. Once again, Albert Hanna voiced the developer's view, arguing that "Chicago's future housing needs should be the issue here, and not the preservation of the neighborhood." He championed the view that downzoning would make lakefront neighborhoods unaffordable to the middle class.[20]

Jared Shlaes echoed these sentiments in a 1980 report, arguing that the city lacked data to substantiate its claims that high-density residential development was detrimental to neighborhoods. The report warned that the downzoning phenomenon, if allowed to continue, would deny the city much needed development along the lakefront, especially between Oak and Addison streets. "Cities cannot freeze at a particular point without dying," he noted in the *Chicago Tribune*, while warning that major housing shortages were imminent.[21] Although this criticism of the reactive posture of the city had merit, history appears to have come down on the side of the community. Astor Street is today a historic district and major tourism attraction, widely known for its old world charm and the distinguished Charnley House by Frank Lloyd Wright.

With more efforts to downzone the Gold Coast and other prime Near North neighborhoods on the horizon in 1982, the city commissioned Philip Zeitlin, a planning consultant formerly on the city staff, to conduct a review of the zoning ordinance. Zeitlin's report concluded that changes to the zoning ordinance tended not to be driven by long-range planning considerations but by apparent crises or narrowly defined local issues.[22] The consequence of these actions, Zeitlin maintained, was an ordinance made up of such disparate components and incentives that it did not foster consistent planning. "When 'hopscotch' downzoning is used to falsely maintain and protect community benefits, the local government no longer may attest that zoning is 'in accordance' with a comprehensive plan," he warned, leaving the city susceptible to lawsuits by developers.[23] The report urged the city to draft a new zoning ordinance that would obviate the need for such extensive rezoning.

A New Downtown Emerges

The backlash against new high-rises in the Gold Coast gave developers added incentive to focus on the Central Area, where downzoning was not an issue. During the late 1980s, it was obvious that buyers would pay premium prices to live in the midst of the hustle and bustle of downtown. In the South Loop, Dearborn Park II and the Central Station development (which attracted the likes of Mayor Richard M. Daley) met with great success, as did a large number of loft and office-building conversions.

A new group, Friends of Downtown, pushed for residential development in the heart of the central business district with an eye toward revitalizing Loop retail activity and nightlife. The construction of a new apartment tower in 1989 at the corner of Lake and Dearborn streets (200 N. Dearborn) was a promising step in this direction, as was the construction of the Huron Plaza Apartments (56 stories) in the River North neighborhood and Presidential Towers (four 49-story buildings) on the west edge of the Loop. All were built in non-residential zoning districts.

When completed in 1989, Presidential Towers was the largest residential development built in the city since Carl Sandburg Village. This four-building complex, built in an area that had been zoned for commercial use, introduced high-rise downtown living to the area immediately west of the Chicago River. (Chaddick collection)

The arrival of thousands of residents into River North infused new life into a declining manufacturing area and spurred the opening of chic galleries, restaurants, and shops. Presidential Towers and the Social Security building were springboards for redevelopment west of the river, contributing to the completion of the city's languishing Near West Side urban renewal project. By the early 2000s, this part of town, once home to skid row, was distinguished by sleek office towers, luxury high-rises, and loft housing, along with upscale restaurants, galleries, and services.

By 2003, there were more than 28,000 dwelling units in the Loop, South Loop, and West Loop—roughly two-and-a-half times the number available just a dozen years before.[24] Today, the city continues to encourage a combination of residential and commercial uses in higher-density areas that can accommodate both uses effectively. One parking space per dwelling unit is today the standard in most zoning classifications that apply to the Central Area.

It is certainly an understatement to say that a great deal has changed since the amendments of July, 1962, were put into effect. New lifestyle choices and rising car ownership have all but eliminated concerns that the city's parking requirements and density limits would stifle the expansion of in-town living. Yet it is noteworthy that what originated as a series of "interim" amendments remained on the books for more than 40 years, surviving until the adoption of the new zoning code in 2004.

The 61-story tower at First National Plaza (now Chase Tower Plaza)—the tallest building inside the Loop—was built with a floor area ratio of 17. Although this plaza earned high praise for providing open space in a congested area, other public spaces, such as the nearby Civic Center Plaza, now Daley Plaza (which is partially visible on the right edge of this August 17, 1989 photograph), were less heavily utilized and drew much criticism. (Photo by Lawrence Okrent)

CHAPTER 9
A City of Skyscrapers

Chicago's skyline is a testament to the famed architects, legendary developers, and astute financiers who incurred great risk in creating some of the world's tallest and most admired buildings. Yet the city's silhouette is also the product of many years of regulation governing the location, height, and contours of its buildings. Although certainly less widely heralded than the city's architectural heritage, these polices—from height limits to floor-area-ratio limits to density "bonuses"—have indelibly affected the city's character and cosmopolitan image.

After the Great Chicago Fire of 1871, the city reaped the benefits of a spectacular expansion of commerce, improvements to transportation, and major advances in engineering. Many fine, multi-story brick buildings sprouted up throughout the central business district to meet the demand. Despite the intensity of development, however, there was still little support for the idea of placing limits on the height or bulk of buildings. Developers were constrained by the necessity of building thick supporting walls of stone or concrete, making structures more than eight stories tall extremely rare. The building boom of the 1870s saw few downtown structures rise in excess of 90 feet.

Circumstances changed as metal framing, new lighting systems, and mechanical elevators made taller structures more feasible. The Home Insurance Building—generally regarded as America's first skyscraper—went up at the northeast corner of Adams and LaSalle streets in 1885.[1] Rising ten stories, this engineering marvel was the first tall building to be supported by a metal skeleton of vertical columns and horizontal beams. With a frame consisting of thin pieces of steel, the Home Insurance weighed less than half as much as a typical ten-story building made of heavy masonry.

The first portion of the Monadnock Building was completed in 1891, rising an awe-inspiring 16 stories. Shortly after the construction of this massive masonry structure, Chicago established a height limit in its building code, a move emulated by many other cities. (Chicago Public Library)

The height and scale of the Home Insurance Building lent credence to the notion that the city needed to draft a set of policies to guide downtown development. Officials were wary not only of the structural integrity of the frames of the tallest buildings, but also the unstable soil upon which these buildings rested and the crowding and congestion they generated on the streets they faced. Public servants envisioned scenarios of streets bereft of sunlight and clogged with manure from horse-drawn carriages.[2] As carriages, pedestrians, and streetcars vied for right of way, the amount of traffic on many corridors already seemed intolerable. Some streets seemed destined to become dark and dangerous "skyscraper canyons" that were incubators for germs.

The completion of a pair of skyscrapers between 1891 and 1893 which reached heights that seemed unattainable only a few years before reinforced the view that the time had come for municipal action. Both the Monadnock Building (53 W. Jackson), which had exterior load-bearing walls, and the metal-frame Manhattan Building (431 S. Dearborn) rose an awe-inspiring 16 stories, putting them among the tallest buildings in the world.[3]

These skyscrapers were icons of Chicago's commercial might, but their size compelled the city to abandon its laissez-faire policy toward tall buildings. Thus began an era of municipal regulation, divisible into four distinct phases, with each phase having a profound effect on the city's skyline.

Height Limits, 1893–1923

The first phase of the city's tall-building regulation began with the adoption of a 130-foot height limit in 1893. This restriction effectively limited the number of floors per building to about ten when many existing structures had a dozen or more floors.

The height limit was apparently the first of its kind in the United States and represented a bold and more liberal interpretation of a municipality's right to adopt nuisance laws to protect public safety.[4] The full effects of the new policy, however, would not be felt for several years.

Permits had already been issued for many buildings exceeding 130 feet, allowing for the construction of several more towering edifices. The grandest of these was the Masonic Temple, which was more than two-and-a-half times the height limit and the tallest office building in the world. This 302-foot giant as well as the Fisher (343 S. Dearborn), Old Colony (407 S. Dearborn), Marquette (140 S. Dearborn), and Reliance (1 W. Washington) buildings (each at least 17 stories tall) greatly expanded the supply of downtown commercial space.

By the mid-1890s, however, height limits had begun to exert a great effect on the supply of office space. As developers built to the maximum, a preponderance of tall, rectangular-shaped buildings arose, standing side by side and seemingly creating a wall along some downtown streets. Some of these buildings helped cultivate the famed Chicago School of Architecture so widely associated with Daniel Burnham, William Le Baron Jenney, John Root, and the firm of Dankmar Adler and Louis Sullivan. Other buildings had a more utilitarian quality.

Developers lobbied intensively for higher height limits as new technologies like electrification systems for streetcar lines moderated pollution and sanitation problems. In 1902, the city doubled the building height limit to 260 feet, only to lower it to 200 feet in the mid-1910s. Some buildings that emerged during this period of rapid growth, such as the Reliance Building, were tall and trim, while others, such as the Federal Reserve Bank at 230 S. LaSalle, the Railway Exchange Building at 224 S. Michigan (see photo on page 16), and the People's Gas Building at 122 S. Michigan, occupied full quarter-blocks but had atriums that allowed light and air to reach interior offices.

By the 1910s, the height limits had altered the city's architectural image. These regulations and the city's grid of streets gave Chicago a preponderance of big, boxy buildings having a large interior light court.[5] Buildings with an "O-plan" (i.e., a courtyard in the center) or a "U-plan" (a courtyard in the rear) allowed developers to maximize the amount of rentable space under the constraint of the height limit. The demand for office space, however, was unremitting, and soon the limits would be revised again.

The Masonic Temple rose 302 feet and was the tallest office building in the world upon its completion in 1894. Although its height greatly exceeded the limit established by the city, the skyscraper was approved before the limit took effect. Located at the corner of State and Randolph streets, this ornate structure was a Loop landmark until its demolition in 1939. (Chicago Public Library)

The 17-story Old Colony Building, completed in 1894 at 407 S. Dear-born Street, was among the last skyscrapers approved before the city's 130-foot height limit took effect. This ornate structure is widely known today for its rounded corner bays. (Chicago Public Library)

A pair of landmarks provides a striking backdrop for motorists traveling south across the Michigan Avenue Bridge, circa 1930. On the right, the Stone Container Building (formerly the London Guarantee and Accident Building) boasts an ornamental tower—a feature made possible by changes in the building code in 1920. Its counterpart on the left, 333 N. Michigan Avenue, has a tower designed to be within the limits of the city's 1923 zoning ordinance. The main part of each building rises to nearly the maximum height allowed by the city at the time. (Chicago Historical Society)

ALLOWANCES FOR TOWERS, 1920–42

The second regulatory phase began in 1920, when the city raised the height limit from 200 feet back to 260 feet and made provisions for the construction of ornamental structures above this new limit rising 400 feet. Although these towers could not be occupied, the new rule cleared the way for more creative designs and less boxy architectural styles, ending the era of "O-" and "U-plan" buildings and giving the city a new set of landmarks. Within a few years, several of these buildings, including the London Guarantee and Accident Building at 360 N. Michigan (later the Stone Container Building), the Wrigley Building, and the Tribune Tower, stood watch over the new Michigan Avenue bridge over the Chicago River. In the heart of the Loop, the Chicago Temple at 77 W. Washington earned the distinction of being the tallest church in the world.

The city experienced few problems with buildings of this size and further liberalized height limits with the passage of the first zoning ordinance in 1923. Although the limit on a building's height only rose from 260 to 264 feet that year, the ordinance allowed more substantial towers to be built above this height. Unlike the ornamental structures authorized in 1920, these towers could have usable floor space and were not subject to a strict height limit. However, the towers could comprise no more than one-fourth of the footprint of the building and no more than one-sixth of the volume of the primary part of the building.

These rules discouraged buildings above 600 feet but made possible the construction of many tall buildings with slender towers, such as the Carbide and Carbon Building at 230 N. Michigan, the Jewelers Building at 35 E. Wacker (later renamed the Pure Oil Building), the LaSalle-Wacker Building at 221 N. LaSalle, Mather Tower at 75 E. Wacker, and the Furniture Mart at 680 N. Lake Shore Drive. The Morrison Hotel at 15–29 S. Clark added a tower of such great height to its existing structure that it reputedly became the tallest hotel in the world. Without the towers, virtually all of these buildings rose vertically to within a few feet of the 264-foot height limit, but with them, several rose in excess of 500 feet.

The Wrigley Building (398 feet) and Tribune Tower (462 feet) are among the most notable products of the regulations governing the design of tall buildings that took effect in 1920. Both have unoccupied towers extending high above the main part of the building. (Chaddick collection)

The Civic Opera House building, completed in 1929, is larger and more impressive than most other buildings constructed during the first decade of zoning. Rising to a height of 550 feet, as prescribed by the zoning law, the tower covers only one-fourth of the lot and represents only one-sixth of the volume of the main part of the building. The 45-floor structure later became known as the Kemper Insurance Building. (Chicago Historical Society)

The towers rising above the 264-foot limit were generally quite striking from the exterior—many rose 17 to 20 stories. Unfortunately, their interior space tended to be underutilized and unattractive to prospective tenants. Architects took note of this and attempted to reduce these problems by experimenting with new designs. One prevalent design featured buildings with step-like setbacks on upper stories, a style similar to the "wedding cake" style widely associated with New York City skyscrapers of this era (see inset later in this chapter).

The requirement that towers built above 264 feet could be no more than one-sixth of the volume of the primary part of buildings was a particularly severe impediment to skyscraper construction. By the late 1920s, however, architects had devised various "massing solutions" to minimize this problem.[6] The results can be seen in such admired structures as the Civic Opera House at 20 N. Wacker (555 feet) and the Palmolive Building at 919 N. Michigan (565 feet), both completed in 1929. These edifices earned accolades for their soaring designs and, like other buildings of the early zoning era, came to be known as "zoning-law towers" in reference to the rules that governed their design. (Others have christened these buildings "Twenties Towers" in recognition of the decade that saw most of this construction.) The Board of Trade, completed in 1930, was even more impressive than its predecessors, surpassing 600 feet and towering above the city's other skyscrapers for nearly a quarter century.

By 1930, this colorful phase of skyscraper development was at a peak. Nearly two dozen "zoning-law towers" now pierced the height limit that had been in place prior to the advent of zoning; many of those buildings rose more than 35 stories. The commercial real-estate market entered a lengthy slump during the Depression, however, leaving the Field Building (today the LaSalle National Bank building) at 135 S. LaSalle in 1935 to mark the end of skyscraper construction for nearly 20 years. This 535-foot office tower was an Art Deco masterpiece, but a casualty of its construction was the old Home Insurance Building.

VOLUME LIMITS, 1942–57

The third phase of the city's regulatory policy grew out of 1942 zoning revisions that instituted a more flexible set of controls on building size. These controls limited the volume (or "cubical content") of the entire structure rather than the height of a building's base or the volume of the tower. For much of downtown Chicago, the maximum volume was capped at a level equal to the size of the lot multiplied by 144 feet. Taking into account prevailing methods of building construction, this would be the equivalent of a FAR of about 12. (A block-like building covering the full site could rise about 12 stories, while a similar structure covering half the site could rise about 24 stories).

The new limit was generally more restrictive—but in some ways more flexible—than the old height and tower regulations that preceded it. This limit was of little consequence through the end of World War II due to the anemic condition of the commercial real-estate market. When work began on the Prudential Building on East Randolph Street in 1952, however, skyscraper construction began anew. To comply with the bulk limit yet maximize height, the developers leased several acres of air rights to enlarge the site; they left much of it empty, thereby meeting the 144-foot-times-the-lot-area limit. Upon its completion in 1955, the 601-foot Prudential was the city's second tallest building, exceeded in height only by the statue at the top of the Board of Trade.[7]

This regulatory phase lasted a mere 15 years. Besides the Prudential, work commenced on only a few tall commercial buildings while these rules were in effect, such the Continental Insurance Building (today's 250 S. Wacker Building) and the Inland Steel Building (30 W. Monroe).

FAR AND BONUSES, 1957–PRESENT

The fourth phase of controls on building height and bulk began when limits on building volume were replaced by caps on floor area ratio (FAR) in 1957. Under this approach, the maximum FAR varied by zoning

The Palmolive Building, completed in 1929, has setbacks similar to those commonly found in New York, but conformed to Chicago's zoning ordinance due to the breadth of the building, which spans an entire North Michigan Avenue block. (Chicago Historical Society)

The tallest of all the city's buildings for nearly a quarter century, the Chicago Board of Trade (1930) soared more than 600 feet in spite of the constraints imposed by zoning. The height of its tower was made possible by setbacks as well as its large base, which featured a pair of wings, each 130 foot high, that had the effect of emphasizing the building's height. (Photo by Lawrence Okrent)

classification but was 16 in downtown office districts, representing roughly a one-third increase in allowable bulk. The FAR approach gave developers a range of options (i.e., from tall slender buildings to short bulky buildings) provided they did not exceed the maximum of 16. Much taller buildings appeared, however, due to a system of FAR bonuses designed to encourage open space and admit light.

The adoption of the FAR approach changed the face of downtown Chicago and allowed the city to reclaim its place as a leader in skyscraper construction. By the end of the 1960s, many buildings of great height and bulk, such as the Civic Center (Daley Center) at 100 N. Dearborn (648 feet), First National Bank (Chase Tower) at 21 S. Clark (850 feet), and the Hancock Center at 875 N. Michigan (1,127 feet), emerged on newly created plazas.

Developers could create structures of such great height by starting with a full-block site but occupying only part of it, and in some instances taking advantage of FAR bonuses. In high-intensity business and commercial districts, the zoning ordinance rewarded developers with a higher maximum FAR if they provided sidewalk arcades and setbacks from the street of 20 feet or more. The city also gave bonuses to developers of buildings with upper-story setbacks and those located next to public open space.

To increase light and air in high-density residential districts, the city similarly rewarded developers who built fewer dwelling units than the maximum permissible number or who built adjacent to public open space—a provision especially important for developers of high-rise buildings along Lake Shore Drive. There was full recognition that developers could not incorporate features like plazas and setbacks without reducing the amount of rentable floor space. It was necessary, therefore, to offer incentives to provide such features in the form of FAR bonuses.

Developers of large-scale residential and commercial projects became quite aggressive in devising site plans with "bonusable" amenities. For many new office buildings, such as the Equitable at 401 N. Michigan (1964), First National Bank at 21 S. Clark (1969), and the IBM Building at 330 N. Wabash (1973), this took the form of a public plaza. By the

An Ordinance Shapes a City: Lessons from New York

The skylines of Chicago and New York stand as testaments to the differing size, geography, and economic history of these rival cities as well as to the effects of zoning.

Much as in Chicago, officials in New York voiced great concern over the heights of buildings in the early twentieth century. In 1915, the construction of the Equitable Building in Lower Manhattan, a massive 42-story office tower casting a deep shadow over neighboring buildings, triggered a particularly vocal outcry over the amount of light and air reaching the streets. When New York adopted its zoning ordinance the following year, it limited the bulk of buildings by requiring a setback at a certain height. At additional heights, additional setbacks had to be provided, until the building occupied no more than 25 percent of its lot site, at which point the building could rise up forever.

The rules governing setbacks differed according to the width of the street and the height district of the site. In a "1½ times district," for example, a building on a street 100 feet wide needed to have a setback when its height reached 150 feet.[8] At greater heights, the ordinance required one foot of setback per three feet of additional height. Such formulas, based on complex equations to assure that sunlight reached the street, generally allowed buildings along the avenues of Manhattan to rise 16 to 18 floors before the first setback; those on side streets generally needed a setback after just 9 to 12 stories.[9]

These requirements spawned the creation of

This bird's-eye view of Wall Street and the East River from the top of the Irving Trust Building, circa 1938, illustrates the setbacks that are prevalent among skyscrapers in New York City's high-intensity zoning districts. (New York Public Library)

many buildings in the "wedding cake" style noted for having distinct tiers, each set back from the one below. The absence of a limit on the height or bulk of towers rising over 25 percent of the lot area, however, made New York's zoning ordinance more amenable to buildings of great height than Chicago's ordinance and opened the door for several of the world's tallest buildings. The 1,046-foot Chrysler Building (1930) and the 1,250-foot Empire State (1931) conformed to zoning by virtue of having an entire city block as their base as well as making extensive use of setbacks. By 1935, there were more than a dozen buildings taller than 600 feet in New York but only one—the 605-foot Board of Trade—in Chicago.

In 1950, New York became the first major city to adopt the use of FAR to control bulk. The city modified its regulations by capping FAR at 15 in 1961 but, like Chicago, awarded developers who included various features into their site plans with FAR bonuses. This system fostered the development of such prominent structures as the World Trade Center towers (1973), the 915-foot Citicorp Center (1977), and the 927-foot Trump World Tower (2001).

In the foreword of Earle Shultz and Walter Simmons's 1959 volume *Offices and the Sky,* Clarence B. Randall notes that "nothing more solidly expresses the American concept of an economy that rests upon individual initiative and responsibility than the skyline of New York or Chicago…"[10] Yet Shultz and Simmons found that New York had a significant advantage in tall-building construction due to the Windy City's height and bulk restrictions between 1893 and 1957. "New York could and did build office buildings to house the great expansion of business. Some of this business wanted to come to Chicago and would have if it could have been accommodated there," they concluded.[11]

Commuters arriving on the Chicago & North Western Railway in 1962 found the central-Loop skyline still dominated by zoning-law towers dating back more than 25 years. From this perspective (facing southeast near Clinton Street), the Randolph Tower at 188 W. Randolph (left), the American National Bank at 33 N. LaSalle (left-center), the 1 N. LaSalle Building (center), and the Field Building (right-center) rise high above the other structures, with the soon-to-be-demolished Morrison Hotel visible between the American National and 1 N. LaSalle buildings. As the contemporary photograph on the following page shows, even the tallest of these buildings are today dwarfed by a veritable sea of modern office towers. (C&NW Historical Society collection)

On October 15, 2005, 43 years after the previous photograph was taken, the evening rush hour on the commuter-rail system is again at its peak. Massive office towers, including the curved 333 Wacker Drive (in the distance behind the Metra locomotive), now dominate the skyline, and there is a mix of commercial and residential properties along the tracks, including the brightly painted Fulton House Condominiums (a loft conversion at left-center; note the added windows since the earlier photo), the sleek Riverbend Condominiums at 333 N. Canal (top-center), and an old industrial building (center) now used by a tire company, having held out remarkably well against the forces of economic change. (Chaddick collection)

early 1970s, several buildings were approved with FAR over 50 percent beyond the code's basic limit, bringing to Chicago three of the world's tallest buildings. The Hancock Center (1969) has a FAR of 26; the Aon Center at 200 E. Randolph (formerly the Standard Oil Building, 1974) has a FAR of 24.6; and the 1,450-foot Sears Tower (1974) has a FAR of 36.[12]

Bonuses, together with city-developer negotiations through the Planned Development process, resulted in the creation of "civic space" amenable to pedestrian movement as well as above-grade setbacks that allowed more sunlight to reach the streets. These designs also helped reduce the canyon effect created by stretches of tall buildings situated side by side.[13] Such designs were accorded considerable aesthetic importance due to city's top FAR (16), which was far more generous than in many other cities. In their highest-density areas, for example, Boston, Los Angeles, Philadelphia, and Washington, D.C. had FAR limits between 10 and 14. New York capped the FAR at 15. Washington, D.C., with its historic plan, imposed a height limit of 130 feet in much of the city, which

The Equitable Building, completed in 1964, was one of the first buildings in the city surrounded by a plaza—a design encouraged by the zoning amendments of 1957. The architecture contrasts sharply with the neighboring Tribune Tower. (Chicago Historical Society)

effectively limited buildings to about 12 stories.[14] Atlanta and San Francisco at one time had higher limits than either Chicago or New York, but each eventually reduced these limits to levels lower than the Windy City's.[15]

ESCALATING CRITICISM OF THE BONUS SYSTEM

The bonuses system fostered the creation of a dramatic skyline, but its deficiencies were quite apparent to architects and urban planners by the early 1970s. The Central Area had become checkered with small, barren, and little-used open spaces; concrete plazas were fast becoming a cliché, and new buildings were becoming taller and taller.[16] In 1967, Lawrence Halprin, a noted landscape architect, warned that the height and design of new buildings in downtown Chicago threatened to "completely destroy what remains of the humane scale of the street."[17]

Several downtown public spaces came to exemplify bonus-eligible amenities that were poorly conceived.[18] The Cook County Administration

A variety of buildings with floor area ratios exceeding the city's basic limit of 16, including the Standard Oil Building (right; FAR of 24.6), First National Bank Building (bottom-right; FAR of 17) and Lake Point Tower, stand out in this 1980 photograph. Work is underway on Doral Plaza at 151 North Michigan (bottom center), an apartment building that will boast a FAR of 33.3, one of the highest in the city. (Photo by Earl L. Kubis, Chicago Historical Society)

Building (formerly the Brunswick Building at 69 W. Washington), built in 1965, is flanked by an almost-unusable plaza. The Sears Tower has a plaza that is swept by high winds and inaccessible from three of its four sides—a public space that the *Tribune's* Paul Gapp called "one of most conspicuous failures in town" in 1975. Gapp added, "I do not think it unreasonable to expect something a bit special on the ground surrounding the world's tallest building."[19] Critics, however, did not uniformly deride all such spaces. Gapp for one gave a favorable critique of the Standard Oil Building plaza, and the plaza next to the First National Bank earned accolades for its pedestrian-friendly design.[20]

Many observers of Chicago's development scene were particularly alarmed by the effects of the bonus system on the effort to preserve historic buildings. The availability of bonuses heightened the incentive for developers to tear down low-rise buildings in favor of sleek towers. When Louis Sullivan's famed Chicago Stock Exchange at 30 N. LaSalle was demolished in 1972, there was a vocal outcry in the preservation community.[21] It was a cruel irony that the new building, which many considered to be lacking architectural merit, received a bonus for a ground-floor setback.

As venerated buildings fell victim to the wrecking ball, attorney John Costonis proposed using a technique called "transfer of development rights" to save the city's remaining historic buildings.[22] His 1972 proposal emulated a New York program that allowed the owners of smaller buildings in areas now zoned for great height to sell their unused air rights to other property owners. The transfer of the air rights to another property gave the buyer the benefit of additional FAR.

Nothing came of Costonis's proposal, but the push for new policies continued unabated. Architects John Macsai and Louis Rocah urged the city to develop a new set of incentives during the 1970s. Rocah said, "we presently give bonuses for open space but don't differentiate between a parking lot and a garden."[23] Architect Jack Hartray, Jr., opined in the *Chicago Tribune,* "What we have here is boomtown zoning that lets you build a Sears Tower on every block."[24] Mary Decker, of the Metropolitan

The marble walls that surround two sides of the Sears Tower plaza (shown here along Jackson Street) have been singled out as examples of the ineffectual designs encouraged by the system of bonuses in place at the time. In 2001, the city changed its bonus system, denying FAR premiums for plazas more than three feet above the sidewalk. (Chaddick collection)

the angels." The Miglin-Beitler Skyneedle, first proposed in the mid-1980s, was to be nearly 2,000-feet tall, surpassing the Sears Tower by more than 500 feet. This sleek skyscraper, slated to occupy the southwest corner of Wells and Madison streets, was to have an extremely narrow white tower that telescoped through several setbacks to achieve a very narrow point at its peak. In addition to "automatic bonuses" for the proposed ground-floor setbacks (which increased the maximum FAR by 5.6) and upper-floor setbacks (which added 9.3 to the maximum FAR), other bonuses were tendered for the plan's interior cultural space (which added two to the maximum FAR), allowing the developer to build to an FAR of 33.1, or more than twice the base FAR of 16.

After the Skyneedle project was scuttled for financial reasons in 1988 (a parking lot today occupies the site), another ambitious proposal came forward in 1998 for a building taller than the Sears Tower. The developer envisioned building a 1,567-foot tower at the southeast corner of Dearborn and Madison, regaining for Chicago the distinction of having the world's tallest building. More recently, as we discuss below, the 1,362-foot Trump Tower on the former Sun-Times Building site received a significant set of bonuses for its setbacks, sight lines, and riverfront improvements.

Despite the imperfections of the bonus system, city planners recognized that it was a powerful economic-development tool. Its usefulness was plainly evident during the early 1980s, when this system helped several major downtown projects move off the drawing board in the midst of a real-estate slump.[26] A boom in office building construction in the late 1980s, however, re-energized the debate about bonuses. Over the course of the decade, developers spent in excess of $10 billion to build more than 75 buildings in the Central Area, including such tall edifices as the AT&T Corporate Center (61 stories), the Chicago Mercantile Exchange (one 40-story and one 41 story tower), the Leo Burnett Building (50 stories), and the NBC Tower (34 stories).

The critique of amenities rewarded with bonuses became quite harsh. One critic opined that many ground-floor setbacks were never intended

Planning Council, made known her view by saying, "We have the most permissive zoning ordinance in America. All developers have to do is include a plaza here, a setback there, and they can build to the angels."[25]

Some developers indeed seemed intent on using bonuses to "build to

The plaza adjacent to the County Administration Building (formerly the Brunswick Building) at 69 West Washington Street, has been roundly criticized for being damp and dark. The city no longer awards bonuses for plazas that open only to the north or that are without landscaping or water features. (Chaddick collection)

developers who provided arcades and plazas that actually detracted from the pedestrian experience.

NEW APPROACHES TAKE ROOT

By the mid-1980s, the city was exploring ways of making bonus-eligible features more genuinely beneficial to the public. Through Planned Development negotiations, the city began to expand bonus options by including such items as interior cultural space, rooftop gardens, and "winter gardens." FAR increases were also given for off-site and "soft" benefits, like financial contributions for neighborhood traffic studies or improvements to transit stops.

Such innovations were certainly helpful, but the city still considered the bonus system to be ineffective in many situations. To avert the most problematic outcomes, it occasionally offered a "bonus waiver," that is, it would give a bonus for a proposed amenity that, by agreement, would not be built if the proposed amenity seemed detrimental to the surrounding area. Common examples included proposals for arcades or setbacks on streets where the continuous facade of buildings gave the street its character. This tactic was used in the case of 190 S. LaSalle and again for City Place (a 40-story office tower at 676 N. Michigan Avenue). Nevertheless, the "bonus waiver" technique was soon discontinued. Instead, the city began asking developers to submit revised plans with more suitable proposals for bonuses.

The ebb and flow of municipal policy pointed to the fundamental tension that existed between two schools of thought on the virtues of the city's system of FAR caps and bonuses. One view held that cities are places where tall buildings and congestion are part of the fabric of life and should be expected. Advocates of this view asserted that the system should be very generous, as the 1957 code was, and afford the public relatively little input on matters pertaining to urban design.

The opposing view emphasized the need for cities to relate to their residents by managing the scale of development. As noted urban design

to create useful public space (their original purpose) but simply distinguish buildings from their neighbors.[27] As Jack Hartray and Jared Shlaes pointed out in a series of talks, bonuses often encouraged and rewarded

By the early 1980s, the city was taking steps to discourage developers from incorporating arcades into their site plan, especially in areas with extensive retail activity. This arcade, completed in 1987, is part of the Chicago Mercantile Exchange complex at 20 S. Wacker. (Photo by J. Kearney)

critic Kenneth Halpern observed, "the intent of zoning incentives only works when the zoning's basic limit is at a threshold where the developers want to build more than that zoning allows."[28] These diverging views exemplified the dynamic tension inherent in city planning—a tension that still exists today.

By 1998, those holding the latter view had greatly escalated their criticism of the bonuses being awarded to developers. The city reviewed the system and issued a report calling for a new and more contextual approach that included clear guidelines for bonus design.[29] Among the items found most worthy of bonuses were public open space, underground parking, and upper-level setbacks. Plazas opening to the north, like that at the Cook County Administration Building, were discouraged due to their deep shade. The report upheld the use of bonuses to encourage "soft benefits" as well.

With input from the American Institute of Architects, the Metropolitan Planning Council, and other civic groups, the city finally codified an expanded list of bonuses, and on October 31, 2001, adopted a new amendment to the zoning ordinance. The list of bonus-eligible amenities included winter gardens, riverwalks, public art, and through-block connections. Developers of as-of-right building projects could still receive bonuses for plazas and setbacks with only the approval of the zoning administrator. Other bonuses, however, required planning department approval. For PDs, the bonus system was now akin to a restaurant menu, allowing developers to choose from a broad list of amenities subject to planning department approval. The list included an "Adopt a Landmark" provision allowing developers to receive a FAR bonus for making investments in the rehabilitation of historic structures—a provision that achieved some of the goals espoused by attorney John Costonis nearly 30 years before.

A notable result of the changes is that the process of awarding bonuses for PDs is more standardized than before. Nevertheless, developers greeted these changes with skepticism. Some voiced concerns that the changes would give City Hall too much control and result in significant reductions in both the scale and number of projects receiving approval.[30] The Chicago Development Council (a consortium of more than 70 builders and property owners) was particularly dubious about the merits of the new policy.[31]

The Trump Tower and Hotel, the first major PD approved after the city adopted its new zoning code in 2004, however, showcased some of the advantages of the new bonus system. The city and the developer engaged in lengthy negotiations before reaching an agreement that promises to greatly increase pedestrian activity along the Chicago River. Through the creative use of bonuses, the developer increased the maximum FAR of the site from 16 to 29. An elaborate three-tier plaza will offer striking views and provide access to a variety of stores in the building's interior, while a pedestrian arcade will shield pedestrians from inclement weather.

Other bold designs will further change the face of downtown Chicago in years to come, raising a new set of planning and zoning issues. Noted skyscraper expert Carol Willis, who has studied the experience of cities with managing tall buildings, observes that "Cities are competitive commercial environments where buildings are businesses and space is a commodity." The principles that give cities order, she notes, "are complex, but comprehensible, and in that, there is great beauty."[32]

The former site of Chicago's Grand Central Station, which was demolished in 1971, remains vacant despite its proximity to prime Loop real estate. This photograph, taken on July 1, 2005, shows the 311 S. Wacker Drive building in front of the Sears Tower with the AT&T Corporate Tower (noted for having twin antennas) in the distance. These grounds (identifiable as BPD no. 481 on the map appearing on page 53) are slated for redevelopment. (Photo by J. Kearney)

This familiar perspective of the Central Area, shown on August 8, 2004, illustrates the division of land uses identified in the Lakefront Protection Ordinance. The ordinance divides the lakefront into the "offshore zone," the "public zone" (extending from the lakeshore to the center of Michigan Avenue in this part of the city), and the "private zone" (the area between Michigan Avenue and Wabash Avenue in this photograph). Development in each zone requires the approval of the Plan Commission, which holds public hearings allowing opinions and protests to be heard. (Photo by Lawrence Okrent)

CHAPTER 10

Aesthetics and Urban Design

Richard F. Babcock once noted that zoning has evolved from "little more than a rational … extension of public nuisance law" to a complex set of requirements intended to resolve a wide range of land-use problems.[1] This is certainly true in Chicago, where the zoning ordinance today has entire sections devoted to protecting the lakefront and riverfront, preserving historic buildings, and improving landscaping, open space, and the appearance of new construction. Although many factors are responsible for this expansion, noted consultant Jared Shlaes wryly summed up the underlying cause when he said, "Cities are like very rich people. They sit waiting for someone to come to them with ideas."[2]

The expansion of zoning to areas unrelated to public health and safety has not been without disagreement or controversy. From the Lakefront Protection Ordinance to special ordinances created to deal with the various forms of automobile-oriented development, the city's push for expanded control over aesthetics and urban design has generated vigorous debate and, at times, heated exchange. The creation and expansion of these controls are notable parts of zoning history in Chicago.

LAKEFRONT PROTECTION

Chicago's early history is a saga of great synergy between its industries and waterways. The Port of Chicago, the lakefront, and the river bustled with commerce during the city's formative years and were important as sources of mechanical power and transportation. Yet the people who surveyed Chicago to build the first inland canal in 1836 understood that the lakefront also had recreational and aesthetic value. They opted not to sell the land along what is today Michigan Avenue between Madison Street and 12th Street, declaring instead that it was "public ground—a common to remain forever open, clear and free of any buildings or other obstruction whatever."[3]

The city, however, could not easily realize this vision. Industrial activity around the harbor spilled out in both directions, and in 1852 the Illinois Legislature granted the Illinois Central Railroad right of way along the shoreline, transforming the downtown lakefront into a terminal area filled with tracks, freight depots, and storage sheds. After the Great Fire, tons of debris were dumped along the shore.

When Montgomery Ward sued the city in 1890 and the court ordered the area cleaned up, a new civic center was proposed for the site, but Ward later sued again to enforce the words "forever open, clear and free of any buildings." The *Plan of Chicago* in 1909 enshrined the idea of the lakefront being a civic resource to be protected as public open space. Over the next 20 years, the city created many acres of new parkland by reclaiming submerged lands along the shoreline, fulfilling some of the goals of the plan.

Many more battles over the lakefront, of course, still lay ahead. The construction of Meigs Field as a commuter airport on Northerly Island (the site of the 1933–34 World's Fair) in 1937 provoked great controversy. The Chicago Plan Commission reaffirmed the idea that the lakefront be protected from development the following year, but pressure to build in this area did not abate. There was more public outcry following the construction of a pair of filtration plants north of Navy Pier in the 1950s and of the McCormick Place convention center in 1960. The convention center was chastised for both its size and opaque facade; many felt that the city should not have allowed such a valuable lakefront parcel to be used for a building having such limited visual appeal.[4]

Still more controversy erupted after the city wrote the *Basic Policies for the Comprehensive Plan of Chicago* in 1964. The report upheld the idea that the lakefront be kept as public open space, and like earlier plans, con-

tained an exception for property near the mouth of the river, which was heavily industrialized. The new plan broke from tradition, however, by omitting the stipulation that the land near the river could be used only for harbor and terminal facilities.

The door was now open for developer Charles H. Shaw to move forward in the mid-1960s with the construction of Lake Point Tower, a 71-story high-rise near Navy Pier. Although the Plan Commission responded with an amendment blocking construction of residential towers east of Lake Shore Drive, it was unable to stop Shaw's project. Several years later, advocates of lakefront protection suffered another setback when the Harbor Point apartment tower—made possible by the previously approved Illinois Center Planned Development—appeared east of the Drive.

Shaw's glistening tower, completed in 1968, quickly became a landmark and earned accolades for its beautiful curved, Y-shaped design. At 645 feet, it was both the tallest reinforced-concrete building in the world and the world's tallest residential building. Despite its intrinsic beauty, Lake Point Tower awakened concerns about lakefront protection. In 1972, the city first adopted the Lakefront Plan, a blueprint for improvements along the shoreline; in the following year, it took the more significant step of adopting the Lake Michigan and Chicago Lakefront Protection Ordinance.

The city envisioned the ordinance as a deterrent to out-of-scale, poorly planned, or architecturally inappropriate development in close proximity to the lake. In support of the lakefront plan, it created an overlay district divided into three zones: the offshore zone (i.e., Lake Michigan itself), the public use zone, which was primarily parkland and beaches along the lake, and the private use zone, which was land further inland. In addition, the ordinance created a special application process that requires an environmental review, a public hearing, and approval by the planning department and the Chicago Plan Commission. The process places a heavy burden on the developer to show that a proposed project does not violate any of the principles or policies of the ordinance.

"We are on the way to saving the most beautiful lakefront in the world," exulted Paul T. Wigoda, alderman of the 49th Ward, to the *Chicago Daily News* when the ordinance was passed. "The mistakes of the past are gone," he optimistically assessed.[5] Others were skeptical. Alderman William Singer, a strong supporter of lakefront protection, complained that "it is an ordinance made for corruption," due to the "discretionary power" it gave to the planning commissioner. Singer lamented that developers "who meet the zoning ordinance requirements will still not know under what circumstances a potential development can or cannot be built."[6]

Over the years, other observers echoed Singer's claim that the principles and policies of the ordinance are so vaguely written that any development falling under its purview could easily be attacked and hampered by lawsuits of dubious merit.[7] Even so, there is a general consensus that the ordinance has achieved some of its intended results. Mandatory public hearings have provided an incentive for negotiation and compromise; in some cases, the hearings compelled developers to make major modifications to site plans, rendering them more acceptable to the surrounding community.

Negotiations surrounding the building at 2960 N. Lake Shore Drive illustrate this point. Originally designed with 42 floors, this project generated vigorous opposition from residents at a series of community meetings. When the project went before the Plan Commission in the late 1980s, many residents went on record protesting its height. Planning commissioner Elizabeth Hollander adopted a novel strategy: inviting residents to meet in one room and the development team in another. After several hours of shuttle diplomacy, the parties reached an agreement that reduced the overall height by four floors, eliminating 40 apartments from the building at considerable cost to the developer. The developer felt that the project was "held hostage" by the community for changes that did little to alter its impact on the area; nevertheless, once modifications were made, the project was allowed to proceed.

The 1968 completion of Lake Point Tower—the tallest residential building in the world at the time—evoked great concern about development along the lakefront. An allowance for development at the mouth of the Chicago River opened the door for this graceful but controversial apartment tower. (Chaddick collection)

A condominium tower at 2960 N. Lake Shore Drive. (Chaddick collection)

ORDINANCES PROMOTING EFFECTIVE URBAN DESIGN

By the early 1990s, strip malls, parking garages, and clusters of townhomes wedged in between older structures were proliferating throughout the city. Newspapers published descriptions of new structures as being "just slightly more attractive than your typical army barracks," "scruffy, vulgar, and loud," and "ugly scars on the urban face of Chicago."[8] Such vociferous complaints resonated with Mayor

After 30 years, the effectiveness of the Lakefront Protection Ordinance is still in question. The deliberations in 2003 about the impending redesign of Soldier Field highlighted the impassioned views of the public regarding large structures near the lake, though it was allowed. Yet the ordinance set a precedent that led to the 1991 passage of the Riverfront Protection Ordinance, which established a similar review-and-approval process for developments along the Chicago River.

Richard M. Daley and his staff, who had sought to curb some of the least attractive urban design practices.

The city has never proposed a design review process—an approach used by many suburbs and several major cities, including San Francisco. Nevertheless, Mayor Daley set out to beautify the city through direct public investment and new regulatory initiatives. Programs to plant trees, clean up brownfields, create rooftop gardens, and install concrete planters, as well as decorative fences resembling the wrought-iron classics of yesteryear, have brought national attention to the city.[9]

Although less heavily publicized, the mayor has also pushed for a variety of new ordinances to foster more attractive design.[10] He pursued these initiatives with the temperament of a pragmatist who apparently eschewed the idea that the city's efforts needed to be orchestrated through an all-encompassing plan. Instead, he pursued small, arguably more achievable initiatives, such as the Landscape Ordinance. Adopted in 1991, this ordinance exemplifies the mayor's beautification goals by directing that the perimeters of parking lots be screened, fenced, or lined with plants to improve their appearance. It also requires that loading docks, service areas, and vehicle storage areas must be screened from public view.[11]

The city took another small step toward "greening" the neighborhoods in 1998, when it adopted the Open Space Impact Fee Ordinance, which requires residential developers to either provide open space for their residents or pay a fee to the city.[12] This ordinance applies only to new development and rehabilitation projects that increase the number of dwelling units and earmarks the fees for creation of new parks or the improvement of existing parks.[13] The impact fee was—in the *Chicago Tribune*'s words—"grudgingly endorsed" by developers.[14]

Also in 1998, the City Council passed the "Townhouse Standards," an amendment to improve the design of the numerous townhome developments springing up in many neighborhoods. The ordinance requires that all new townhomes have a private yard with attractive landscaping and parking spaces that are accessible through an alley or a shared driveway—

This image of a townhome development with a blank wall facing the street was published by the city in 2002 to show the need for contextual zoning. (City of Chicago)

a move the city indicated was necessary in order to prevent driveways from "taking over the sidewalk." Townhomes must also have an attractive front façade—with real or faux doors and windows; no longer could developers create unadorned walls facing public thoroughfares.[15] This ordinance also created a new zoning category with setback requirements and other standards appropriate for townhomes.[16]

Community groups and aldermen, meanwhile, voiced great displeasure about the proliferation of strip malls (a string of small retail shops with a common parking lot), a form of development some lamented was leading to the "suburbanization" of the urban streetscape. These retail outlets were an especially serious concern in the Lincoln Park and Lake View neighborhoods, where developers built strip malls with setbacks to provide customers the convenience of parking within view of the front door.

In 1999, the City Council passed an amendment that set design standards for strip smalls, giving the city the authority to review and approve such plans to ensure that their design blended with the surrounding neighborhoods.[17] The Strip Center Ordinance regulates building materi-

als, access, parking, buffers and screens, landscaping, and signs. It also sets standards for lighting and requires that walls facing a public thoroughfare have windows, doors and brick detailing, thus eliminating unsightly barren walls along the street.

Clearly, an overarching goal of the measure is to preserve the sense of continuity between storefronts, sidewalks, and city streets. The ordinance requires that developers create pedestrian walkways and mandates that driveways be situated away from any nearby residential properties; it also restricts the setbacks of strip centers and confines parking lots to the sides of retail buildings in neighborhoods with an established streetscape. Concerns about safety precluded the city from limiting parking lots to the rear of buildings—a design alternative that had been successfully used in other cities.

These efforts to foster attractive urban design, while important to the city, did not compare in scale to those undertaken by many suburbs or even by several large cities. Several of Chicago's suburbs, including Des Plaines, Evanston, and Skokie, all adopted far more ambitious policies that enlist the input of design review committees. San Francisco created urban design guidelines in 1971 to protect its streetscape from unwanted forms of development. Spurred in part by public backlash against the 853-foot TransAmerica Building (completed in 1972), San Francisco's regulations govern not only the height and bulk but also the color of new buildings and their effect on "view corridors" (i.e., sight lines).

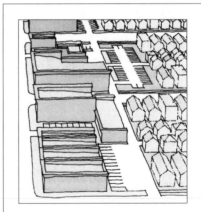

This graphic was used by the city to illustrate a traditional street-oriented retail district with an alley in the rear. (©Farr Associates Architecture | Planning | Preservation, Chicago, Illinois)

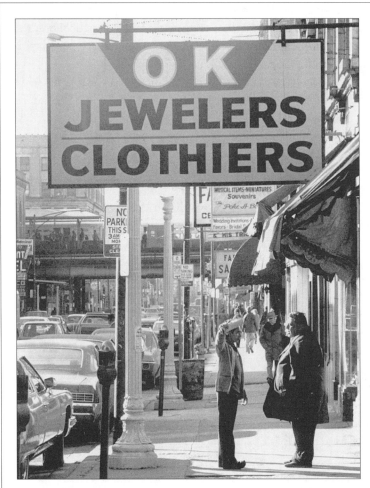

The 900 block of West Belmont Avenue (note the CTA Belmont Station on today's Red Line in the distance), circa 1974, is an example of a "pedestrian friendly" environment that several of the ordinances passed by the city in the 1990s were intended to protect. A mix of storefronts along a narrow street in close proximity to transit stops make this North Side business area attractive to those traveling on foot. (Courtesy of the American Planning Association)

Chicago was a pioneer, however, in negotiating agreements directly with major retailers to protect the visual character of its retail districts. For example, during the late 1990s the city and Walgreen Co. agreed on a set of design guidelines that precludes the construction of concrete-block façades lacking architectural detail—a style typical among the pharmacy's earlier outlets. Under the terms of the Walgreen agreement, any new store will be "street-oriented" and "articulated with rhythm and texture." This initiative came in response to complaints that the stores being built by Walgreens and other retail chains detracted from the visual quality of the neighborhood.

Similarly, an amendment passed in 1999 set design standards for parking garages in order to make these facilities more compatible with the character of the surrounding area.[18] In addition to imposing façade and landscaping requirements as well as mandating that parked cars not be visible from the street, the amendment requires that automobiles be directed away from residential and pedestrian areas and street locations susceptible to traffic problems. Enforcing these special ordinances gave the city insights and experience that were instrumental in the effort to rewrite the zoning code in 2004.

Only time will tell how well some of these urban design policies have achieved their goals. When critiquing the scope of contemporary zoning, Richard Babcock lamented that "Instead of simplifying, we've made everything terribly complex," fearing that such complexity stifles development and brings unintended consequences.[19] In Chicago, however, the expansion of zoning into new areas has occurred incrementally and generally with the benefit of broad public support.

CHAPTER 11

Aldermen and the Community

In the city's earliest days, Chicago's aldermen ruled their wards like fiefdoms. "They were first and last the tribunes of the neighborhoods, less concerned with governing than dividing the largesse," says Donald L. Miller in describing the nineteenth-century City Council. "When an alderman rose in council chambers to speak for a 'courtesy' for his district, he invariably got the support of his fellow[s]; 'aldermanic privilege,' it was called."[1] Although much has changed since those turbulent years, Chicago is still widely known for its rough-and-tumble politics—a reputation attributable in no small way to aldermanic prerogative in zoning decisions.

The power that aldermen have wielded over development in their wards is a well-chronicled part of the city's past. Historian Robin L. Einhorn notes that during Chicago's earliest days, "Alderman were ... trustees of the 'private affairs' of their propertied constituents."[2] Through the early twentieth century, the aldermen filled the void left by the absence of established procedures to review and approve large-scale developments. Some were likened to "little mayors" because of their ability to set an agenda for their wards. Anyone seeking to construct a building in a ward generally contacted the ward office.

The expansion of city government gradually changed the nature of the aldermen's work. As a matter of political expediency, many city departments established the practice of deferring to the requests of aldermen. "Aldermen regularly intervened in city departments seeking such favors for voters as tree cutting, alley cleaning, and permits for driveways and for building conversions," notes Richard Thale in the *Encyclopedia of Chicago*.[3] Bill and Lori Granger provide a more critical

The front rows of the Chicago City Council chambers are filled to capacity in 1947. It was a busy year for planning activity, which included the creation of the Chicago Land Clearance Commission, extensive urban renewal, and the election of Mayor Martin Kennelly, who ran on a platform of revitalizing the city. (Chicago Historical Society)

synopsis: "Political corruption was wide-open in nineteenth-century Chicago, and it merely changed its form as the twentieth century took shape."[4]

The granting of favors by aldermen to ward constituents was a key feature of Chicago politics. Aldermen won votes by doling out patronage jobs, building permits, zoning changes, and other material incentives that enabled them to cultivate individual relationships with voters. For most of Chicago's aldermen, serving constituents and accruing power took precedence over policymaking.

With the advent of zoning regulations, the general presumption was that the politics of land-use decisions would be swept away and replaced with a more scientific approach guided by the principles of effective city planning. In actual practice, Chicago's "strong-council/weak-mayor" system virtually insured that aldermen retained a high degree of control over zoning decisions. Authority to amend the zoning ordinance was lodged in City Council, and politics held sway. Aldermen not only used their power to make amendments to the zoning map at the request of their constituents, they exerted significant influence over the Zoning Board of Appeals (ZBA). On matters pertaining to zoning in their wards, members of the City Council were tacitly given veto power by fellow councilmen.[5] Out of this tradition, "aldermanic privilege" was refined, allowing members of the City Council to initiate or block actions by the full council on matters concerning their wards.[6]

CHANGING TIMES

During both the Great Depression and World War II, the number of requests for zoning changes and variations dropped sharply. The flow of investment into new construction declined, leaving zoning out of the spotlight. After the war, however, the quickening pace of real-estate investment made zoning changes more urgent. The number of requests for zoning amendments and variations skyrocketed, putting the aldermen in a position of great power. Developers were on the move, encouraged by Mayor Martin Kennelly's efforts to modernize the city.

Leon Despres (right) at a campaign meeting in 1955. Elected alderman of the 5th Ward (Hyde Park) that year on a ticket of reform, Despres served on the City Council through 1974 and on the Chicago Plan Commission during the terms of Jane Byrne and Harold Washington. An outspoken advocate of open and honest government, his vigilance often put him at odds with aldermen trying to use zoning changes to their maximum advantage. (Chicago Historical Society)

Eager to meet the pent-up demand for new housing, developers curried favor with aldermen for zoning changes, creating an environment in some wards ripe for graft and corruption. The Chicago Home Rule Commission observed in 1954 that aldermanic privilege led to "allegations of political favoritism and of an uncoordinated system [whereby] changes … were made according to no plan or design…"[7]

Complaints about the influence of aldermen, the number of amendments they approved, and the effect of these amendments on the integrity of the zoning ordinance revealed the tarnished image of zoning. To counter this, the City Council established a requirement in 1954 that the Plan Commission review any proposed amendment. Compliance with commission recommendations was generally good at first, but aldermen still had room to maneuver. Proposals disapproved in committee, for example, were placed "on file" rather than killed, allowing an alderman to "take the amendment from the file at any time and 'slip it through' on an omnibus roll call."[8] This practice was finally abolished in late 1954.

Although aldermen could push routine zoning changes in their wards through the City Council, many were systematically excluded from the more notable zoning decisions of this era. When Leon Despres began his first term as alderman of the 5th Ward in 1955, proposals for zoning changes submitted to the Building and Zoning Committee were always "taken under advisement" rather than acted upon at once, even if a public hearing had been held. The committee rarely met in open forum; instead, decisions were made by the chairman and select members behind closed doors and then adopted by the full council. Aldermen within the inner circle had the benefit of being part of the decision-making process, but aldermen on the outside—even those serving on the committee—were often reduced to asking the chairman for information.[9]

The Zoning Ordinance must be kept Attuned to Public Needs

Cartoon reprinted from *… And on the Eighth Day: The Last Word on City Planning and Planners,* by Richard Hedman and Fred Bair, Jr., American Society of Planning Officials, 1961.

The dynamics of zoning changed markedly after Richard J. Daley unseated Martin Kennelly in 1955. Daley gradually centralized control over many city functions and consolidated power through the patronage system, giving him control over some 35,000 jobs in Chicago and the rest of Cook County, as well as great influence over aldermen and city services. Daley was astutely aware of the vicissitudes of city politics and assembled a majority bloc in the City Council that was unfailingly loyal to him.[10] Chicago's political machine was reenergized and remained a major force until the 1980s, long after other big city machines had ceased to function.

The creation of the Department of City Planning in 1956 and the completion of the ambitious efforts to overhaul the zoning ordinance the following year further strengthened Daley's authority over planning and zoning. The work of the planning department sharply reduced the role of the Chicago Plan Commission, which became primarily an advisory body, prompting its chairman to resign in protest.[11] Equally significant, the massive zoning changes of 1957—especially the provisions for Planned Development (see Chapter 6)—put the city's planning staff at the negotiating table on major developments in the city.

These changes ushered in an era marked by extensive involvement of city staff in planning, zoning, and development decisions. The planning department became the place where major deals were negotiated. Aldermen now had reason to think twice before breaking ranks with the mayor and his staff. When embarking on major projects, developers understood that they needed to approach an alderman *and* the planning department at an early stage. New sources of public funds as well as the growing use of various creative-financing techniques insured that the mayor and his staff had a prominent place at the table.

Nevertheless, the mayor afforded aldermen considerable discretion over routine zoning changes in their wards, recognizing that this would enhance their loyalty to him.[12] Indeed, the ability to secure zoning changes for constituents was the basis for much of an alderman's clout. Joel Rast sums it up this way: "As long as a particular alderman was loyal to the mayor and votes for the machine were being delivered in the ward

in question, Daley was unlikely to interfere in something as minor as a zoning variance."[13]

Although the City Council deferred to the mayor on important issues, it remained standard practice for this legislative body to defer to aldermen on day-to-day zoning matters in their wards. Rarely did fellow aldermen cast "no" votes when an alderman proposed a routine zoning change in his ward, even when neighborhood residents staunchly opposed such changes.

TWO ILLUSTRATIVE CASES

The heavy-handedness of many zoning decisions during the late 1960s is illustrated by two examples of zoning amendments approved by the City Council. One example involves Ritchie Court, a short street in the historic Gold Coast neighborhood; the other, curiously enough, involves an alley in the Loop commercial district.

Gold Coast residents cried foul in 1967 when a developer acquired several parcels on Ritchie Court and applied for a zoning change from R7 to R8 to increase the size of a proposed high-rise apartment building on a site occupied by a series of Victorian brownstones. Prominent residents living in the area hired an attorney to fight the zoning change. Although the city scheduled a public hearing (as required by the zoning ordinance),

The high rise at 1313 Ritchie Court, shown above from the foot of Stone Street, was the source of controversy in the Gold Coast during the late 1960s. (Chaddick collection)

William S. Singer.

the hearing was postponed until both sides could prepare testimony.[14] Despite simmering neighborhood opposition, the hearing was never held and, a year later, the Building and Zoning Committee approved the zoning change. The amendment then sailed through the City Council, with the committee chairman Ralph Metcalfe defending the action by pointing out that the planning department had recommended the change.

When asked about the hearing, Metcalfe claimed he had simply overlooked the "promise" to hold a hearing due to his health-related absence from office.[15] A court ruling later overturned the amendment on grounds that there had not been a hearing. Nevertheless, the City Council still had the upper hand and gradually exhausted its opposition. Over the objections of recently elected Alderman William Singer, who strongly opposed the measure, it passed a new amendment upzoning the site in 1971.[16]

The second example involves an east-west alley between Madison and Monroe streets in the Central Area. In early 1969, Alderman Fred Roti sponsored an amendment to rename this alley as a street, Arcade Place, even though it was not being opened to traffic or in any way improved. With this action, the developers of 230 W. Monroe qualified for a FAR bonus (in return for a 20-foot, first-floor setback from the new "street"), allowing for the addition of 12 percent more floor area (over 50,000 square feet) to their proposed building. Alderman Roti candidly told a *Chicago Daily News* reporter, "Nobody talked to me about this. I walk around the Loop all the time and I noticed this alley. It's Arcade [Place] east and west and it didn't make sense to me to be an alley here."[17]

Reform-minded public servants were aghast at the prevalence of these types of zoning changes. In 1969, while challenging a package of proposed zoning amendments, Aldermen Leon Despres and Seymour Simon accused their fellow council members of using zoning changes to enrich developers and charged that frequent "piecemeal zoning amendments … are drastically changing the city." Despres and Simon drew attention to the fact that the Building and Zoning Committee made its decisions at secret meetings with no notice to the public. Although Simon recognized that he was violating the "aldermanic courtesy" through his criticism of actions outside of his ward, he was outraged that gasoline stations and drive-in restaurants were being permitted in residential areas. Their efforts did not persuade many of their colleagues to disregard the "courtesy," however; the City Council overwhelmingly passed the package of zoning changes.[18]

Members of the media and professional planners gradually shed light on the unspoken rules that seemed to govern the City Council's policies on zoning changes. In 1970, columnist Mike Royko, a particularly prominent critic, wrote: "In Chicago, the secret of alchemy is shared by a handful of real estate operators, big investors, aldermen and other top city officials.… When they cast their rezoning spell on a piece of real estate, things grow that never grew before."[19]

Attorney Richard Wexler voiced his concerns over the tendency of the Zoning Board of Appeals to defer to the aldermen. "Petitioners commonly solicit their aldermen to appeal to the Board and the question of 'how your alderman feels about the variation' is one frequently asked," he concluded.[20] Some aldermen used this

Arcade Place, shown here at the intersection with Franklin Street, was reclassified from an alley to a street in 1969 in order to provide a developer a floor-area-ratio bonus. (Chaddick collection)

influence to solicit campaign contributions and other favors from the recipients of zoning variations.

Richard Babcock expressed deep concerns in 1973 about the ability of individual aldermen to use zoning changes to deliver favors to constituents. "I have a very hard time justifying it [as public policy]," he lamented, "but I don't know how you're going to end that."[21] Echoing the sentiment voiced by others, Babcock believed that the adoption of a comprehensive plan could help make zoning change more rational and systematic. Although Chicago has published many plans over the decades—some being general policy proposals and others being somewhat more specific guides for development—few were linked to zoning.

By the mid-1970s, it was apparent that aldermen had become quite comfortable with the zoning practices at work in the city and would resist efforts to promote reform. The ordinance's permissiveness, together with the heavily amended nature of the zoning maps, left the door open for more spot changes. Accustomed to the malleable, pro-development nature of the zoning ordinance, many aldermen considered the ability to make zoning changes one of their job entitlements; some used their power to win favors for friends or family members.[22] More than a few were sent to jail for taking bribes in exchange for influencing zoning changes or for the issuance of building permits.[23]

Calls for more accountability became more difficult to ignore as community organizations grew larger and more sophisticated. The city's newspapers also took an interest in the issue. In 1987, the *Chicago Sun-Times* reviewed 400 rezoning cases and found "a pattern of campaign contributions for aldermen who held veto powers over rezoning."[24] Lerner Newspapers conducted a random review of 92 cases before the City Council Zoning Committee in 1991 and found that the committee, without exception, deferred to the aldermen. Although the zoning department recommended rejecting 26 of these cases, the committee readily approved 23 of them and deferred the remaining three, which it eventually approved. "The advice of the Zoning Department appears to have a tenuous effect on the aldermen," noted reporter Jonathan H. Marshall at the time.[25]

AN ERA OF GREATER TRANSPARENCY

Structural and procedural changes, along with the decline of Chicago's political machine, have had the effect of making aldermen more accountable in recent years. Although the City Council still generally defers to the local alderman when voting on zoning measures in his or her ward, the process of amending the zoning ordinance has become more transparent. Due to the increased complexity of building and zoning issues and the heightened awareness of concerned citizens in many Chicago wards, local elected officials now have less latitude than they had in the past.

Several wards now have zoning advisory bodies or hold public hearings on proposed changes to solicit citizen input. Dick Simpson, who was elected alderman of the 44th Ward in 1971, created the first such body. Called the "community zoning board," this volunteer group reviewed all proposed zoning changes, and the alderman was bound to abide by its decision.

The board was successful enough that a group of independent aldermen led by Simpson sponsored an ordinance in 1974 to create similar entities in all 50 wards. With Leon Despres, William Singer, and several others signed on as co-sponsors, the measure envisioned establishing a community zoning board in any ward in which signatures were gathered from just two percent of all registered voters. Each board would have seven appointees selected by the mayor from a list of ten nominees.[26]

Many aldermen and the city's planning department opposed the idea. Assistant planning commissioner Martin Murphy objected on the grounds the some decisions "have to be made on a citywide basis." Murphy supported his position by referring to the opposition the city had to overcome to allow for the construction of

Dick Simpson.

City council considers local zoning control

Headline appearing in the *Austin News* in 1974.

the Brickyard Shopping Center.[27] Although the ordinance was defeated, many aldermen have since voluntarily created community zoning boards. Not all aldermen have ceded power to the same degree, but several have given these groups considerable influence over zoning decisions.

Developments such as these signal a new era of accountability for the city's aldermen. In recent years, a growing number of aldermen lacking ties to the machine have been elected to the City Council. Particularly in gentrifying neighborhoods—where most residents have little need for or interest in requesting favors from the ward office—aldermen are more open to community input and take a broader view of zoning and other public policy decisions.

Rising community awareness has also limited the discretion of aldermen and created an atmosphere of accountability. In one outstanding case, residents of the 35th Ward placed a referendum on the ballot in November, 2002, requiring the alderman, Vilma Colom, to hold public hearings on any proposed zoning change. Residents were incensed when Colom granted a zoning change against the community's wishes after she made statements implying that she agreed with the residents' position. Following the referendum, which passed overwhelmingly, proposals for zoning changes in the ward faced intense challenges. Two such proposals drew sharp negative reactions, a petition drive, and even picketing of Colom's office. The alderman's failure to fully implement the public-hearing requirement was apparently a decisive factor in her being voted out of office in 2003.

The democratization of zoning changes was also the basis for a new citywide requirement imposed in 2001 whereby property owners seeking zoning amendments, special uses, and variations must post a large sign on the site (see discussion in Chapter 13). These black-and-red alert signs made it easier for neighborhood residents to monitor proposed zoning changes in their ward.

Due to increased transparency and greater community involvement, the "aldermanic courtesy" with respect to zoning is not now as durable as it once was. In May, 2004, many aldermen broke ranks with a pair of fellow aldermen in whose wards Wal-Mart was seeking zoning changes. Encountering intense opposition from residents and businesses in their own wards as well as labor groups voicing concern about the superstore's non-union practices, many council members ignored aldermanic courtesy and simply voted *no*. By a narrow margin, one of the proposed zoning changes passed and the other failed. It is significant that the successful proposal was supported by an alderman who not only worked hard but also reminded colleagues of the "courtesy" before the votes were cast.

EMPOWERING COMMUNITY ORGANIZATIONS

The ability of community groups to sway an alderman's position on zoning issues has rankled some in the development community. There are claims that some aldermen have surrendered control over zoning issues to the people they represent in a less-than-appropriate way.[28] Critics also accuse aldermen of allowing neighborhood groups to hold development projects hostage until their demands are met.

Should residents have a voice in rezonings?

Headline appearing in the *Lincoln-Belmont Booster,* 1975.

A recent case involving DePaul University illustrates how the neighborhood can be the driving force in decisions about development. The university considered a large site near the school's Lincoln Park campus an attractive location for student housing and, in concert with a private developer, proposed construction of a multi-story dormitory to house 500 students. The community was adamant that the proposed building was too large, had too little parking, and would aggravate traffic problems. After lengthy negotiation, the developer reduced the density, took steps to increase parking and control traffic, and added ground-floor retail space to enliven the street.

Concerns about aldermanic practices surfaced again as the city launched its effort to write a new zoning ordinance in 2001. The media and representatives of business and civic organizations urged the city to revisit the policy.[29] For a brief period, the city appeared ready to consider taking steps to lessen the effect of aldermanic prerogative. In the end, however, no significant changes were made.

Recent history suggests that the level of neighborhood vigilance on matters pertaining to zoning and development will continue to rise. The effort by residents living on or near North Michigan Avenue in 2005 to block a proposed high-rise tower behind Fourth Presbyterian Church not only illustrates this point, but also raises the question of whether downtown development should be subject to the same political process as development in other parts of the city.

It may still be true in some wards, as political observer Milton Rakove noted in 1978, that "stability, continuity, adaptation, subordination of private interests to party needs, and practical politics are still the watchwords in Chicago and Cook County Democratic politics."[30] As the voice of the community grows stronger, however, local elected officials are more vulnerable to shifting public opinion than they were years ago.

Such neighborhood dynamics bring to mind Edward Bassett's observations about zoning in New York more than 80 years ago. "It is remarkable to what extent the zoning plan becomes what the property owners of each district want it to be," he wrote, hinting at his frustration with the malleability of that city's ordinance.[31] Although circumstances differ sharply between wards, a similar observation could certainly be made about Chicago today.

Mayor Richard J. Daley (seated at right) has dinner with (from left) Harry Chaddick, an unidentified man, luminaries Frank Bogart (mayor of Palm Springs, California) and Phil Regan, and P.J. Cullerton (former chair of the Chicago City Council's zoning committee) during the 1960s. Cullerton and Mayor Daley made regular visits to Chaddick's Palm Springs resort. (DePaul Special Collections and Archives)

CHAPTER 12
Stalemate:
The 30-Year Struggle to Overhaul Zoning

As we have seen, barely ten years after the overhaul of Chicago's zoning ordinance in 1957, many citizen groups were voicing criticisms that the city's zoning policies had once again become outdated and inconsistent with local needs. Rising congestion, unanticipated new building styles, and the exploitation of loopholes by developers raised questions about the city's land-use controls. Yet the vagaries of city politics, the sudden deaths of two mayors, and the scope of the task itself all prevented the city from initiating a second, comprehensive revision of the ordinance for more than three decades.

By 1967, more than 1,000 text and map changes to the ordinance had been adopted. Given the ease and frequency of amendments adopted by the City Council and the city's failure to enforce some of its policies, the image of zoning suffered. Indeed, the architects of the 1957 ordinance scarcely imagined that the policies they created would hold sway for nearly a half-century. Several among them championed the view that the ordinance had to change.

The amortization schedule created to eliminate nonconforming uses and structures was eventually deemed a failure, although the consequences of this failure were less serious than some had anticipated. Vigorous enforcement of the building code had eliminated thousands of substandard dwelling units from the city, and private investment was flowing into some of the city's more desirable neighborhoods. Due to the city's failure to enforce its own policies, however, many called into question the city's commitment to the zoning ordinance.

A large enough number of issues had been raised in various quarters that Mayor Richard J. Daley launched a major rewrite of the ordinance in early 1967. He created the Zoning Ordinance Review Committee and once again turned to Harry Chaddick to lead the effort. Chaddick, then serving as chairman of the Zoning Board of Appeals, made a telling comment to the *Sun-Times:* "I know I'm opening up a Pandora's box."[1] To serve as staff for the project, the committee hired two zoning consultants: George Kranenberg (who had been technical director of the 1957 effort) and Ron Peters (formerly Cook County's assistant zoning administrator).

Chaddick and other members of the Zoning Ordinance Review Committee made notable strides in their first months of work. At one time, there were ten full-time city employees working under the direction of Chaddick, who worked without pay.[2] In October, 1967, the committee issued a preliminary list of seven priority areas in the zoning ordinance that needed further review.[3] The team also identified more than 60 potential problem areas, such as off-street parking, signs, floor area ratio, and residential uses in business districts, that were worthy of more attention by policymakers.[4] The amendments that resulted from this effort were relatively minor in scope and provoked no major disagreements; nevertheless, many people anticipated that more significant initiatives would be forthcoming as the effort continued.

To the disappointment of Chaddick's committee, this was not the

Lewis Hill, city planning commissioner, 1967–78.

case. In January, 1968, the city's urban renewal and planning departments merged to create the Department of Planning, City, and Community Development (DPCCD). This powerful agency was put under the leadership of Lewis Hill, who made the case that the Zoning Ordinance Review Committee should be under its purview.[5] When the

Robert J. Boylan, advocate of zoning modernization and planner for Harry F. Chaddick.

mayor asked that the committee no longer report to him but to Hill instead, both Kranenberg and Peters resigned.[6] Each had strong disagreements with Hill about the function of zoning and held critical views about the process being employed by the city to approve zoning changes.[7]

The committee staff felt that zoning must be based on planning in order to *regulate* development. Hill wielded considerable influence in Daley's administration and viewed zoning as a tool that should be adaptable to *encourage* development. He felt that the city should be open to negotiation and ready to respond to opportunities presented by developers and financiers. Other influential public servants shared Hill's view, including urban renewal director Phil Doyle, who appreciated the high degree of flexibility needed to give birth to Lake Meadows, Sandburg Village, and other inner-city redevelopments. These officials favored high-rise construction and the mixing of residential and business uses, which collided with the vision of various committee members. "We were only going through mental gymnastics," complained Kranenberg to a *Chicago Daily News* reporter.[8]

The city made the best of the departure of Kranenberg and Peters by hiring Barton-Aschman Associates to provide technical assistance. Barton-Aschman named its zoning expert, Robert Boylan, who had been deeply involved in the creation of the 1957 ordinance, to head the project. Chaddick lauded Boylan's skills but soon tendered his own resignation due to differences of opinion with Hill. The committee then dissolved, and the opportunity to revise the ordinance was lost.[9]

The late 1960s were a trying time for the residents of many neighborhoods. Deteriorating housing conditions, the decline of local retailing, and "white flight" all had devastating effects. Manufacturing fell onto hard times and the high hopes that had surrounded the massive investments of urban renewal programs began to fade. Large tracts of vacant land lay idle in blighted areas and the city's industrial and manufacturing districts. Protests against urban renewal began to occur.

Mounting unrest during the civil rights movements of the 1960s forced the city to deal with new social and political problems. Riots erupted in Chicago following a 1966 accident involving a fire engine that killed an African-American woman. The segregation of African-Americans, who were concentrated in poorly maintained housing on the South and West sides, triggered an outcry to end housing discrimination. Dr. Martin Luther King's protest marches in Chicago were periodically disrupted by violence. The riots following the April, 1968, assassination of Dr. King and during the Democratic Party's National Convention in Chicago that summer hurt the city's image.

Mayor Daley continued his call for zoning reform, but with less fanfare. In 1969, the Office of Zoning Review, housed within the DPCCD, was charged with facilitating comprehensive zoning-map revisions and text changes. Its staff drew heavily on the work of Boylan and Barton-Aschman who, between late 1969 and mid-1970, conducted a detailed parcel-by-parcel land-use inventory of the entire city.[10]

In June, 1970, the Office of Zoning Review prepared extensive reports dealing with many technical aspects of development control in the city. Prepared with the assistance of zoning lawyers Richard Babcock and Fred Bosselman, these reports expounded upon the need for new regulations governing residential floor area ratio, drive-in establishments, sign content and size, special-use standards, and the elimination of nonconforming buildings. They contained specific recommendations for zoning text changes and modifications to the zoning maps in 14 critical areas.

Planning commissioner Hill, who did not want to make zoning more rigid and restrictive, allowed these recommendations to languish. Hill felt that the zoning review staff was infringing upon the authority of aldermen by making frequent negative recommendations on proposed map changes.[11] In February, 1971, the Office of Zoning Review was dissolved. Although 18 major amendments were submitted, only seven were adopted, none of which involved the suggested map amendments.[12] As a result, yet another opportunity to modernize the zoning ordinance slipped away.

Top official calls city's zoning law outmoded

Politics, economics, history resist zoning code revamp

Critical Look At Chicago Zoning

City needs new zoning law

Let's curb zoning ordinance

Daley Calls For Brand New Zoning Law

Zoning law feeds disaster, rather than development

Newspaper headlines appearing between 1967 and 1987. (Chaddick collection)

Mayor Harold Washington and Alderman Edward Vyrdolyak have a humorous exchange in the City Council chambers. Former Alderman Leon Despres is in the foreground. (Chicago Public Library)

THE STALEMATE CONTINUES

Daley's reign as mayor was nearing an end by 1976, when he launched his last effort to modernize the zoning ordinance. Despite earlier differences, Chaddick and Hill agreed to co-chair the new Zoning Review Commission. As suggested by a headline in the *Chicago Daily News*—"Total Rezoning of City Slated"—this effort was expected to be a large-scale initiative.[13] The commission included many prominent figures, including Board of Appeals Chairman Jack Guthman, Zoning Administrator Harry Manley, Corporation Counsel William R. Quinlan, and Aldermen Michael Bilandic, Wilson Frost, and Edward Vrdolyak. The death of Mayor Daley on December 20, 1976, however, derailed the project. The group dissolved and no further efforts were made in this direction for several years.

In 1979, Jane Byrne became mayor, elected on a platform of revitalizing the city and shoring up its infrastructure. To demonstrate her commitment to improve living conditions, Byrne briefly lived in the Cabrini-Green public housing complex. During her term, she also established a blue-ribbon committee to review the zoning ordinance as well as the city's development and planning policies. Yet it appears that this committee failed to meet.

Harold Washington defeated Byrne in 1983. Washington, like Byrne, brought many policy-oriented staffers to City Hall who had a strong commitment to better housing, neighborhood improvement, downtown development, and public open spaces. It even appeared that zoning might return to the agenda in September, 1983, when Alderman Edward Vrdolyak set up a new Zoning Review Commission to investigate the need for a comprehensive rezoning effort. A rift between the aldermanic factions loyal to Vrdolyak and Washington, however, grew to extraordinary proportions, so nothing came of this zoning effort.

After being reelected in 1987, Mayor Washington announced that one of his chief priorities was to review and overhaul the city's zoning ordinance and building code. A coalition of civic organizations, including the Metropolitan Housing and Planning Council, Friends of Downtown, and the Landmarks Preservation Council, urged him to appoint a task

U.S. Rep. Danny K. Davis, former alderman of the 29th Ward.

Graham Grady, zoning administrator, 1989–94.

force to review the zoning ordinance.[14] Alderman Danny K. Davis, chairman of the City Council Zoning Committee, made known his intention to spearhead zoning reform but felt that a new comprehensive plan was needed first.[15] Once again, however, fate intervened with Mayor Washington's sudden death on November 25, 1987, interrupting a process that had just begun to gather momentum.

The push for major revisions to the ordinance was fueled by a rising tide of criticism from planning specialists and the general public about the deteriorating reputation of zoning in the city. Robert Boylan was especially vocal in expressing his concern that Chicago lacked updated land-use information to assist with planning decisions, stating that the city needed a workable system for updating maps after authorizing changes in the zoning of individual properties. The absence of up-to-date zoning and land-use information, he felt, fostered an environment of inconsistent and ineffective planning and invited more spot amendments.

Even lawyers whose work focused on representing the interests of developers seeking zoning changes criticized the ordinance for being outdated and ineffective. Noted zoning attorney Jack Guthman spoke out, advocat-

ing zoning reform as a way to improve the level of predictability for developers and the community. Guthman argued in a 1984 *Tribune* editorial that amendments being adopted to the ordinance were only "temporary patches" that could not adequately address the modern needs of the city.[16] His perspective was broad, since he served on the Zoning Board of Appeals from 1970 through 1987 and was its chairman from 1975 onward.

Several aldermen, including Danny K. Davis and William J. Banks, at various times head of the City Council zoning committee, also called for an update to the ordinance. Local newspapers joined the chorus of critics by editorializing about Chicago's "Band-Aid" approach to dealing with zoning and emphasized the need for a new zoning ordinance. *Chicago Tribune* urban affairs columnist John McCarron spotlighted the antiquated character of the ordinance and its cumbersome content, writing "every Chicago mayor from Richard J. Daley to Harold Washington has promised zoning reform, yet none of them produced it."[17]

In 1989, Richard M. Daley (son of the late Richard J. Daley) was elected mayor. He had a strong interest in urban planning and demonstrated

Jack Guthman, chairman of Zoning Board of Appeals, 1975–87.

John McCarron, *Chicago Tribune* columnist.

his responsiveness to community concerns about development by opposing a plan to build low-rise buildings to replace the Hancock Center's open plaza. Daley was not yet ready to overhaul the zoning ordinance, however, when Harry Chaddick sent him an unsolicited proposal in 1991—replete with a mission statement, budget, and timetable—calling for an overhaul of the Chicago zoning ordinance.[18] Chaddick, who was now 88, considered this his last good shot to prod the city into action and enlisted the support of Richard Babcock, Robert Boylan, and others, to no avail.

Daley's first zoning administrator, Graham Grady, also pushed to modernize the ordinance. Bringing fresh perspective and experience as a zoning attorney to the position, Grady identified sections of the ordinance most urgently needing attention and worked to establish priorities for municipal action. Grady also drafted a widely circulated proposal for a comprehensive rewrite of zoning.

AN URBAN RENAISSANCE

In the early 1990s, Chicago witnessed a residential building boom. Condominiums and townhomes, even new communities, appeared in many neighborhoods. Developers found opportunities to demolish outdated buildings along commercial streets and replace them with three- and four-story condominiums. New enclaves of townhomes also emerged, in some

Elizabeth Hollander, city planning commissioner, 1984. (Photo by Jessie Ewing)

instances with curb-cuts for driveways that interrupted local traffic flow. Residents and organizations often objected to these radical changes in the density and appearance of their neighborhoods.

Public appreciation of the link between planning and quality of life gradually increased as tall buildings sprouted up along homey side streets, casting the older residences in deep shade. In some areas, neighborhood streets developed a "canyon effect" as multi-story condominium buildings arose side by side.

Manufacturers also felt the impact of neighborhood change. Converting aging industrial buildings to residential units became a trend, creating new conflicts that spurred the creation of Planned Manufacturing Districts, an innovation designed to protect these areas that is summarized in Appendix A. The city began to address the most prominent zoning issues one at a time, taking action on a series of fronts.

Some observers nevertheless questioned whether the city would ever muster the political will to embark on an overhaul of the ordinance. Planning commissioner Elizabeth Hollander observed in *Crain's Chicago Business* in 1989 that "zoning reform is a cause without a constituency."[19] Hollander went on to surmise that a constituency would eventually emerge when enough residents felt the effects of an outdated zoning ordinance—and when the resources became available in City Hall. By the century's end, events had proved her correct.

CHAPTER 13

A New Zoning Ordinance

As the twentieth century drew to a close, the city's population rose for the first time in nearly 50 years, and tens of thousands of housing units were added to its tax rolls.[1] Many neighborhoods that had seen little construction in several generations underwent a metamorphosis. New development was changing the feel of neighborhoods everywhere, and people who never thought about zoning before began complaining about the lack of restraint. As more and more amendments were adopted, often taking residents of affected areas by surprise, the general public grew increasingly cynical about the politics of zoning.

The residential building boom that began in the 1970s was refueled in the 1990s, shifting the contours of development in the city. Three forces—interest rates at historically low levels, a dramatic fall in crime rates, and a spectacular rise in property values—converged, giving residential property owners strong incentive to pay attention to zoning.

After years of sluggish appreciation in property values, tens of thousands of city dwellers suddenly found themselves in possession of enormously valuable real estate. The growing interest of maturing baby boomers and empty nesters in an urban lifestyle fueled the market for upscale homes. Between 1993 and 2000, the number of zoning requests processed by the City Council more than doubled, rising from about 300 per year to more than 600.

With this development boom came changing attitudes about the purpose and role of zoning. The conversion of factories into lofts and the construction of new residential units in distressed commercial areas suggested that the city was not always best served by an ordinance promoting the strict separation of land uses. In many neighborhoods, different

This view of the Central Area on July 5, 2001, shows the density of development between the Hancock Center, partially visible at left, and the Sears Tower, on the far right. The North River Industrial Corridor is visible on the right, with the Goose Island Planned Manufacturing District nearby at the lower right-hand corner. (Photo by Lawrence Okrent)

land uses in close proximity, without buffer zones or other contextual measures, were creating appealing new environments.

Around the country, new paradigms, including "smart growth" and "the new urbanism," elevated awareness of more flexible approaches to land-use planning. Many communities adopted zoning ordinances intended to foster compact development, neighborhoods with a mix of land uses, and pedestrian-friendly environments. In densely built cities, planners championed the benefits of transit-oriented development, the pedestrian aspect of neighborhood streets, and the conversion of nonresidential property into housing.

Some of the underlying concepts could be traced to the pioneering work of Jane Jacobs, who challenged conventional wisdom about the value of high-rises and the benefits of the strict separation of land uses. In her 1961 book *The Death and Life of Great American Cities*, she describes healthy cities as an amalgamation of diverse and ever-changing land uses and calls for a reassessment of traditional planning premises. To promote healthy variety, Jacobs exhorts urban planners to create neighborhoods with multiple "primary functions," saying, "the point of cities is multiplicity of choice."[2] Even where an area had office space, residential living,

or retail activity as the principal function, she urges planners to make allowances for restaurants, parks, and cultural facilities.

A dramatic expansion in the use of tax-increment financing (TIF) also pushed development in new directions. By using TIF, the city could select targeted areas for improvement and make investments capable of attracting new development. By the year 2000, more than 13 percent of Chicago's entire property tax base fell within TIF districts.[3] Many of these districts cultivated a mix of residential and commercial activity that appealed to city dwellers.

Several of the initiatives launched in the 1990s laid a foundation for a general reassessment of the city's land-use policies. As we described in Chapter 10, new ordinances governed the construction of townhomes, strip malls, and parking garages, as well as the creation of special districts. New policies for FAR bonuses aligned the city's development incentives more closely with its urban-design priorities. Sensing the city was ready to take action, the Chicago Development Council, the Metropolitan Planning Council, and other civic and professional groups intensified their push for a more comprehensive set of changes.

DALEY TAKES ACTION

In early 2000, Mayor Daley announced that he wanted to rewrite the zoning ordinance; in July of that year he appointed a 21-member Zoning Reform Commission headed by Alderman William Banks and attorney John R. Schmidt (who was later succeeded by former planning commissioner David Mosena). The panel also included aldermen Burton Natarus, Bernard Stone, and Ray

Alderman William Banks.

Accompanied by former planning commissioners David R. Mosena and Valerie B. Jarrett, Mayor Richard M. Daley makes an announcement at City Hall in August, 1996. (Courtesy of the American Planning Association)

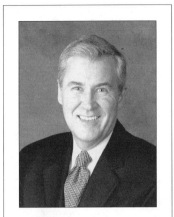

Edward J. Kus.

Suarez, as well as Plan Commission chairman Peter C.B. Bynoe, planning commissioner Christopher R. Hill, and Gerald Roper, head of the Chicagoland Chamber of Commerce, along with other civic and business leaders.[4] Zoning staff in the planning department developed a series of recommendations to support the commission's work.

Seasoned observers warned that the city would face entrenched opposition at every step of the way. Several days after the mayor's announcement, *Chicago Tribune* columnist John McCarron noted, with some exaggeration, "It won't be easy changing a zoning code with rules so generous you could build a Sears Tower on every downtown block."[5] The editorial writers of the *Chicago Sun-Times* expressed concerns that developers would hijack the process and raised the question, "A rewrite is certainly overdue, but whom will it benefit?"[6]

Naming Edward J. Kus as the commission's executive director, Mayor Daley charged the commission to substantially revise both the text portion of the zoning ordinance and the zoning map. To streamline its work, the Zoning Reform Commission was asked to exclude from its consideration the Lakefront Protection Ordinance and the Landmark Preservation Ordinance, whose modification would be awkward and politically difficult.[7] Kus was well prepared to lead this effort. Since beginning his career as an attorney in the city's law department in 1979, Kus had accumulated extensive experience in land-use and zoning law, and had worked on such high-profile projects as Navy Pier, Central Station, and Millennium Park.

In the autumn of 2000, the commission held a series of public meetings to obtain input from individuals and groups. The feedback focused on a number of concerns, including insufficient parking, excessive density, and a zoning code that was too malleable, inaccessible, and difficult to understand. Another concern was the current process for notifying residents of zoning changes in their neighborhoods. Although applicants requesting zoning changes were already required to notify by certified mail all property owners within a 250-foot radius, many residents and community groups found this measure to be grossly inadequate. The commission responded by drafting an ordinance, adopted by the City Council in early 2001, that requires a large red-and-black sign to be posted on any property under consideration for either a zoning change, a variance, or a special use—such as a parking lot, a business serving alcohol, or a drive-through establishment.[8]

The city held six more public meetings during May and June, 2001. Feedback continued to flow at these well-attended meetings. Many community representatives pushed for zoning changes to protect the character of neighborhoods. Developers and zoning attorneys voiced their hope that a new ordinance might reduce the level of confrontation they faced with the community. In particular, they called for an ordinance that would provide more durable zoning classifications and foster more predictability. Others observers were somewhat dubious about the process in view of the fact that the city had identified many priorities for change well before the hearings.

The rezoning effort gained visibility after the city issued

a heavily illustrated report, *Principles for Chicago's New Zoning Ordinance*, on June 4, 2002. Supplemented with maps, diagrams, and color photographs, the report outlined the concepts under consideration for the new ordinance. The glossy document was aimed at the informed voter (rather than professional planners) with the goal of persuading the public of the merits of the process.

Over the next several weeks, media outlets, including the *Chicago Sun-Times*, the *Chicago Tribune*, *Crain's Chicago Business*, and WTTW's *Chicago Tonight*

New Voices

The move to revise the zoning ordinance launched in 2000 was led by a new generation of planners and civic organizations whose training and vision differed from that of Harry Chaddick and his team. There was considerable agreement at various levels about the kinds of changes that were needed, but weighty questions about how to codify them, how to redesign the ordinance, and how to bring the public into the process had to be answered. The commission took the view that it could learn from other cities' experiences and worked closely with several consulting firms to find outside assistance in developing an effective new code.[9]

The city hired Duncan Associates, a company based in Austin, Texas, to direct the effort, which entrusted its leadership on the project to Kirk Bish-

Kirk Bishop.

op, head of the company's Chicago office. Drawing upon his past consulting work, which included efforts to modernize the zoning ordinances of Detroit, Minneapolis, and Pittsburgh, Bishop stressed the relevance of learning from other cities. His experience and affable style enabled him to keep the project moving while remaining attentive to the diverse views of the Zoning Reform Commission. Bishop worked closely with city zoning administrator Ed Kus and planning department staff (including Alicia Mazur Berg, commissioner; Jack Swenson, deputy commissioner; Tom Smith, assistant commissioner; Tim Barton; Erik Glass; and Jill Murray).

The Metropolitan Planning Council (MPC) remained an active participant and pushed hard for a more predictable and enforceable zoning ordinance. Led by its executive director, MarySue Barrett, and vice president, Peter Skosey, MPC convened eight neighborhood focus groups during the summer of 2001, evaluated various national models of zoning and prepared an educational CD-ROM for distribution to the general public.[10] In 2002, the organization presented nine "priority recommendations"—

Peter Skosey and MarySue Barrett of the Metropolitan Planning Council. (Metropolitan Planning Council)

addressing issues such as housing options, urban design, open space, and transportation—to the commission and pushed the city to focus on new ideas like transit-oriented development. MPC's leadership was reminiscent of that of the Chicago Real Estate Board during the effort to create the 1923 ordinance.

The 190 S. LaSalle building, noted for its distinctive roof (right center), and the Chicago Temple (upper center) are among the most prominent structures in this aerial photograph of the Loop, which the city used to depict the areas assigned the new Downtown Core (DC) zoning classification. (City of Chicago)

program, expounded at length upon the *Principles* report, drawing public attention to the topic of zoning in a way reminiscent of 45 years earlier. Blair Kamin of the *Chicago Tribune*, who noted that the "recommendations

reflect a marked shift from the Cadillac-with-tail-fins days of 1957," wrote favorably of the report, as did other journalists.[11] Ed Keegan used his position as architecture critic on Chicago Public Radio (WBEZ) to make known the significance of the proposed changes.

In the *Principles* report, the city made its case for launching a broad range of initiatives, many of which emphasized concerns about appearance and density in residential areas near the city's center. Echoing reports from the 1950s, the document emphasized that the city still has far more commercial frontage than could be reasonably supported by the marketplace; a section within the report outlined the need to creatively re-use these areas. Other sections described the advantages of zoning classifications that allow for a mix of residential and retail uses as well as the creation of new zoning districts tailored to the needs of downtown.

With its emphasis on conservation and quality of life, the report generally evoked favorable responses from planners and watchdog groups, especially from those championing pedestrian-friendly environments. A study by Clarion Associates concluded that the changes would not discourage new construction.[12] Developers, however, were quick to voice their concerns. The Chicago Development Council prepared a critique of the *Principles* report taking exception to recommendations it deemed hostile to development. It found the report to be based on "a preconceived notion that density and high-rise development are intrinsically bad notwithstanding that Chicago's high-rise lakefront skyline is one of its most admired features." The letter also expressed concern that there was no language calling for reopening discussion about the city's newly adopted system of bonuses, which, in its words, "substituted subjectivity for predictability."[13]

In late 2002 and early 2003, the city made modifications in response to the feedback the commission collected and began to unveil various chapters of the zoning text for public review. As awareness of the effort spread, crowds in excess of 100 people gathered at meetings in Lincoln Park, on the Northwest Side, and in the 48th Ward (Uptown). Input from the Zoning Reform Commission also led to a variety of changes, and on May 26, 2004, the city formally adopted the text portion of the new ordinance, which took effect the following November 1.

Legal-sounding language was replaced with instructive narrative. Entire pages of text were replaced with simple tables displaying the requirements of various zoning districts. The rules governing each type of zoning district were put in a single section to allow readers to find answers to their questions more easily and to understand the differences. Although the ordinance remained a large and complex document with more than 300 pages of text, the changes reflected Ed Kus's belief that "the average person should be able to pick up the zoning code and understand what can and can't be built in his neighborhood."

Enhancements to the city's Internet site also helped make the zoning ordinance more accessible. Previously, the city had relied on a private publisher to print the zoning code each year. In 2003, however, the ordinance was made available in both print form and electronic form on the municipal web site; the latter version was equipped with a versatile search tool and updated regularly to reflect amendments passed by the City Council.

A variety of new features, including links to aerial photography, gave the ordinance a more dynamic quality.

As summarized in the inset box on page 128, the ordinance approved in 2004 has a clear bent toward conservation, both of the existing building stock and of the prevailing density of neighborhoods. The new code embraces many new concepts, several of which represent a repudiation of zoning practices that were bedrocks of zoning just a few decades ago. Finally, it expands appreciably the city's control over several certain aspects of the development process.

After adoption of the zoning text, attention turned to the creation of new zoning maps. By early 2006, the city had completed the maps for the Central Area (a process abetted by the completion of a master plan for this area in 2003) and industrial parts of the city. The city made clear that it would work closely with aldermen to facilitate the mapping process—an approach met with concern by some in the development community, who feared that this method would encourage downzoning. Some observers warned that the mapping phase of the project would be difficult, recalling how opposition to changes to zoning

---

17-4-0405 Floor Area Ratio

17-4-0405-A   Standards

All development in "D" districts is subject to the following maximum *floor area ratio* standards:

Dash Designation	Maximum Base Floor Area Ratio	FAR Bonuses Allowed?
–3	3.0	No
–5	5.0	Yes (affordable housing and adopt-a-landmark bonuses only)
–7	7.0	Yes (affordable housing and adopt-a-landmark bonuses only)
–10	10.0	Yes (affordable housing and adopt-a-landmark bonuses only)
–12	12.0	Yes
–16	16.0	Yes

(See Sec. 17-17-0305 for rules governing the measurement of *floor area ratio*.)

17-4-0405-B   Bonus Floor Area

Under the provisions of Sec. 17-4-1000, development in dash 12 and dash 16 districts is eligible for floor area bonuses, over and above the stated maximum *base floor area ratios* of Sec. 17-4-0405-A. Floor area bonuses for affordable housing and "adopting" an historic landmark may be approved in any dash 5, dash 7, dash 10, dash 12 or dash 16 "D" district, subject to the provisions of Sec. 17-4-1004 and Sec. 17-4-1022, respectively.

Floor area ratio table for downtown (D) districts in the 2004 Chicago Zoning Ordinance. (City of Chicago)

maps had hampered an effort to modernize the zoning code in New York several years earlier.

There was also concern that the mapping phase would be driven by a political rather than analytical process. MPC shared this concern and created a program called "Zoning Change Strategy" aimed at training residents to make meaningful contributions to the map revisions. A pilot program in the Rogers Park neighborhood was successful, but funding was not available to expand the program citywide. The planning department partially filled the void, emulating MPC's program in several other wards. Nevertheless, there is continuing concern that the process for creating new maps lacks structure and is open to subjectivity.

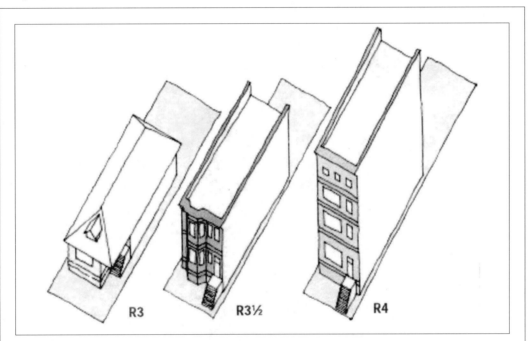

This drawing appears in the *Principles* document to illustrate the type of neighborhoods where the new R3.5 zoning classification is appropriate. In these areas, it is common to have two dwelling units per 25-foot lot with the parking garage in the rear. (©Farr Associates Architecture | Planning | Preservation, Chicago, Illinois)

renew the city during the 1950s, and the desire to preserve and even showcase Chicago's distinctive urban character after the turn of the twenty-first century.

History shows how difficult it is to anticipate the kinds of regulation needed to protect cities from poorly conceived or undesirable development. Shifting development patterns, the march of technological innovation, and the changing preferences of consumers constantly present situations that are not foreseen by the architects of zoning. The city's experience with zoning exemplifies the need for cities in the future to revise and refresh zoning ordinances more often than they have done in the past.

Chicago's first zoning ordinance of 1923, drawing upon

LESSONS FROM THE PAST

When evaluated in its entirety, Chicago's zoning story reaches well beyond the geographic limits of the city. It is a saga that should be remembered for the visionary leaders of the 1920s, the great push to

the lessons of New York, was important in spite of its simplicity. It ushered in a new era of skyscrapers with upper-level towers, altering the design and density of downtown buildings while addressing concerns about light, health, and safety. While its two-map system was the forerunner to an era of greater sophistication in land-use control, the ordinance's shortcomings became obvious by the late 1930s. It was too permissive to have a major effect on land-use patterns, allocated too much land for industrial use, and failed to produce the benefits many had expected.

The amendments of 1942 were the precursors to an era of great experimentation with new zoning concepts. The adoption of bulk limits for downtown opened the door to new building design, while the new emphasis on eliminating nonconforming uses underscored a more vigorous effort to achieve uniformity within districts. These amendments also reduced the amount of land allocated to apartments and businesses and established standards pertaining to parking for apartments. Nevertheless, these changes were insufficient in the robust postwar economy. Demand for new housing types, the opportunities of urban renewal, and new construction in the downtown area required more innovative or novel approaches.

The spirited effort to modernize the ordinance in the 1950s was arguably the finest hour in Chicago's zoning. The amendments approved

Inside the 2004 Ordinance

The ordinance adopted in 2004 is notable for its emphasis on conservation, its introduction of a variety of new zoning concepts, and the heightened level of control it affords city hall.

Bent toward Conservation. The 1957 ordinance facilitated bold new designs that swept away older housing and commercial buildings; the 2004 code reverses that direction. To protect neighborhoods from development practices that had been controversial in the past, there are height limits on residential buildings, requirements governing setbacks and green space in rear yards, restrictions requiring traditional front yards, and new rules governing driveways and curb cuts.

In residential districts, the ordinance establishes new "½ step" districts with regulations on FAR and density that fall between those found in the 1957 code. The addition of R3.5, R4.5, R5.5, and R6.5 districts as well as some business step-districts allows zoning to more closely match the scale of existing development. In addition, a new front-yard setback

requirement promotes more uniform streetscapes, as does the requirement that at least 17 percent of the street facade be windows and doors, to prevent blank walls along streets. The ordinance also reduced the maximum permitted size of some signs in some instances by as much as 75 percent.

The replacement of the highest-density residential districts (R7 and R8) with the new R6.5 district reduced the maximum FAR in some areas from as high as 10 to 6.6. This change in particular "ratcheted down" allowable density of new development in some of the city's most congested neighborhoods, correcting what was widely seen as a fundamental flaw in the 1957 amendment.

New Concepts. The 2004 ordinance introduces many concepts that have been tested elsewhere but never employed in a city as large as Chicago, which is known for the intense involvement of many community and professional organizations. This makes Chicago's new ordinance of national significance in the evolution of zoning.[14]

Through the creation of new "downtown zoning districts" (downtown core, mixed use, residential, in 1957 moved Chicago to the forefront of zoning practice, including such innovative techniques as minimum lot-area requirements for dwelling units to control density and FAR to control bulk. The city's industrial performance standards became a prototype for zoning ordinances nationwide, and its sophisticated system to deal with "economic compatibility" for commercial uses was a significant contribution to the planning profession.

Soon enough, however, complaints and criticisms were heard again. Dense high-rise development along the north lakefront in the 1960s led to a great outcry. Rather than accommodating a growing population, development seemed to occur in a free-for-all fashion. The backlash that ensued culminated in downzoning and a multiplicity of ad-hoc zoning changes. Yet several decades would pass before the city marshaled the resources and political will to systematically revisit its approach to zoning.

The zoning changes of 2004 reflect many of the same goals as those of 1942—putting constraints on dense development in certain areas and reducing heights in residential districts. The end result, however, is

and service areas), the city put into place a new system for regulating land use in the Central Area. (The changes are quite significant in residential and service zones but less so in core and mixed-use zones). Development along designated "pedestrian" and "mobility" streets is now guided by a new set of standards. On designated "pedestrian streets," gas stations, drive-through restaurants and banks, and similar auto-dependent uses are prohibited. And for the first time, the city has parking maximums; when parking exceeds a maximum, it is counted against that building's FAR.

Although the types of business and commercial districts were reduced by half, falling to just six, a new "Neighborhood Mixed Use" zoning district (B2) allows for ground-floor residential uses in commercial areas without special approval—a provision intended to make it easier to redevelop properties along underused commercial corridors. This classification allows development to mimic the typical look of a century ago, when corner stores and service shops near homes and apartments were common.

The addition of a new FAR bonus for affordable housing provides developers an incentive to offer a mix of dwelling types.

In manufacturing districts, the new code limits the number, types, and size of non-manufacturing uses with the goal of protecting the city's industrial and employment base. Due to the belief that state and federal regulation sufficiently controls pollution, the ordinance abolished the industrial performance standards created in 1957 but introduced new screening and buffer requirements.

There were also notable *administrative* innovations. A new "Type 1 Rezoning" process was established for zoning changes that have particularly significant implications for density or patterns of land use. More rigorous standards apply to "Type 1" changes than "Type 2" changes.

Heightened Municipal Control. The ordinance affords City Hall greater control over many large and mid-size developments. Many construction projects that otherwise could have proceeded as-of-right without extensive city involvement now must be submitted as Planned Developments, enabling the city to seek changes in appearance, design, landscaping, traffic enhancement, and the overall pedestrian experience.

Buildings in the highest-intensity zoning districts of the Central Area, for example, are automatically made Planned Developments when their heights exceed 440 feet, as opposed to the previous 600-foot limit. For the first time, residential developments in certain lower-density zoning districts are automatically Planned Developments if they exceed a specified number of dwelling units. In zoning districts where such "triggers" were already in place, the threshold was revised downward, forcing more projects to become PDs. New language governing FAR bonuses also gives the city more control over high-intensity developments.

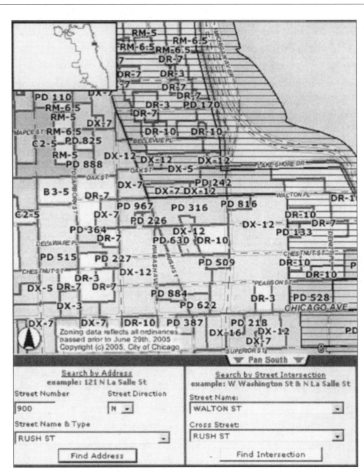

This zoning map obtained from the city's on-line search tool in 2005 shows the widespread use of the newly created downtown mixed-use (DX) and downtown residential (DR) categories in the Gold Coast neighborhood. (City of Chicago)

distinctly different. While allowing for innovation, Chicago's new ordinance is also designed to help preserve existing neighborhoods and echo

the styles of earlier eras. With the elimination of the highest-density residential classifications, the creation of "pedestrian streets," and incentives for transit-oriented development, the new ordinance places emphasis on scale and context.

The city now has more control over certain aspects of the development process, but centralizing control is not without its risks. The experiences of Philadelphia and San Francisco, where the zoning ordinances are riddled with complex controls, have not been encouraging. The challenge that Chicago faces, therefore, is to exercise its powers judiciously, consistent with larger plans and objectives, and to assure that zoning is predictable yet nimble enough to support neighborhood goals.

The Chicago Development Council has made known its view that the new "triggers" for Planned Development could create an excessive workload for the city, causing severe delays and possibly discouraging development, a credible concern.[15] Although the volume of work has increased dramatically due to heightened review requirements, the size of city staff has been reduced through budget cuts and early retirement, resulting in the loss of many experienced people. Much of the institutional knowledge about the evolution of zoning has left City Hall; much of that which remains rests with a few individuals. More than 1,000 zoning changes are now processed annually, placing a heavy burden on the staff.

LOOKING AHEAD

If history is a guide, unanticipated development trends and social changes will soon raise a civic outcry for another round of zoning changes. The unpredictability of such trends was overlooked by early advocates of zoning, who had a static view of the city and unrealistic expectations about zoning's economic and social benefits. Yet, despite the fierce political environment in which zoning decisions take place, it seems clear that this method of land-use control has paid dividends to this city.

Early proponents of zoning believed that imposing uniformity within districts would preserve and augment the value of real estate holdings. Today, some economists maintain that the benefits of zoning can be measured almost exclusively by looking at how it affects property values. Recently, however, a new view has taken root, holding that the evaluation of zoning must account for the benefits accruing to residents who value the characteristics of the neighborhood beyond that reflected by the market price.[16] The willingness of Chicago residents to invest enormous amounts of time and energy to protect subtle aspects of a neighborhood's character lends credence to this view.

It is hard to imagine a time when zoning will cease to be the source of civic debate, litigation, and intrigue, perhaps even cynicism, or when aldermen will no longer wield great influence in land-use matters. Developers will surely persist in their efforts to build to the limits allowed by zoning laws, stirring up great controversy. To this end, developers will continue to cultivate relationships with elected officials and city staff in hopes of influencing zoning.

Few planners today would go so far as to say—as Charles Nichols did more than 80 years ago—that zoning has the capacity to ensure that citizens "dwell together in comfort and contentment,"[17] yet zoning still guides development in Chicago and most American cities. Opinions about whether zoning should be rigid or fluid will continue to diverge, and new techniques regulating the use of land will emerge. The politics of zoning will continue to swirl. As Richard Babcock and Charles Siemon, wrote, "Often zoning is put down as being political. So, what else is new? Of course it is highly political; perhaps that is why it is so exciting a game."[18]

APPENDIX A

Planned Manufacturing Districts

Just months before Chicago adopted a zoning ordinance, city public health commissioner Charles B. Ball wrote that "The principal advantage [of zoning] will be the security against invasion of home districts by factories and stores."[1] Ball's comment was characteristic of the 1920s, when officials pushed hard for zoning to protect residential property owners from the nuisances associated with heavy industry and other incompatible land uses.

Less apparent to the pioneers of zoning was the potential for land-use conflicts to create problems for *industrial* land uses. As history would show, however, the encroachment of residential land uses on manufacturing areas can create safety problems, traffic congestion, and political pressure for more restrictive zoning. Residents near industrial areas may demand limitations on pollution, noise, and the storage of materials, all of which can drive up the cost of doing business.

In some situations, industry can shield itself from these problems by locating in industrial districts where residential development is strictly prohibited. During the early twentieth century, consortiums of private entities created the Clearing Industrial District and the Chicago Manufacturing District on the city's Southwest Side. By the early 1920s, the CID and CMD were home to more than 10,000 jobs and among the largest districts of their type in the country.[2] Both were off-limits to housing developments.

Such privately managed industrial districts, however, have never accounted for more than a small portion of the city's industrial output. During Chicago's early years, residential areas regularly abutted industry, a commingling of land uses that was scantly altered by the 1923 ordinance. Due to the demand for new housing after World War II, residential developers gradually made inroads into areas zoned for manufacturing. The creators of the zoning revisions of 1957 took steps to protect residential areas from the impact of industry. By establishing performance standards that regulated noise, vibrations, and emissions, these revisions provided the basis for legal challenges initiated against industries by, or on behalf of, nearby residents.

Conflicts between residential and industrial land uses came into sharp focus as rapid real-estate development accelerated in the North River Industrial Corridor (the area along the North Branch of the Chicago River) in the early 1980s. Residential and commercial developers

Drawing prepared for the city to illustrate the problem of land-use conflicts. (City of Chicago)

eyed this property due to its proximity to the greater downtown area. Some offered to pay high prices for the land to entice manufacturers to sell at a profit and relocate. The industrial uses that remained often faced rising property taxes, growing traffic congestion, and complaints from nearby residents about noise, smoke, and other problems.

By the mid-1980s, these conflicts had greatly intensified. In many instances, the City Council responded by simply rezoning manufacturing areas for residential or commercial use. Such changes were to some extent inevitable due to the abundance of land zoned for industry in the city at a time when manufacturing was rapidly declining. Nevertheless, the city gradually became more sympathetic to the plight of industry. Between 1972 and 1988, the number of manufacturing jobs in the city plummeted from 389,000 to 258,012, and the number of jobs in metal works dropped by more than half.[3] Many factories closed or relocated to the suburbs or other regions, or simply ceased production, as the Midwest's industrial sector underwent a dramatic transformation.

Strong demand for loft space and other types of housing in changing areas of River North raised questions about the future of even the most

successful industrial facilities in the area. Critics maintained that the City Council and the Zoning Board of Appeals systematically gave precedence to residential and commercial uses over manufacturing in zoning decisions.[4] Watchdog groups expressed the view that many zoning amendments reclassifying industrial land as residential were costing the city industrial jobs. Officials from the Harold Washington administration, initially hesitant to take a position on the issue, eventually grew more supportive of industrial retention.

A NEW STRATEGY UNFOLDS

Retaining industrial jobs was central to the mission of the Local Economic and Employment Development (LEED) Council, a nonprofit formed in 1982 at the New City YMCA in the North River Industrial Corridor. In 1986, the Council, together with the city and a student from the University of Illinois at Chicago, produced a study calling for new policies to preserve city land for industrial development, including the creation of Planned Manufacturing Districts.

Proposals for high-profile commercial and residential projects in the North River Corridor, meanwhile, made such protection more urgent. In the autumn of 1986, a developer requested a zoning change to allow for the conversion of an industrial building on Goose Island (which had been a scrap smelting plant) into a mixed-use development called River Lofts. Further north, plans were underway for Riverpoint Center, a large shopping center at the corner of Fullerton and Clybourn.

Although the developers of both projects obtained the requested zoning changes from the City Council (with certain stipulations), there was strong opposition. One major manufacturer threatened to leave Chicago if nearby land were rezoned residential. Concern about such changes galvanized neighborhood organizations, manufacturers, labor unions, and others concerned about the future of manufacturing in the city. As a result, proposals for the creation of PMDs gained political traction.

The City Council approved the 115-acre Clybourn Corridor PMD in

1988, thereby protecting 24 industrial firms that employed about 1,400 workers. In doing so, Chicago joined Boston, Massachusetts, and Portland, Oregon, as pioneers in the development of this planning tool. Two other districts, the 170-acre Elston Corridor PMD and the 146-acre Goose Island PMD, were added to the zoning map in 1990.

The two new districts were divided into core and buffer zones, while Goose Island was made entirely a core zone. Industrial uses were heavily concentrated in the core zone; residential and commercial uses were prohibited in this area, while the buffer zone was reserved for commercial and industrial uses. This policy reflected the belief that the expansion of commercial uses tends to be less disruptive to industry than residential development. Allowing commercial uses in the buffer zones, it was felt, would support nearby residents without posing a threat to manufacturers.

The Montgomery Ward distribution center and the adjacent railroad yards flank the North Branch of the Chicago River at Chicago Avenue, just south of Goose Island (left center), circa 1926. The city designated Goose Island its third planned manufacturing district in 1990. (Chicago Historical Society)

An important, if unstated, goal in creating PMDs was to take zoning decisions in manufacturing areas out of the control of local aldermen. PMDs are a distinct zoning classification. They are not created as amendments to the zoning maps and are not subject to routine amendment. They are "off limits" to traditional rezoning efforts. Over time, speculators realized that rezoning in PMDs would be extremely difficult. As their interest waned, property values stabilized and many industrial businesses began to feel more confident about investing and expanding in these areas.

THE FUTURE OF PMDs

Although the city's experience supports the idea that PMDs can abet industrial retention, it also demonstrates the difficulty of using land-use controls as a form of industrial policy. By the mid-1990s, it was clear that PMDs, too, were vulnerable to the winds of industrial change. Large areas of land

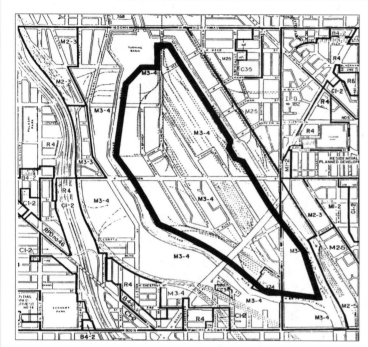

A zoning map shows the boundaries of the Goose Island Planned Manufacturing District. (City of Chicago)

set aside for manufacturing in PMDs remained idle. As in other American cities, macroeconomic, financial, and geographic forces precipitated a drop in industrial activity. In some PMDs, there was simply not enough demand for manufacturing space to effectively utilize all of the land. In 1997, the editorial writers of the *Chicago Tribune*, who had long been skeptical of PMDs, noted in an editorial that "Communism may have fallen, but Chicago still has central planners who know best where industry must go."[5]

The city was by this time quite judicious in the creation of PMDs and established only a handful of additional districts over the next several years. In 1998, the city established the Kinzie Corridor PMD. In 2001, the city created a similar district along the Chicago River at Chicago Avenue and Halsted Street. Several more PMDs were established in 2004.

The effort to use zoning to preserve manufacturing jobs has generated significant research. Joel Rast offers the most comprehensive assessment in *Remaking Chicago: The Political Origins of Urban Industrial Change*. Some of Rast's more recent analysis suggests that job growth within the Goose Island PMD has been strong, abetted by the natural buffer separating it from nearby residential populations. A partnership between the LEED Council and the city allowed for the creation of the 25-acre Goose Island Industrial Park. With infrastructure improvements and environmental cleanup paid for through tax-increment financing, the industrial park has attracted such tenants as Republic Windows and Doors (450 jobs), River North Distributing (100 jobs), and Federal Express (330 jobs). As a result, employment in the PMD increased from 950 workers when the PMD was created in 1990 to just over 2,000 workers in 2004, although many of these jobs were relocated from elsewhere in the city and are in warehousing and distribution rather than traditional manufacturing.[6] Industrial employment in the Elston Corridor PMD has not appreciably changed, but it remains the home of some 1,500 jobs, roughly the same as when the PMD was created in 1990.

Several of the city's PMDs have been less successful. Manufacturing employment within the Clybourn Corridor, for example, has plummeted, partially due to the enormous expansion of retail activity in its buffer zone.[7] Industrial jobs fell from 1,146 in 1988 to 336 in 2004.[8] Overall, however, Rast has found "cause for optimism" in recent PMD employment trends.[9]

APPENDIX B

Hyde Park: A Fountainhead of Research on Zoning

Many urban historians are familiar with Hyde Park's role as a university community, its lengthy struggle with racial integration, and its pioneering role in the urban-renewal movement.[1] The neighborhood also deserves recognition, however, for being fertile ground for research about the economic, cultural, and social implications of zoning and other policies affecting urban development. Perhaps no other neighborhood in the world can claim such an impressive record of scholarship—either as the place of research or point of publication—on matters relating to the spatial character of cities as this South Side area.

Several years after a school of the same name had failed, a new University of Chicago opened in 1892 with the support of industrialist John D. Rockefeller. The school became an institutional anchor of the Hyde Park neighborhood, which had recently been annexed into Chicago. Hyde Park and nearby Woodlawn were in the midst of a great transformation at the time, enjoying the benefits of a growing population and improvements being made in anticipation of the Columbian Exposition in Jackson Park. This celebrated world's fair, held in 1893, attracted international attention and stimulated much interest in the aesthetic, economic, and social effects of urban forms. (As we discuss in Appendix D, among the visitors was a young lawyer named Edward Bassett, who later earned distinction as the "Father of Zoning.") Daniel Burnham's City Beautiful Movement grew out of this great exposition and was rooted in the idea that city planning could both inspire and enhance the quality of civic discourse.

While Burnham worked to educate citizens and civic leaders, the faculty at the University of Chicago immersed themselves in more theoretical issues associated with the character and shape of cities. By the late 1910s, a group of sociologists—part of the famed "Chicago School of Sociology"—had made many scholarly advances in this area. The Chicago School gained worldwide fame for exploring the evolution of the causes, effects, and implications of urban growth. Robert Ezra Park and Ernest W. Burgess brought considerable prominence to the university by developing a cohesive theory of urban growth. Their 1925 book, *The City*, soon earned distinction as one of the most influential books about urban development ever written up to that time.[2]

Louis Brownlow lifts the first shovel of dirt at the groundbreaking ceremony for the four-story building later named the Merriam Center. Standing next to Brownlow (from left to right) are Marshall Dimock, William F. Ogburn, and Robert M. Hutchins. (Courtesy of the American Planning Association)

Later, in *The Gold Coast and the Slum,* Harvey Zorbaugh explored the changing land-use patterns in Chicago's Near North neighborhoods and eloquently described the dynamic qualities of urban economies.[3] His work contrasted sharply with that of his colleague, political scientist Charles Merriam, who served as a local alderman and focused his research on the necessity of zoning. As we described in Chapter 3, Merriam—a decisive figure in the establishment of Chicago zoning—drafted legislation authorizing the use of zoning in the state legislature in the late 1910s.

By the late 1920s, many public servants were disillusioned with zoning, feeling that it had failed to live up to earlier promises. Several faculty members at the university, including political scientist Ernst Freund, were instrumental in raising awareness of the need for a reform of the administration of zoning. Freund called for greater fairness in zoning and advocated a system that would allow residents to bring their objections and concerns to the courts rather than the Board of Appeals.[4] Among those influenced by his work was Richard Babcock, a law student at the university many years later who became one of the country's most respected authorities on zoning (see Appendix C).

By the early 1930s, the University of Chicago had built an international reputation as a leader in the study of cities, especially on issues relating to allocation of urban land. Although many of the school's publications during this fruitful period had a theoretical bent, the institution strengthened its link to the practice of planning in 1938, when the four-year-old American Society of Planning Officials and a dozen other organizations moved into a new building on its campus. This facility would likely never have been built were it not for Merriam, who helped persuade the Spelman Fund of New York to provide financing for the building.

These efforts paid dividends for both the university and the planning profession as a whole. The American Society of Planning Officials, the Public Administration Clearing House—an entity led by Louis Brownlow, a renowned expert on city management—and other professional organizations became the country's leading sources of research on municipal governance. For the next 60 years, the organizations housed in this building made enormous contributions to the debate about zoning and the evolution of American cities.

Amid the struggle to find improved methods of city administration, Louis Wirth, a sociologist who studied under Burgess and Park, emerged as a prominent critic of racial restrictive covenants—a method of exclusion supported by the university at the time to forestall racial changes in its immediate neighborhood. Wirth's dissertation, *The Ghetto*, was published as a book by the university and recognized as a classic in the field. In the 1940s and early 1950s, many of Wirth's students wrote theses on race, housing, and restrictive covenants in Chicago, docu-

The Merriam Center at 1313 E. 60th Street on the University of Chicago campus. (Courtesy of the American Planning Association)

menting the extent of racial restrictions and helping to accelerate the demise of various exclusionary practices.

pioneering book *Cities and Housing*, through the school's press), together with Edwin Mills of Northwestern University and William Alonso of Harvard, developed frameworks to evaluate the spatial character of cities. Their works became classics in the urban economics field and sparked a great deal of scholarship.[5] This rich body of research offered new perspectives on the economic forces contributing to the centralization of employment in the city and illuminated the tendency for property values and population densities to decline as one moved further from a city's core.

The American Society of Planning Officials, meanwhile, gradually expanded its research on zoning and planning. By the early 1970s, the writings of Jack Noble, the longtime editor of the society's *Zoning Digest* (launched in 1949 and later renamed *Land-Use Law & Zoning Digest*), combined with monographs published through the society's Planners Advisory Service, made it arguably the country's leading source of published material related to zoning. In 1978, the society merged with the American Institute of Planners to form the American Planning Association, which expanded its research agenda as well as its visibility in the professional community. In 1993, after a fiery debate about a possible relocation to Washington, D.C., the American Planning Association left Hyde Park and settled into a new downtown

THE POSTWAR ERA DAWNS

After World War II, other scholars with connections to the university made more pathbreaking discoveries about the allocation of urban land. In the 1960s, Richard Muth of the University of Chicago (who published his

Library at the Merriam Center (circa 1960). (Courtesy of the American Planning Association)

office on the 16th floor of the old People's Gas Building at 122 S. Michigan Avenue, a landmark designed by Daniel Burnham and Co.

The University of Chicago has also been part of the career of some of the nation's most notable critics of zoning. Longtime Chicago attorney Bernard H. Siegan, who earned his law degree at the school in 1949,

authored *Land Use Without Zoning* in 1972, a classic in the literature on the limits of municipal regulation. Robert C. Ellickson echoed this theme in a path-breaking article, "Alternatives to Zoning: Covenants, Nuisance Rules, and Fines as Land Use Controls," in the *University of Chicago Law Review* the following year. Ellickson then spent a year on campus as a visiting professor, exploring the idea that a system of penalties and fines as well as court-enforced restrictive covenants could effectively govern how land can be used—approaches widely used in Houston, the nation's largest city without a zoning ordinance.

Much of the criticism directed at zoning in recent decades has its roots in the University of Chicago, especially in the interdisciplinary field of "Law & Economics," which gained prominence at the university after the 1960 publication of Ronald Coase's article, "The Problem of Social Cost," in a quarterly journal published by the University of Chicago Press.[6] Coase joined the faculty of the university's law school several years later and earned the Nobel Prize in economics for this work in 1991. The writings of Coase, Richard A. Posner, and other faculty at the university influenced an entire generation of scholars exploring zoning and other forms of land-use regulation. Among them was Richard Epstein, a professor of law at the university who has written extensively about the constitutional problems associated with centralized approaches to land-use planning. Drawing upon some of the same themes as Ellickson and Siegan, Epstein explores opportunities for greater reliance on nuisance laws enforced by the courts and less emphasis on zoning and other traditional forms of regulation.[7]

Hyde Park's role in research about zoning is today less prominent than it was years ago. The legacies of the Columbian Exposition, the Merriam Center, and the University of Chicago's research, however, live on in the planning profession. Their contributions to the study of zoning will be felt for generations to come.

APPENDIX C

The Legacy of Richard Babcock

Richard Babcock, born on November 3, 1917, in Evanston, is today a towering historical figure in zoning and land-use law. His career spanned many decades and touched the lives of hundreds of planners. His best-known book, *The Zoning Game: Municipal Practice and Policies*, is said to have changed an entire profession.

Babcock earned a B.A. degree in 1940 from Dartmouth College and served in the army during World War II. He then pursued a law degree at the University of Chicago, serving as editor in chief of the university's law review. He received his J.D. in 1946 and earned an M.B.A. from the university's School of Business in 1950.

Babcock's interest in zoning grew out of his law school experience. Searching for a subject for a law review note, he came upon the work of Ernst Freund, well-known as a professor at the university before the war. Babcock, duly impressed by Freund, was surprised to learn that few appreciated the contributions of this scholar's seminal article, "Some Inadequately Discussed Problems of the Law of City Planning and Zoning."[1] In 1947, Babcock made his own scholarly contribution

Richard Babcock. (Photo by Jessie Ewing)

by writing a critical assessment of the Illinois Supreme Court's position on land-use laws.[2]

When starting his professional career at the law firm of Sidley and Austin, Babcock worked primarily on railroad mergers, but he continued to pursue his interest in zoning whenever time permitted. Babcock sought to identify ways in which zoning could be applied fairly for everyone and concluded that the lack of uniformity and supportive direction from the courts were driving a wedge between the theory of zoning and its practical application.[3]

In the early 1950s, Babcock's insights into and knowledge of zoning were in high demand. As the city of Chicago worked to review and update its outdated zoning ordinance, Harry Chaddick turned to him for assistance. Babcock's experience with the city reinforced his view that zoning was being held back by poorly conceived judicial opinions and outdated statutes.

Already known as a practitioner and teacher of land use at universities across the country, Babcock became a prolific writer. His first book, *The Zoning Game*, quickly became a classic in the planning field. Considered by some experts to be one of the most influential books on zoning ever written, *The Zoning Game* was required reading for students in planning schools through the country. Its sequel, *The Zoning Game Revisited*, written with Charles Siemon, offered new insights into the political dimensions of zoning.[4] Babcock also wrote, with Fred P. Bosselman, a pioneering treatise on the exclusionary effects of zoning—the tendency for zoning to discriminate against minority and low-income groups by preventing their integration into the general society. Babcock ended his career as a managing partner at the Chicago law firm Ross, Hardies, O'Keefe, Babcock and Parsons (now known as Ross and Hardies).

The gulf between the research and practice of zoning was once a matter of great concern to Babcock. "I used to feel sad," he wrote in *The Zoning Game*, "that so youthful a technique would so early establish a formidable stable of dogma." But, he added, "My reaction has now changed to one of perplexed admiration that the confusion which characterizes zoning thrives in the same culture in which the myth flourishes so abundantly."

Babcock died on September 13, 1993. Brian W. Blaesser, a partner in the law firm Rudnick & Wolfe, who is a noted expert on zoning, observed, "Richard Babcock was, in a word, compelling. By the force of his personality and intellect, and through an engaging writing style crafted from practical experience, he captured and held the national stage of land use and planning law until his death. His performances enriched us all."[5]

APPENDIX D

Edward Bassett: "The Father of Zoning"

"I cannot come to Chicago and tell you how to solve your problems. These things cannot be done by imitation," noted zoning specialist Edward M. Bassett, a New Yorker, at a Chicago Real Estate Board event on June 20, 1920.[1] Offering such advice was typical of Bassett, who traveled ceaselessly to share his expertise with cities considering the adoption of zoning.

Regarded in planning and administration circles as "The Father of Zoning," his tenacity and legal acumen were critical to the movement's success. Although Bassett's contributions to New York's zoning movement have been widely documented, his support of zoning efforts in Chicago was critical as well.

Born in New York City in 1863, Bassett earned degrees from Amherst College and Columbia Law School before beginning his legal career securing land-use rights and easements for new public water works in several cities in New York. After marrying, he returned to Brooklyn in 1892 and established his law practice.

In 1903, Bassett began his one term in the U.S. House of Representatives. Five years later, he accepted an invitation to join the National Conference on City Planning.[2] At the Conference, Bassett pushed cities to

Edward M. Bassett

adopt a broader concept of police power to achieve municipal planning goals, and he aggressively promoted the idea of zoning (or districting). He earned

143

distinction as one of the nation's foremost champions of zoning and eventually became chairman of New York City's Heights of Building Commission. He led that city's effort to adopt a zoning ordinance and was named chairman of its newly formed Citizen's Zoning Committee in 1916.

Over the years, Bassett cultivated strong connections with Chicago. His first visit to the city was apparently to see the World's Columbian Exposition in 1893, which seemed to fuel his interest in the future of American cities. In 1909, he published an article about rapid transit in the *Chicago City Club Bulletin*. In 1911, he hosted Daniel Burnham and Edward Bennett in New York City and gave them and other luminaries a tour of Brooklyn. His friendship with Burnham and Bennett lasted for many years and generated extensive written correspondence. In October, 1916, Bassett shared his expertise with a team of leaders from Chicago who had been dispatched to New York to study the practice of zoning. The group came home eager to implement a program that drew upon the lessons they had learned from Bassett.

Over the next several years, Bassett was a familiar figure in Chicago zoning circles. He served as legal counsel for the Chicago Real Estate Board as it drafted the city's first zoning ordinance. In 1919, his speech before an audience of 400 in the Morrison Hotel ballroom helped galvanize the city's zoning movement, and his insights about the importance of zoning won over many skeptics. In particular, Bassett drew attention to the potential legal problems stemming from the city's reliance on the Glackin Law, which created wide disparities in land-use regulation between neighborhoods.

Bassett worked closely with Chicago Real Estate Board officials on the preparation of Chicago's zoning ordinance and contributed a great deal of material to the newly created City Planning and Zoning Library at City Hall, helping it become one of the largest libraries of its kind. Although his name would be synonymous with zoning for another quarter-century, his work began to shift to other cities around the country until his death in 1948.[3]

Perhaps Edward Bassett's contributions to zoning are best summarized in this quote from Frederick Law Olmsted, son of the famous landscape architect and Bassett's longtime friend, who in 1937 wrote a letter congratulating Bassett on the third printing of his widely read book, *Zoning*: "Your wise, persistent guidance alone…saved the movement from shipwreck when the flood of popular enthusiasm broke loose in the wake of the New York Ordinance."[4]

APPENDIX E

Enforcing the Ordinance

One of the most difficult problems facing the framers of Chicago's first zoning ordinance was finding a way to deal with nonconforming uses and nonconforming structures. Without a mechanism to grant relief to the owners of such properties in extenuating circumstances, any requirements that called for the elimination of nonconformities would invite legal challenges. Such challenges would put the city at risk of unfavorable court rulings that could undermine the enforcement of zoning.

The solution was to create the Zoning Board of Appeals (ZBA). In 1923, the city spelled out 17 types of variations that that its newly formed ZBA could grant, which ran the gamut from allowing nonconformities to persist, allowing them to be modified, and even in some situations allowing new nonconformities to be introduced. The ZBA was also given the authority in certain circumstances to authorize changes in land-use classifications, such as a change from residential to commercial use. (This power today is reserved for the City Council.)

In the early years of zoning, the city's Department of Buildings had the day-to-day responsibility for zoning enforcement. All applications for a building permit were required to have a plot plan—drawn-to-scale, with dimensions—that showed how a building would sit on the lot. A reviewer then determined if the proposed structure complied with the building and zoning codes. If it did not, the building department could either deny the application or give the applicant a chance to make adjustments. An applicant denied a permit could apply to the ZBA for relief. However, the criteria for granting variations were not explicitly defined, giving the ZBA considerable leeway.

Dealing with nonconforming uses that had monopoly power in neighborhoods was a particularly sensitive issue. If the ZBA rejected applications for new nonconforming uses in these neighborhoods, it would deny consumers the benefits of competition. If it granted variations liberally, it would violate the spirit of the ordinance and possibly undermine the uniformity of land uses in the neighborhood. On the other hand, if it forced the discontinuation of an established nonconforming use, it risked being sued for "taking without compensation." So problems would occur regardless of the city's policy.

A compromise to this predicament was to "grandfather" existing nonconforming uses and give the ZBA

A drawing from the city's *Zoning and You* pamphlet illustrates the judicial orientation of the ZBA. (City of Chicago)

the authority to allow for the creation of new nonconforming uses in specific situations. One such situation was where the same type of use already existed on the block. For example, if a grocery store operated on a block zoned for residential use, the ZBA could approve the creation of another grocery. Similarly, in situations where a zoning amendment had already allowed manufacturing uses within 125 feet of a residential area, the ZBA could permit more such uses in the area. It also could authorize the *expansion* of a nonconforming use if another existing nonconforming use already exceeded the volume limit imposed by the ordinance.

Such a permissive policy opened the door to ad-hoc rulings that had the potential to greatly affect the character of neighborhoods. Adding to the ZBA's power was its authority to process applications for *amendments* to the zoning maps. All of its recommendations for variations and amendments, however, had to be adopted by the City Council to take effect. If at least 20 percent of the surrounding owners protested, such an amendment could only be adopted by a two-thirds vote of the City Council.

At its inception, the ZBA had five members appointed by the mayor. Despite efforts to assure that it had a high level of technical expertise—

by law, the board had an architect, a structural engineer, and a realtor— the ZBA apparently was quite sympathetic to the grievances of appellants. In all likelihood, some variations were granted as favors. Such a permissive philosophy invited legal challenges and was the impetus for new policies adopted in 1934 that brought greater formality and more rigidity to the ZBA's work.

The changes of 1934 made an explicit reference to the enabling legislation passed by the Illinois legislature. This landmark bill authorized the creation of ZBAs but stipulated that the decisions of these entities needed to be ratified by the local government (i.e., the City Council) and were subject to administrative review in court. The new language apparently had the effect of reining in the decisions of the ZBA and making its decisions more judicious.

The composition of the ZBA also changed. A majority of members was now required to have relevant professional or governmental experience. Although only three members had previously constituted a quorum (allowing recommendations to be passed with a mere two votes), all recommendations were now required to have at least four votes.

Considering that nonconformities still accounted for the bulk of the ZBA's work during the late 1930s, it was clear that this problem was not going to disappear without more vigorous enforcement. The city took aggressive action in 1942 by stipulating that any nonconformity which was not grandfathered should be discontinued over time. New restrictions were also put on the enlargement and improvement of nonconformities, and an amortization schedule was adopted with a strict timetable for their elimination. All nonconforming uses now had to be discontinued upon a transfer of ownership, the termination of a lease, or after a specified period. The ability for the ZBA to grant certain types of variations was also scaled back.[1]

These same wartime amendments also gave the ZBA the responsibility of hearing applications for proposed special uses, including airports, streetcar barns, cemeteries, carnivals, and various public-service facilities. Applications for special uses were made subject to a public hearing before the ZBA. Previously, the building commissioner had authority over these requests.

In low-density neighborhoods, special uses were limited to less invasive facilities, such as parks and community centers, as well as transportation terminals for bus or railroad lines. In apartment districts, the ordinance allowed for a wider range of special uses, including hospitals, public-utility substations, and parking lots. Some objected to giving the ZBA authority over special uses. For example, noted zoning lawyer Richard Babcock later criticized this decision, arguing that "the special use is a different breed than a variation" and thus "should be a function of the Planning Department and City Council."[2]

THE ZBA ENTERS A NEW ERA

The creation of the Office of Zoning Administrator and the Bureau of Zoning in 1956 and the zoning revisions of 1957 were milestones in the administration of zoning and helped the city deal with a surge in urban redevelopment activity. At the time, officials envisioned that they could eliminate most nonconforming uses through vigilant enforcement by an expanded number of city inspectors.

The 1957 code swept away the sprawling list of variations adopted in 1942 and created a new list of just ten, all of which remain in place today. The list included variations providing relief from the yard-size or lot-size regulations in the zoning ordinance as well as relief from parking requirements. The ZBA could now relax parking requirements by up to 20 percent and authorize an increase of 10 percent or less in maximum floor area ratio for business, commercial, or manufacturing establishments.

No longer could the ZBA simply grant variations to protect existing nonconformities or allow for the creation of new ones. Its decisions were now expected to be based on a set of *standards*, which required that the applicant spell out the hardships created by zoning and demonstrate that the property could not otherwise yield a reasonable return. Applicants also

Visiting the site of a proposed zoning amendment, apparently in 1959, are (left to right) Ira J. Bach, planning commissioner, Leroy J. Ziegele, chief of Zoning and Project Division, Department of Planning, and John P. Maloney, Zoning Administrator. (City of Chicago)

had to show that their plight was unique and that the hardship was more than an inconvenience. Requests could not be based solely on a desire to make more money, nor could the hardship be created by the applicant.

If someone wished to upgrade a building on an irregular lot, or build one too close to the alley or sidewalk by contemporary standards, the board could rule that a hardship existed and grant a variation. If a building on a lot contained four apartments but could offer parking for only three cars, relief could be granted. A buyer of a building that is nonconforming because of its lack of yard space could obtain relief, but the buyer of a lot who simply wanted to exceed the allowable FAR might not.

The variation could not alter the character of the surrounding area, harm the public welfare, diminish light and air, increase traffic, or impair property values in the neighborhood. All of these standards remain in place today.

The ZBA retained authority over special use permits, but now all applications were subject to planning department review. Moreover, there was now an established list of permitted special uses for each zoning classification, thus narrowing the ZBA's authority. The changes made in 1957 curtailed the ZBA's power to review proposed zoning amendments and eliminated the requirement that members have professional expertise. Significantly, however, members of the ZBA now received a salary and its decisions on appeals and variations were final and not subject to action by the City Council.

Despite the changes, the ZBA's permissiveness remained the source of great concern in the planning and design community. The ZBA often took the position that "a man's home is his castle," a position that was certainly defensible in many situations but also a source of concern when it came to decisions about investment property. Richard Babcock considered the wholesale granting of variations as an affront to effective zoning. "The history of the variation procedure in Illinois is a story of confusion and abuse," he said.[3]

This sentiment was echoed in a study by attorney Richard L. Wexler for the Metropolitan Housing and Planning Council. Wexler's analysis, published in 1967, showed that the ZBA granted 95 percent of all variations requested between 1958 and 1962. In eight months during 1965,

it granted 97 percent. He found that the owners of nonconforming properties were using the ZBA to avoid the amortization provisions of the code. Wexler noted that in blighted areas, the board granted most of the requests for variations, despite city efforts to condemn and demolish structures that were nonconforming or badly deteriorated in those areas. Believing that its procedures were too informal and slipshod, not to mention vulnerable to being overturned in court, Wexler concluded, "City policy and that of the Board of Appeals passed each other like ships in the night."[4]

REPUTATION OF THE ZBA IMPROVES

The image of the ZBA improved after Harry Chaddick became chairman in May, 1967. During the preceding four months, the board had granted 86 percent of all requests submitted to it. Between May and August, however, it granted only 49 percent of such requests and turned down most requests in blighted areas. The number of applications to the ZBA also reportedly fell as word spread about its tougher stance on variations.[5]

Chaddick strengthened the administration of the ZBA by hiring court reporters and by having trained staffers conduct preliminary casework. These changes were retained by his successor, Morgan M. Finley, who became chairman in 1972. The ZBA earned more accolades after zoning lawyer Jack Guthman began his 12 years of service as chairman in 1975. In 1978, the *Chicago Tribune* quoted a local political scientist saying that "Both critics of the Democratic machine and long-time organization stalwarts feel that the Zoning Board of Appeals is democratic local government at its best."[6]

Today, much of the ZBA's workload centers on requests for variations from the owners of older homes. It handles several thousand applications each year for additions to homes that require relief from yard requirements and height limits. The ZBA generally approves such requests, based on the justification that improvements to older homes help retain residents and improve the neighborhood.

The 2004 zoning code provided a new option for neighboring property owners who feel harmed by a decision made by the Zoning Administrator. Neighboring property owners can file an appeal if the zoning administrator grants an exception to an applicant for changes that would significantly increase the bulk or height of an existing building. In such cases, the ZBA would apply the same standards as if the owner seeking the exception were the applicant.[7]

AMENDMENTS

Those who drafted the 1923 code undoubtedly thought the fruits of their labors would last a lifetime. Apparently acting on the presumption that there would be a high level of goodwill in future zoning transactions, they created only cursory standards for ZBA proceedings. It also appears that they anticipated relatively few amendments to the ordinance. As a result, there were no guidelines as to how amendments should be evaluated.

The limits of these assumptions were evident by the late 1920s. Yet it was not until 1944 that the ZBA lost its power to process amendments. From that point forward, proposed amendments had to be submitted to the City Council Buildings and Zoning Committee.

Concerns about the influence of aldermen, the extent to which amendments undermined the intent of the ordinance, and the sheer number of amendments being processed gradually took their toll on the image of zoning. In 1954, the City Council imposed a requirement that the Plan Commission review all proposed amendments to provide a professional opinion. When the Department of City Planning was established in 1956, the review of proposed amendments was delegated to its Office of Zoning Review, which helped develop the 1957 amendments. The Zoning Administrator and the planning department were required to review all proposed map amendments and make recommendations to the City Council Committee on Zoning. The 1957 ordinance also stipulated that a public hearing be held on all proposed amendments, a practice which continues today.

City to act on zoning violators

Chicago Daily News headline, May 10, 1971.

Standards for evaluating amendments were established in September, 1957, in the wake of an important zoning case heard by the Illinois Supreme Court. LaSalle Bank appealed an order of the Cook County Zoning Board of Appeals, which refused to grant a requested amendment to rezone a parcel of land in suburban Des Plaines. The trial court ruled in the bank's favor. Although the county appealed, it lost the case on the grounds that its decision was not supported by evidence showing that the applicable zoning was related to the public health and welfare.

Following this landmark decision, Chicago's planning department adopted standards for the review of any proposed zoning amendment. The standards require that the proposed use be: (i) consistent with area plans adopted by the city; (ii) consistent with changes in the area related to zoning and development; (iii) compatible with surrounding uses, zoning, density, and scale; and (iv) compatible with existing infrastructure.

These standards, which remain in place today, have the effect of adding a degree of rigor to decisions on amendments. Many observers, however, consider them too general to assure that neighboring property owners receive adequate protection from some poorly conceived zoning changes.

THE OFFICE OF THE ZONING ADMINISTRATOR

The 1957 ordinance created the Bureau of Zoning, under an administrator appointed by the mayor, to respond to an increasing workload and the need to have a high level of technical knowledge of zoning on staff. The work of the bureau was supported by a new chapter in the ordinance that spelled out detailed regulations governing nonconforming uses, such as criteria about when they could be repaired or improved, and when their use must be terminated. Several inspectors were assigned to inspect such properties to enforce the law.

During the 1960s, the city stepped up its enforcement of the zoning code, both in designated Conservation Areas and in other neighborhoods. Such activity kept the newly expanded roster of zoning and building inspectors busily occupied. Their work helped to gradually reduce the number of illegal and nonconforming uses and structures, particularly those dangerous to life and health. Where necessary, the city used condemnation and demolition to rid neighborhoods of these nonconformities.

By 1981, a growing workload warranted creation of the Department of Zoning. The volume of petitions to the ZBA had become so great that a new category of permitted relief was defined under the zoning administrator's jurisdiction: exceptions from the requirements of the ordinance. These exceptions include: (i) certain reductions in yard requirements for pre-existing buildings not meeting those requirements, as well as certain reductions in off-street parking requirements, (ii) granting the use of a previously illegal dwelling unit in certain circumstances and if it will otherwise meet code requirements, and (iii) a reduction of up to ten percent in lot size to accommodate an otherwise legal use. The list has grown over time largely in response to the rising volume of applications.

APPENDIX F

The Recollections of Harry F. Chaddick

arry F. Chaddick's description of his experiences in his autobiography, *Chaddick! Success Against All Odds*, underscores the complex political environment in which his team conducted its work during the mid-1950s.[1]

"In the midst of our zoning project, there was a dramatic change in Chicago politics. The Democratic ward committeemen were clearly dissatisfied with Martin Kennelly as mayor and were determined that he not be elected for a third four-year term in the Spring of 1955. The chairman of the Democratic Central Committee was Richard J. Daley, the Cook County Clerk and committeeman of the 11th ward which included the Bridgeport community on the city's near Southwest Side....

"I had known Daley as an attorney and as an astute politician but I was not involved in the political maneuvering that was about to take place and the bitter campaign that followed. My concentration at the time was on the mammoth rezoning task.

"In December of 1954, the Democratic Central Committee had voted 49–1 to support Daley to succeed Kennelly. The incumbent fought hard but, in the

Harry F. Chaddick.

end, it was Daley who prevailed in the Democratic primary that following February. Two months later, in April of 1955, he was elected mayor and a dynamic era in Chicago's history began. It was to last more than 21 years. As those years progressed, the new mayor and I became great friends. It was a friendship I cherish to this day.

"Shortly after taking office, the new mayor invited me to meet with him. He assured me that he supported everything I was doing to reform the city's zoning code. I could count on him, he said, for his total backing.

"Five months later, in October 1955, the proposed ordinance was ready for public presentation to the City Council. The proposal was greeted by a newspaper headline which proclaimed: 'Vast Rezoning Plan Aims At "New City."'

"Among the features of the 'new city' would be the rezoning of more than 1,000 miles of business streets for residential use. The city was detrimentally overzoned for business and commerce. There were 2,712 miles zoned for business and 511 for commercial uses but, of these, only 413 miles were actually used for business and only 79 for commercial. In an era when the automobile had long been king, Chicago was still zoned for needless miles of strip-shopping created at a time when most people walked or took streetcars to shop or do business. All of this unproductive land, with block after block and, sometimes, even mile after mile of vacant stores, could be usable as residential property under the proposed zoning. . . .

"Many months of work followed, explaining the document to civic organizations and everyone with an interest in it. The zoning team members providing this information, answering questions and participating in public discussions, in addition to myself, included Alderman Pacini, Ted Aschman, George H. Kranenberg and Dan Ferrone. We spoke in just about every neighborhood and before every group we could find and we addressed all of the issues. . . .

"As might be expected when 643,000 parcels of land are involved, there are many, many opinions about the ordinance. The overwhelming sentiment, however, was highly supportive. This was especially true of the proposals relating to residential uses. Arthur Rubloff, a longtime Chicago realtor, was but one of the many people in the real estate industry who strongly backed the provisions calling for much of the over-zoned business uses to be converted to residential. 'If 90 percent of existing vacant property were to be zoned for homes,' Rubloff said, 'we would have a sensible balance of land use.'

"The *Chicago Tribune* hailed the work we had done: 'The new ordinance,' the paper stated editorially, 'is a courageous attempt to undo some of the mistakes of the past and to plan orderly future development.' It cited my staff and me and said we deserved credit for 'one of the best planning jobs in history.'"

Map of Community Areas

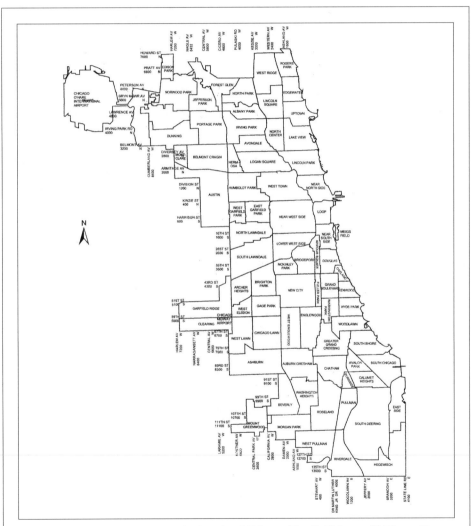

This map shows the various neighborhoods of Chicago. The Gold Coast, Old Town, River North, and Streeterville are part of the area labeled the Near North Side. (City of Chicago)

Administration of Chicago's Zoning Ordinance

DEPARTMENT OF BUILDINGS

The Department of Buildings (for a time called Department of Inspectional Services) has responsibility for implementation and enforcement of the building code, which included limits on the height of downtown buildings through 1923. The department had responsibility for the implementation and enforcement of the zoning ordinance from 1923 to 1957.

Commissioners:

Charles Bostrom	1915–22
Frank E. Doherty	1923–26
C.P. Paschen	1927–30
John E. Ericsson	1931–34
Richard E. Schmidt	1934–42
Paul J. Gerhardt, Jr.	1942–47
Roy T. Christiansen	1947–54
Richard Smykal (Acting)	1954–55
George L. Ramsey	1955–62

ZONING ADMINISTRATORS

The Office of the Zoning Administrator was created along with the formation of the Bureau of Zoning in 1957. The office remained part of the bureau until the newly created Department of Zoning was given responsibility for the zoning ordinance in 1981.

Zoning Administrators:

John P. Maloney	1957–71[1]
Harry Manley	1971[1]–83
James Wilkes (Acting)	1983–84
Maurice Parrish (Acting)	1984–88
Larry W. Parkman (Acting)	1988–89
Graham C. Grady	1989–94
Paul Woznicki	1994–2001
Edward J. Kus	2001–04
Thomas Smith (Acting)	2004–

ZONING BOARD OF APPEALS

The Zoning Board of Appeals was created in 1923 to allow variations in cases of "particular hardship," hear requests for amendments to the ordinance, and hold public hearings on proposed amendments. Today, it hears appeals and requests for variations.

Chairmen:

Allen B. Pond	1923–27
Eva H. Hamilton	1927–31
A.A. Sprague	1931–35
James H. Gately	1935–45
Charles E. Fox	1945–48
Samuel T. Lawton	1948–61
B. Emmet Hartnett	1961–66
Harry Chaddick	1967–72
Morgan M. Finley	1972–75
Jack Guthman	1975–87
Lawrence E. Kennon	1987–90
Joseph J. Spingola	1990–2003
Brian Crowe	2003–present

CHICAGO PLAN COMMISSION

The Chicago Plan Commission was involved with the creation of the city's zoning ordinance and its revision, and now acts in an advisory capacity to the Department of Planning and Development.

Chairmen:

Charles H. Wacker	1909–26
James Simpson	1926–35
Albert A. Sprague	1935–40
George T. Horton	1940–44
Aubrey H. Mellinger	1944–48
Nathaniel A. Owings	1948–51
William M. Spencer	1951–56
Clair M. Roddewig	1956–61
John L. McCaffrey	1961–63
Edward C. Logelin	1964–69
Patrick L. O'Malley	1969–73
Julian H. Levi	1973–79
George Cullen	1979–80
Miles L. Berger	1980–85
E. Wayne Robinson	1986–90
Reuben L. Hedlund	1990–97
Peter Bynoe	1997–2004
Linda Searl (acting)	2004–present

DEPARTMENT OF PLANNING AND DEVELOPMENT

On July 12, 1956, the City Council adopted an ordinance creating a Department of City Planning, which on January 1, 1957, assumed responsibility for the technical and staff work formerly done by the staff of the Plan Commission. The Plan Commission became an advisory and policy-initiating unit of City Planning as well as a reviewing agency concerned with the zoning ordinance, sites of community facilities and the urban renewal program.

The Department of City Planning was divided into six divisions, one of which was the Office of Zoning and Project Review. It merged with the Department of Urban Renewal in 1980 to create the Department of Planning, City, and Community Development. The unit was later renamed the Department of Planning and Development.

Commissioners:

Ira J. Bach	1957–65
John G. Duba	1965–67
Lewis Hill	1967–78
Thomas Kapsalis	1978–79
Martin R. Murphy (Acting)	1979–80
Martin R. Murphy	1980–83
Elizabeth Hollander	1983–89
David R. Mosena	1989–91
Valerie B. Jarrett	1991–95
Joseph Boyle, Jr.	1995–97
Christopher R. Hill	1997–2000
Alicia Mazur Berg	2001–04
Denise M. Casalino	2004–05
Lori Healey	2005–present

CITY COUNCIL COMMITTEE ON ZONING

The City Council Committee on Zoning, previously called the Committee on Buildings and Zoning, determines whether to grant amendments to the zoning ordinance, such as changes in the zoning regulation or to the classification of a particular parcel of land.

Chairmen:

William R. O'Toole	1922–31
Dorsey R. Crowe	1931–41
William A. Rowan	1941–43
Parke Cullerton	1943–53
Emil V. Pacini	1953–63
Paul T. Corcoran	1963–64
Daniel J. Ronan	1964–65
Ralph H. Metcalfe	1965–70
Kenneth E. Campbell	1970*
Thomas Fitzpatrick	1970–75
Edward R. Vrdolyak	1975–83
Theris M. Gabinski	1983–87
Danny K. Davis	1987–89
William J. Banks	1989–present

*Died December 1970

CHICAGO ZONING COMMISSION

Individuals involved with the creation of the 1923 zoning ordinance.

Charles Bostrom
Chairman
William R. O'Toole
Vice-Chairman
Charles H. Wacker
Secretary
Edward H. Bennett
Consultant on Zoning
William E. Parsons
Consultant on Zoning
H.T. Frost
Chief of Staff

Members

Charles J. Agnew
Edward R. Armitage
William Artingstall
Frederick H. Bartlett
James E. Bowler
Herman N. Bundesen, M.D.
Charles S. Duke
Samuel Ettelson
Michael J. Faherty
Charles W. Ferguson
John P. Garner
E.R. Graham
Scott M. Hogan
Benjamin Kulp
Thomas B. Maginniss
Robert J. Mulcahy
Oscar H. Olsen
Andrew Ringman
Richard W. Wolfe

Personnel of the Staff

Clarence W. Farrier
City Planning Engineer
Pierre Blouke
Designer
Frank E. Collins
Chief Draftsman
Ralph Galke
Field Foreman
Eugene S. Taylor
Executive Secretary of the Commission
W.C.P. Phillips
Industrial Survey Foreman
Henry Riedl
Statistician
A.W. Truedson
Statistician
Isabel Jarvis
Staff Secretary
Leon Hornstein
Attorney, Assistant Corporation Counsel
Edward M. Bassett
Attorney, Legal Consultant

CITY COUNCIL COMMITTEE ON BUILDINGS AND ZONING: REZONING PROGRAM

Individuals involved with the creation of the 1957 zoning ordinance.

Alderman Emil V. Pacini
   Chairman
Harry F. Chaddick
   Director
Alderman Joseph P. Immel
   North Sector Chairman
Alderman William J. Lancaster
   West & Central Sector Chairman
Alderman Paul M. Sheridan
   South Sector Chairman

Technical Staff
George H. Kranenberg, Jr.
   Technical Director
Daniel J. Ferrone
   Chief Planner
Anna M. Rantala
   Associate Research Planner
Stephen A. Doyle
   Administrative Assistant

Executive Committee
George L. DeMent
   Commissioner, Department of Public Works
James C. Downs, Jr.
   Housing and Redevelopment Coordinator
Paul Gerhardt, Jr.
   City Architect
Paul van T. Hedden
   Acting Executive Director,
   Chicago Plan Commission
Lloyd M. Johnson
   Commissioner,
   Department of Streets and Sanitation
Gen. Samuel T. Lawton
   Chairman, Zoning Board of Appeals
John P. Maloney
   Secretary, Zoning Board of Appeals
John C. Melaniphy
   Corporation Counsel
Richard L. Nelson
   Real Estate Research Coordinator
George L. Ramsey
   Commissioner, Department of Buildings

The Mayor's Zoning Reform Commission Appointed in 2001

William J.P. Banks, *Co-Chair*
Alderman, 36th Ward
Chairman, Committee on Zoning

John R. Schmidt, *Co-Chair**
Partner, Mayer Brown & Platt

Alicia Mazur Berg*
Commissioner, Department of
Planning & Development

Peter C.B. Bynoe
Chairman, Chicago Plan Commission

James Capraro
Executive Director, Greater Southwest
Development Corporation

Lorraine L. Dixon
Alderman, 8th Ward
Chairman, Committee on Budget
and Government Operations

Michael Fitzgerald
Business Manager, International Brotherhood
of Electrical Workers Local 134

Lori Healey
Principal, Perkins & Will

Diane Legge Kemp
President, DLK Architecture, Inc.

Lester McKeever
Managing Principal, Washington Pittman &
McKeever
Federal Reserve Board of Chicago
Metropolitan Planning Council

David Mosena
President, Museum of Science and Industry
Chairman of Landmarks Commission

Burton F. Natarus
Alderman, 42nd Ward
Chairman, Committee on Traffic Control

David Perry
Professor and Director of the Great Cities Institute,
University of Illinois at Chicago

John Rogers
President, Ariel Capital Management, Inc.

Gerald Roper
President and Chief Executive Officer,
Chicagoland Chamber of Commerce

Christine Slattery
Director, Trust for Public Lands

Bernard L. Stone
Alderman, 50th Ward
Chairman, Committee on Buildings, Vice-Mayor

Ray Suarez
Alderman, 31st Ward
Chairman, Committee on Housing & Real Estate

Cherryl T. Thomas
Chairman, Railroad Retirement Board

Paul Woznicki
Zoning Administrator, Department of Zoning

Edward J. Kus
Executive Director

Principal Consultant: Duncan Associates
Other consultants included Clarion Associates, Dyett & Bhatia, Lane Kendig, Camiros, Ltd., Farr Associates, Applied Real Estate Analysis, and Jacobs/Ryan Associates.

*At the beginning of 2001, Alicia Mazur Berg replaced Christopher Hill, who had been the city's planning commissioner since 1997, and Edward Kus replaced Paul Woznicki, who had been the city's zoning administrator since 1997. Also during 2001, David Mosena, the long-time civil servant, replaced John Schmidt as co-chair of the commission.

Notes

CHAPTER 1

1. Ann Lunde, "Chicago Drafts New Zoning Ordinance to Update, Protect City's Land Use," *Edison-Norwood Times Review* (Norwood, IL), 7 January 1987.
2. Charles M. Nichols, *Zoning in Chicago: Containing the "Glackin" Enabling Act, and Recommendations of Law Department of the City of Chicago, as to How to Proceed Under This Act* (Chicago: Chicago Real Estate Board, 1919), 3.

CHAPTER 2

1. For an analysis of legal antecedents of zoning in Chicago, see Andrew King, *Chicago: A Prehistory of Modern Zoning* (New York: Garland Publishing, 1976). In this chapter, we focus primarily on the economic, political, and social forces that led to the adoption of zoning.
2. Province of Massachusetts Bay, *Province Laws* (1692–93), 23, cited in Charles M. Haar, *Land-Use Planning* (Boston: Little Brown & Co., 1959), 129.
3. Ibid.

4. Harold M. Mayer and Richard C. Wade, *Chicago: Growth of a Metropolis* (Chicago: University of Chicago Press, 1969), 3–15. For additional information on Chicago's early history, see William Cronon's *Nature's Metropolis: Chicago and the Great West* (New York: W.W. Norton, 1991); and Donald L. Miller, *City of the Century: The Epic of Chicago and the Making of America* (New York: Simon & Schuster, 1996).
5. "Primary Sources in Chicago History" (Chicago: DePaul University Department of History, 2002). http://www.condor.depaul.edu/~history/chicago/primary.html (accessed October 20, 2002, last modified June 1, 2001).
6. Mayer and Wade, *Growth of a Metropolis*, 3–15.
7. Fred P. Bosselman, "The Commodification of Nature's Metropolis: the Historical Context of Illinois' Unique Zoning Standards," *Northern Illinois University Law Review* 12 (Summer 1992): 545–546.
8. Robert J. Spinney, *City of Big Shoulders: A History of Chicago* (DeKalb, Ill: Northern Illinois University Press, 2000), 36.
9. Chicago Municipal Code, Sections 6.6 and 28.22.

Notes from Chapter 2, continued

10. Andrew J. King, *Law and Land Use in Chicago: A Prehistory of Modern Zoning* (New York: Garland Publishing, 1976), 164.

11. David M. Young, *Chicago Maritime: An Illustrated History* (DeKalb, Ill: Northern Illinois University Press, 2001).

12. David M. Young, *The Iron Horse and the Windy City: How Railroads Shaped Chicago* (DeKalb, Ill: Northern Illinois University Press, 2005), 22–24.

13. Spinney, *City of Big Shoulders*, 49–51.

14. Karen Sawislak, *Smoldering City: Chicagoans and the Great Fire, 1871–1874* (Chicago: University of Chicago Press, 1995), 124.

15. Robin L. Einhorn, *Property Rules, Political Economy in Chicago, 1833–1972* (Chicago: University of Chicago Press, 2001), 207.

16. Chicago Municipal Code, Section 33.

17. Einhorn, *Property Rules*, 207.

18. Mayer and Wade, *Growth of a Metropolis*, 106.

19. Bosselman, "Nature's Metropolis," 549–550.

20. Chicago Citizens' Zone Plan Conference, *Report of Proceedings* (City of Chicago, 1920), 64–91.

21. King, *Law and Land Use*, 215–217.

22. Oscar Wilde, *Picture of Dorian Gray* (1891).

23. David M. Young, *Chicago Transit: An Illustrated History* (DeKalb, Ill: Northern Illinois University Press, 1998), 21.

24. See King, *Law and Land Use*, Chapter 3 (79–114), for a discussion of the evolution of judicial practices related to nuisances.

25. Ibid.

26. King, *Law and Land Use*, 123–126.

27. David M. Young, *The Iron Horse and the Windy City*, 161; see also King, *Law and Land Use*, 194–212.

28. King, *Law and Land Use*, 218.

29. "Primary Sources in Chicago History" (Chicago: DePaul University Department of History, 2002). http://www.condor.depaul.edu/~history/chicago/primary.html (accessed October 20, 2002, last modified June 1, 2001).

30. Mayer and Wade, *Growth of a Metropolis*, 193–194.

31. Lois Wille, *Forever Open, Clear and Free* (Chicago: University of Chicago Press, 1991), 23.

32. Robert L. Wrigley, Jr., *Introduction to Planning History in the United States*, ed. Donald A. Kruekeberg (New Brunswick, N.J.: Center for Urban Policy Research, Rutgers University, 1983), 59.

33. Ibid.

34. Mayer and Wade, *Growth of a Metropolis*, 274–278.

35. Wrigley, *Introduction to Planning History*, 67.

36. Mayer and Wade, *Growth of a Metropolis*, 272–274.

37. Ibid.

38. This definition is derived from Michael Davison and Fay Dolnick, *A Glossary of Zoning, Development, and Planning Terms* (Chicago: American Planning Association, 1999), 188.

39. A discussion of notable court rulings on racially restrictive covenants appears in Chapter 4.

40. King, *Law and Land Use*, 229–235.

41. King, *Law and Land Use*, 229–235; Bosselman, "Nature's Metropolis," 571–572; Robert J. Boylan, "History of Chicago Zoning for Harry F. Chaddick Foundation," 1991 (Special Collections, John T. Richardson Library, DePaul University, Chicago), 1.

42. King, *Law and Land Use*, 245.

43. King, *Law and Land Use*, 248–249; Bosselman, "Nature's Metropolis," 569–571.

44. See King, *Law and Land Use*, 248.

45. Bosselman, "Nature's Metropolis," 571.

46. King, *Law and Land Use*, 5–6.

47. Bosselman, "Nature's Metropolis," 572.

48. The court further contended that the efforts of residential property owners to prevent retail stores from opening in their neighborhoods were motivated strictly by aesthetic considerations. Their actions, consequently, were not supported by legal precedent. For a discussion of

the court decision, see Bosselman, "Nature's Metropolis," 572.

49. Bosselman, "Nature's Metropolis," 573.

50. See Richard F. Babcock, *The Zoning Game: Municipal Practices and Policies* (Madison, Wis: University of Wisconsin Press, 1966), 4–5, for a discussion of this idea.

51. Readers interested in the economic and sociological dimensions of land-use regulation may wish to consult one of several works devoted to these topics, including: William Fischel's *The Economics of Zoning Law: A Property Rights Approach to American Land Use Controls* (Baltimore: Johns Hopkins, 1985), Martin A. Garrett's *Land Use Regulation* (Westport, Conn.: Praeger, 1987), and Robert Nelson's *Zoning and Property Rights* (Cambridge, Mass.: MIT Press, 1977).

52. Citizens' Zone Plan Conference, *Report of Proceedings* (City of Chicago, 1920), 64–70.

53. Spinney, *City of Big Shoulders*, 174–175.

54. See, especially, Nichols, *Zoning in Chicago*, 10–12.

55. Chicago Real Estate Board, "Final Report of the Library, City Planning and Zoning Committee of the Chicago Real Estate Board on Zoning in Chicago," 1923 (Municipal Reference Collection, Harold Washington Library, Chicago), 11–12; King, *Law and Land Use*, 364.

CHAPTER 3

1. Nichols, *Zoning in Chicago*, 2.

2. This idea is evident in Nichols, *Zoning in Chicago*, 2–4.

3. Bosselman, "Nature's Metropolis," 573.

4. Ibid.

5. King, *Law and Land Use*, 365–366; Bosselman, "Nature's Metropolis," 573.

6. Bosselman, "Nature's Metropolis," 569.

7. Chicago Real Estate Board, Final Report, 7; King, *Law and Land Use*, 365.

8. King, *Law and Land Use*, 373–374.

9. King, *Law and Land Use*, 377–378.

10. Chicago Real Estate Board, Final Report, 6.

11. Nichols, *Zoning in Chicago*, 3.

12. King, *Law and Land Use*, 386.

13. Chicago Real Estate Board, Final Report, 6–7; King, *Law and Land Use*, 386–387.

14. See King, *Law and Land Use*, 388–389.

15. Chicago Citizens' Zone Plan Conference, *Report of Proceedings*, 64–70.

16. Chicago Zoning Commission, *Zoning Chicago*, 1922 (Municipal Reference Collection, Harold Washington Library, Chicago,), 10.

17. King, *Law and Land Use*, 389.

18. Chicago Real Estate Board, Final Report, 14; King, *Law and Land Use*, 390.

19. Chicago Real Estate Board, Final Report, 13–14; King, *Law and Land Use*, 390–391.

20. Chicago Real Estate Board, Final Report, 14–15; King, *Law and Land Use*, 399.

21. Bosselman, "Nature's Metropolis," 575–577.

22. "Council Votes Zoning Law at Final Session," *Chicago Tribune*, 6 April 1923.

23. The city also estimated the amount of lot frontage devoted to various purposes to be as follows: 777 miles devoted to single-family homes, 484 miles of two-flat building frontage, 263 miles of apartment building frontage, and 286 miles of business frontage.

24. Chicago Zoning Commission, Final Report of the Chicago Zoning Commission Together with a Proposed Zoning Ordinance for the City of Chicago, 1923 (Municipal Reference Collection, Harold Washington Library, Chicago), 1.

25. Chicago Zoning Commission, *Zoning Chicago*, 3–11.

26. The zoning commission held meetings with local organizations, businesses, and property owners to review its progress to date. The

Notes from Chapter 3, continued

commission used these July gatherings to assure the public that zoning would not be retroactive (that is, it would not require significant changes to existing buildings and land uses) and to provide a glimpse of the notable features of the ordinance under consideration.

27. Chicago Zoning Commission, Final Report, 1–5.

28. Chicago Zoning Commission, Final Report, 7.

29. "Council Votes Zoning Law at Final Session," *Chicago Tribune*, 6 April 1923.

30. One commission member, Alderman James Bowler, pushed for an amendment requiring that all salvage dealers be excluded from streets with streetcar lines, while acknowledging that it would not be possible to require all existing junk dealers to relocate to side streets. See "Council Votes Zoning Law at Final Session," *Chicago Tribune*, 6 April 1923.

31. For a discussion of the rise of lakefront apartment living, see Neil Harris, *Chicago Apartments: A Century of Lakefront Living* (Somerset, U.K., Acanthus Press, 2004).

32. Wrigley, *Introduction to Planning History*, 69.

33. Wrigley, *Introduction to Planning History*, 64.

34. For a discussion of this ruling, see Edward M. Bassett, *Zoning: The Laws, Administration and Court Decisions During the First Twenty Years* (New York, Russell Sage Foundation, 1947), 40.

35. In 1925, the Illinois Supreme Court, in *City of Aurora v. Burns,* ruled that prohibiting new uses in an area in which existing uses were allowed to continue was discriminatory. However, a petition by the losing party ultimately led the court to reverse this decision on the grounds that Aurora's zoning plan had set aside other areas for those uses that were excluded from a particular zoning district. See King, *Law and Land Use*, 401–402; Bosselman, "Nature's Metropolis," 576–577.

36. Herbert Hoover, *Zoning Primer* (Washington, D.C.: Department of Commerce, 1922), 1.

37. John McDonald and Daniel McMillen, "Could Zoning Have Increased Land Values in Chicago?" *Journal of Urban Economics* 33 (1993): 168. The authors offer this quote from Final Report of the Library, City Planning and Zoning Committee of the Chicago Real Estate Board on Zoning in Chicago (1923): "Zoning will not only stabilize land values, but, in the opinion of experts, it will increase the total value of real property in Chicago by *One Billion Dollars* during the next twenty five years." [emphasis in original]

CHAPTER 4

1. For a discussion of the increases in property values that were anticipated, see John McDonald and Daniel McMillen, "Could Zoning Have Increased Land Values in Chicago?" 168. For a discussion on the disillusionment associated with zoning during the 1920s and 1930s, see Ernst Freund, "Some Inadequately Discussed Problems of the Law of City Planning & Zoning," *Illinois Law Review* 24, no. 135 (1935): 43.

2. See Chapter 11 for a discussion of this issue.

3. Chicago Home Rule Commission, *Chicago's Government: Its Structural Modernization and Home Rule Problems,* (Chicago: University of Chicago Press, 1954), 150. See also Appendix E.

4. Joseph P. Schwieterman and Martin E. Toth, *Shaping Contemporary Suburbia: Perspectives on Development Control in Metropolitan Chicago* (Chicago, Law Bulletin Publishing, 2001), 5–25.

5. Wendy Plotkin, "Deeds of Mistrust: Race, Housing and Restrictive Covenants in Chicago, 1900–1953" (Ph.D. dissertation, University of Illinois at Chicago, 1999).

6. Roger L. Rice, "Residential Segregation by Law, 1910–1917," *The Journal of Southern History*, Vol. 34, No. 2 (May 1968), 179–199, 181–182. For a detailed description of Atlanta's and St. Louis's racial zoning initiatives, see Flint, "Zoning and Residential Segregation"

(Ph.D. dissertation, University of Chicago, 1977). See also David Delaney, *Race, Place and the Law, 1836–1948* (Austin: University of Texas Press, 1998), Chapter 4.

7. Flint, "Zoning and Residential Segregation," 310–312; 316–317. On *Buchanan v. Warley* (245 U.S. 60), in addition to the sources cited by Flint, see Clement Vose, *Caucasians Only: The Supreme Court, the NAACP, and the Restrictive Covenant Cases* (Berkeley: University of California Press, 1959); "Colloquium: Rethinking *Buchanan v. Warley*," in *Vanderbilt Law Review* 51 (May 1998); and Delaney, *Race, Place & the Law*, Chapter 5. The Supreme Court invalidated racial zoning on the grounds that it violated the rights of whites to dispose of their property freely, rather than as an outgrowth of the Constitution's protections of African-Americans.

8. Plotkin, "Deeds of Mistrust," 30.

9. Ibid.

10. Vose, *Caucasians Only*, passim; Thomas Philpott, *The Slum and the Ghetto: Neighborhood Deterioration and Middle-Class Reform*, Chicago, 1880–1930 (New York: Oxford University Press, 1978), 259–269; Plotkin, "Deeds of Mistrust," 238–243.

11. Flint, "Zoning and Residential Segregation," 323–324.

12. Morris Lewis to George W. Gross, April 10, 1923, Reel 1, John H. Bracey, Jr., and August Meier, ed. *Papers of the NAACP, Part 12: Selected Branch Files, Series C: The Midwest.* See also "Residential District to Become Commercial," *Chicago Defender*, 10 February 1923, 4, asking "whether the people of Chicago will allow a business wedge to be driven into the Race residential section or whether they will show the zoning commission the necessity of preserving Grand boulevard as one of the desirable residence streets on the South Side."

13. "Citizen Rights and Community Rights: What A Zoning Plan Is and Its Relation to Negro Housing," *Opportunity* 1 (1923): 12–14, cited in Flint, "Zoning and Residential Segregation," 324. Flint notes that the Women's City Club was "one of the leading organiza-

tions that worked for zoning." See also "Chicago Lags Among Zoned Cities of Land," *Chicago Defender*, 10 February 1923, for a positive assessment of zoning in its summary of a report by the U.S. Department of Commerce.

14. "Birmingham Can't Force Segregation," *Chicago Defender*, 27 January 1923. The *Defender* also reported on the use of zoning to bolster racial segregation in other cities, such as Berkeley, Illinois, in "Change Zone Law to Head off Building," *Chicago Defender*, 23 June 1923, 10.

15. Flint, "Zoning and Residential Segregation," 346.

16. Ibid., 348, 349.

17. Ibid., 357.

18. Ibid.

19. Chicago Plan Commission, "Master Plan of Residential Land Use of Chicago," 1943 (Municipal Reference Collection, Harold Washington Library, Chicago), 10.

20. Hugh E. Young, "Paper on Need for and Some Practical Method of Rezoning Urban Areas," presented at the meeting of the City Planning Division, American Society of Civil Engineers. New York City, 21 January 1937 (Municipal Reference Collection, Harold Washington Library, Chicago).

21. Homer Hoyt, *One Hundred Years of Land Values in Chicago* (Chicago: University of Chicago Press, 1933), 440.

22. Hugh E. Young, "Rezoning Urban Areas," 1–3.

23. Ibid.

24. Ibid., 3.

25. Chicago Plan Commission, "Master Plan," 9–11.

26. Ibid.

CHAPTER 5

1. Chicago Plan Commission, *A Study of Blighted Vacant Land Prepared for the Chicago Land Clearance Commission*, May 1950, 5.

Notes from Chapter 5, continued

2. Betty Blum, *Oral History of John Cordwell* (Chicago: Art Institute of Chicago, 1993), 116.
3. Committee on Buildings and Zoning, City Council of Chicago, "Rezoning Chicago," 1952 (Municipal Reference Collection, Harold Washington Library, Chicago), 2–5.
4. Harvey M. Karlen, *The Governments of Chicago* (Chicago: Courier Publishing, 1958), 110; Richard Babcock, "New Chicago Zoning Ordinance," *Northwestern University Law Review* 52 (1957), 174–201.
5. Ibid.
6. Babcock, "New Chicago Zoning Ordinance," 1957, 190.
7. Robert J. Boylan, interview with the authors, 1999.
8. Harry Chaddick, *Chaddick: Success Against All Odds* (Chicago: Harry F. and Elaine M. Chaddick Foundation, 1990), 52.
9. Boylan, "History of Chicago Zoning," 2–3.
10. Ibid., 53.
11. See City Council of Chicago, "Rezoning Chicago," for a discussion of this issue.
12. Chaddick, *Success*, 54–56.
13. Chaddick, *Success*, 60.
14. Babcock, *Zoning Game*, 175–178.
15. Boylan, "History of Chicago Zoning," 2.
16. Babcock, *Zoning Game*, 178–181; Chaddick, *Success*, 60–61.
17. Among the individuals involved in this effort were Robert J. Boylan, Dan Ferone, George Kranenburg, and John Murray.
18. Babcock, *Zoning Game*, 181–186; Chaddick, *Success*, 62–64.
19. Chaddick, *Success*, 64.
20. Committee on Buildings and Zoning, City Council of Chicago, *An Amendment to the Chicago Zoning Ordinance for Off-Street Automobile Parking Facilities*, 1952 (Municipal Reference Collection, Harold Washington Library, Chicago); City Council of Chicago, Committee on Buildings and Zoning, "Zoning for Off-Street Parking and Off-Street Loading," 1953 (Municipal Reference Collection Harold Washing-ton Library, Chicago), 3.
21. Karlen, 110.
22. Committee on Buildings and Zoning, City Council of Chicago, *Off-Street Automobile Parking Facilities*.
23. Ibid.
24. Chaddick, *Success*, 56–58.
25. Ibid.
26. Boylan, "History of Chicago Zoning," 2.
27. Ibid.
28. City Council of Chicago, *Proposed Comprehensive Amendment to the Chicago Zoning Ordinance* (Municipal Reference Library Collection, Harold Washington Library, Chicago), 22.
29. See City of Chicago, "Proposed Comprehensive Amendment to the Chicago Zoning Ordinance," January 1954, 25–26. The calculations provided in this document suggest that the creators of the 1957 ordinance intended to make changes that would significantly reduce the allowable density of development.
30. Blum, 116.
31. Chaddick, *Success*, 67–71; Boylan, "History of Chicago Zoning," 2.
32. Boylan, "History of Chicago Zoning," 2.
33. Babcock, "New Chicago Zoning Ordinance," 190.
34. Chaddick, *Success*, 67.
35. Billboard companies retained legal counsel to oppose the provisions. Controversy erupted when local newspapers discovered that the city had been issuing permits for signs that would not conform to the proposed ordinance (the old ordinance had no explicit regulations on the size of signs). Embarrassed by its seemingly contradictory behavior, the city withdrew the permits it had issued for the problematic signs and billboards. See Chaddick, *Success*, 75–77; Chicago Zoning Ordinance (1957), sec. 11.10.6.
36. Committee on Buildings and Zoning, City Council of Chicago, "Proposed Comprehensive Amendment to the Chicago Zoning

Ordinance" 1955 (Municipal Reference Collection, Harold Washington Library, Chicago), I.

37. Chaddick, *Success,* 77. Robert J. Boylan recalled in an interview that the public meetings in the Belmont/Central area, Humboldt Park, Marquette Park, and Uptown were particularly vocal gatherings.

38. Babcock, "New Chicago Zoning Ordinance," 174.

39. Alderman E.V. Pacini, Chicago, Illinois, to members of the City Council, 3 December 1956, (Municipal Reference Collection, Harold Washington Library, Chicago).

40. Chaddick, *Success,* 77.

41. "Council Votes Far Reaching Zoning Laws," *Chicago Tribune,* 30 May 1957.

42. Ibid.

CHAPTER 6

1. Jay McMullen, "New Silhouette for Chicago?" *Chicago Daily News,* 23 July 1973.

2. Jay McMullen, "PUDs: A Way to Duck Tough Zoning Rules?" *Chicago Daily News,* n.d., collection of the Municipal Reference Library, City of Chicago.

3. Babcock, *Zoning Game,* 133.

4. Paul Gapp, "Proposed Zoning Law Could Lift the City's Face," *Chicago Tribune,* 8 August 1973.

5. It is also noteworthy that Crown Hall on the IIT campus also earned National Landmark status in 2002.

6. Miles Berger, *They Built Chicago: Entrepreneurs Who Shaped a Great City's Architecture* (Chicago: Bonus Books, 1992), 244–58.

7. Gapp, "Proposed Zoning Law Could Lift the City's Face."

8. "Fight Seen on New Building Law," *Chicago Tribune,* 20 February 1974.

9. Gapp. "Proposed Zoning Law Could Lift the City's Face."

10. McMullen, "PUDs: A Way to Duck Tough Zoning Rules?"

11. Ibid.

12. The Lakeview-based Campaign to Control High-Rises was among the organizations supporting the measure. See Stanley Ziemba, "City Council Unit OK's Plan to Control Builders," *Chicago Tribune,* 21 February 1974, section 1A, p. 2.

13. This estimate is based on the Chaddick Institute's analysis of all planned development approved between 1957 and 2000.

14. Mark Caro, "Chicago's Mr. Insider Made Sure 'Baby' Happened," *Chicago Tribune,* 27 February 2005.

15. Interview by the authors with Jane Heron, May 2005.

16. One notable example is the Millennium Centre at 33 W. Ontario Street, completed in 2000. Through the use of a creative design that limited the tallest portion of the development to only one part of the site, the developer was able to build a 58-story structure as-of-right, avoiding the PD track. Yet this avenue was not simple; pursuing it was still costly and time-consuming.

17. For the city, a notable advantage of PDs is the ability to precisely limit the scale of development. Although developers sometimes presented plans that, in effect, are "R3½" density (i.e., they have densities between R3 and R4), they need to try to obtain R4 zoning in the absence of a PD, which would allow them to build to greater density than the city felt appropriate. PD agreements, however, allowed the city to precisely specify the maximum FAR.

18. McMullen, "New Silhouette for Chicago?"

CHAPTER 7

1. Devereux Bowly, Jr., *The Poorhouse: Subsidized Housing in Chicago: 1895–1976* (Carbondale: Southern Illinois University Press, 1978), 127.

2. This estimate is based on the authors' analysis of a data set of all

Notes from Chapter 7, continued

buildings at least 12 stories in height provided by Emporis Research.

3. Donald J. Bogue, *An Estimate of Metropolitan Chicago's Future Population: 1955 to 1965* (Prepared as a report to the Chicago Plan Commission and the Office of the Housing and Redevelopment Coordinator, 2 February 1955).

4. Mayor's Zoning Reform Commission, *Actual Chicago Population Trends Compared by Periodic Population Forecasts,* 2003.

5. Delia O'Hara, "Up with High-Rises, Consultant's Report Urges," *Chicago Sun-Times,* 1 August 1980.

6. Shlaes and Company, "Chicago's Lakefront Downzoning: Too Much Too Soon?" April 1980 (Municipal Reference Collection, Chicago Public Library), 1–28.

7. Fred Orehek, "Daley to Sponsor High-Rise Controls," *Chicago Tribune,* 13 November 1974.

8. Scott Jacobs, "Families Ask Space in New Town," *Chicago Sun-Times,* 28 April 1974; Nancy Todd, "LV Residents Air Downzoning Views," *The Lerner Newspaper* (Chicago), 1 February 1975.

9. Orehek, "High-Rise Controls."

10. Lester Jacobson, "Sheridan Downzoning Sought," *North Town* (Illinois), 17 September 1975.

11. Elizabeth Brenner, "Zoning Controversy Spreads North," *Chicago Tribune,* 30 September 1979, section 1.

12. Jack Houston, "Chaddick Reviews Zoning Criticism," *Chicago Tribune,* 26 August 1971.

13. Ibid.

14. This estimate is based on the authors' analysis of a data set of all buildings at least 12 stories in height provided by Emporis Research.

15. Martin Oberman, interview with Joseph P. Schwieterman on 18 May 2005.

16. The Wrightwood Neighbors adopted a Long Range Plan to guide development in 1977. This plan was in effect for 25 years until it was replaced with a new plan in 2002.

17. John McCarron, "High-Rises Shoot Through the Roof: Chicago's Zoning Ordinance Shoves Open Spaces into the Shadows," *Chicago Tribune,* 20 September 1987.

18. The policy of not counting the ground-level and below-grade uses as a story of the building created multiple problems related to both the building code and zoning code. Four-plus-ones, for example, narrowly qualified for "ordinary construction" under the building code, which allowed developers to use masonry materials rather than steel frame construction.

19. "Work on '4 Plus 1' Apartment Snagged by City Building Code," *Chicago Tribune,* 25 April 1969.

20. Roger Flaherty, "4-Plus-1 Talk 'Frank,'" *North Town* (Illinois) (Lerner Newspapers), 19 October 1969.

21. Don Kazak, "Daley Agrees: 4 Plus 1 Is 'Bad,'" *Chicago Tribune,* 28 July 1969.

22. Douglas Schroeder of the Park West Community Association, Dan Crowe and Louis Rocah of the South East Lake View Neighbors, Don Lerner, executive vice president of Lerner Newspapers, representatives of Citizens for Better Housing, and representatives of the North River Commission soon joined Lincoln Park's Pat Feely in the chorus of criticism over four-plus-ones. Source: Kazak, "Daley Agrees."

23. Kazak, "Daley Agrees."

24. "Those Four Plus Ones," *Chicago Tribune,* 26 July 1971.

25. Earl Moses, "Neighbors Fight 4 plus 1's," *Chicago Sun-Times,* 5 January 1969.

26. Jay McMullen, "4 Plus 1 Buildings," *Chicago Daily News,* 20 July 1971, 3.

27. "'4 Plus 1' Curtailment Challenged," *Chicago Tribune,* 4 June 1971.

28. Ibid.

29. Cornelia Honcher, "Tougher '4 Plus 1' Rules Also Hit High-Rise Costs," *Chicago Tribune,* 10 April 1971.

30. Ibid.

31. Ibid.

32. Interview of William S. Singer by Joseph P. Schwieterman, 22 June 2005.

33. Jay McMullen and James Kloss, "City Council Votes Easier Codes for 4 Plus I Buildings," *Chicago Daily News*, 22 June 1971.

34. Four-plus-ones remain part of the streetscape, providing moderately priced housing to thousands, but also eliciting unkind words from architectural historians. The American Institute of Architects describes them as "cheaply constructed apartments" in the 2002 edition of its Chicago guidebook, noting: "These buildings are poorly suited for conversion into condominiums or upgrading. Some have been adequately maintained and even aesthetically improved over the years, continuing to provide small apartments at modest rents. Others have fallen into poor condition and may become problematic to the city."

35. Delia O'Hara, "Lakefront Zoning Debate: Up Down or All Around," *Chicago Sun-Times*, 15 August 1980.

36. Ibid.

37. Mayor's Taskforce on Neighborhood Land Use, *High-Rise High-Density*, 1987 (Municipal Reference Collection, Harold Washington Library, Chicago), 1–14.

38. City of Chicago, *Principles for Chicago's New Zoning Ordinance: Recommendations for Preserving, Protecting and Strengthening Chicago's Neighborhoods* (Chicago: Mayor's Zoning Reform Commission, City of Chicago, 2002), I.

CHAPTER 8

1. Frank A. Randall and John D. Randall, *History of the Development of Building Construction in Chicago* (Urbana: University of Illinois Press, 1999), 25.

2. Berger, *They Built Chicago*, 165.

3. Randall, *Development of Building Construction*, 25.

4. Richard Pavia, interview by Jane Heron, December 2004.

5. The complex has earned its share of criticism for its lack of connectedness with the surrounding streetscape. Urban design writer Kenneth Halpern, for example, called it an illustration of the "urbanistic consequences of the lack of sound zoning, planning and urban design policy in Chicago" in *Downtown USA: Urban Design in Nine American Cities* (New York: Whitney Library of Design, 1978), 85. Despite the sharp differences about the impact of its presence, the complex remains a prominent and heavily photographed city landmark.

6. *Development Plan for the Central Area of Chicago* (Chicago: Department of City Planning, August 1958), 26–28.

7. "Action Needed on Zoning Law," *Chicago Sun-Times*, 20 June 1962.

8. Ruth Moore, "Ban on Skyscraper Jungle OKd," *Chicago Sun-Times*, 22 June 1962.

9. Ruth Moore, "Civic Units Urge City Curb Bid Downtown Apartments," *Chicago Sun-Times*, 21 June 1962; Thomas Buck, "High Rise Apartment Zoning Under Study," *Chicago Tribune*, 24 October 1962.

10. Jack Meltzer Associates, "Zoning for Residential Development in the Central Area, 1963," (Municipal Reference Collection, Harold Washington Library, Chicago), 3.

11. Ibid., 1–4.

12. Ibid.

13. Jack Meltzer Associates, "Zoning for Residential Development," 3–4; Buck, 24 October 1962.

14. McMullen, "New Silhouette for Chicago?"

15. Jack Meltzer Associates, "Zoning for Residential Development," 3–4.

16. The Melzer report summarized its conclusions as follows: "The primary requirements of heavy residential growth are light, air, view, privacy and horizontal and vertical open space. These requirements are interdependent and their achievement is most closely related to the provision of adequate daylight."

Notes from Chapter 8, continued

17. For a summary of Shlaes' arguments, see Shlaes and Company, "Lakefront Downzoning."

18. Ruth Moore, "City to Tighten Controls for Apartment Hotels," *Chicago Sun-Times*, 4 February 1969, 24.

19. This estimate is based on our analysis of a data set of all buildings in the Gold Coast neighborhood at least 12 stories in height provided by Emporis Research.

20. Michelle Stevens, "Council Unit OK's Ban on New Gold Coast High-rises," *Chicago Sun-Times*, 17 August 1979.

21. Shlaes and Company, "Lakefront Downzoning," 1–28.

22. Philip Zeitlin Associates, *Chicago Zoning Ordinance Review*, 1982 (Municipal Reference Collection, Harold Washington Library, Chicago), 1–13.

23. Ibid., 8.

24. For a discussion of housing trends since the mid-1990s, see John R. Jaeger, "Are Central Cities Coming Back?" Center for Urban Real Estate, University of Illinois at Chicago, 28 September 2001.

CHAPTER 9

1. Berger, *They Built Chicago*, 61-62; Carol Willis, *Form Follows Function: Skyscrapers and Skylines in New York and Chicago* (New York, Princeton Architectural Press, 1996), 127–28.

2. Alice Sinkevitch, *AIA Guide to Chicago* (Fort Washington, Pa.: Harvest Books, 2004), 14.

3. Ibid.

4. Willis, *Form Follows Function*, 64.

5. Chicago Real Estate Board, *Final Report*, 3.

6. Willis, *Form Follows Function*, 64.

7. Willis, *Form Follows Function*, 73.

8. Ibid.

9. Clarence B. Randall, quoted in Earle Shultz and Walter Simmons,

Offices in the Sky (Indianapolis: Bobbs-Merrill, 1959), 7.

10. Shultz and Simmons, *Offices*, 7.

11. See Halpern, *Downtown USA*, 79, for a discussion of the city's early experience with plazas.

12. Ibid.

13. City of Chicago, Department of Planning and Development, *A New Zoning Bonus System for Chicago*, 1998 (Municipal Reference Collection, Harold Washington Library, Chicago), 4–5.

14. The amendments to Philadelphia's ordinance in 1960 capped FAR in its central area at 12; Boston's 1964 amendments capped FAR at just 10; Los Angeles, established a maximum FAR of 13; Minneapolis adopted an FAR limit of 14 while Washington, D.C., turned to a maximum FAR of 10 (while still employing height limits to limit the scale of new construction).

15. In 1954, Atlanta established an exceedingly generous FAR limit of 25, but the city eventually reduced the limit to 10, where it remains today. In 1960, San Francisco established an FAR limit of 20 (25 on corner lots), in the densest part of the city, only to reduce it several years later to 16 (20 on corner lots). In the late 1960s, San Francisco capped the FAR at 14 for office buildings, 10 for retail and general commercial buildings, and seven for support facilities.

16. Halpern, *Downtown USA*, 79–80.

17. Halpern, *Downtown USA*, 81.

18. City of Chicago, Department of Planning and Development, *A New Zoning Bonus System for Chicago*, Draft for Public Review and Comment, 18 December 1998, 9.

19. Paul Gapp, "Taking a Critical Walk Thru Three Plazas: One Sweet and Two Sour," *Chicago Tribune*, 13 July 1975.

20. Ibid.

21. Sinkevitch, *AIA Guide to Chicago*, 22.

22. Halpern, *Downtown USA*, 87–88.

23. John McCarron, "Chicago Needs Zoning Reform to Help New

Growth Complement the Old," *Chicago Tribune*, 20 December 1987.

24. Ibid.

25. Ibid.

26. The construction of the building at 190 S. LaSalle illustrates this point. See discussion in Chapter 6.

27. See Halpern, *Downtown USA*, page 129, for a discussion of this issue.

28. A discussion of the problems posed by arcades along Michigan Avenue appears in City of Chicago, Department of Planning and Development, *New Zoning Bonus System*, 12–13, 17.

29. Halpern, *Downtown USA*, 236.

30. David Roeder, *Chicago Sun-Times*, 22 February 1999.

31. The Chicago Development Council, for example, sent a letter outlining its concerns about the city's new bonus policy in 1999.

32. Willis, *Form Follows Function*, 182.

CHAPTER 10

1. Babcock, *Zoning Game*, 4–14.

2. The quote appears in Delia O'Hara, "Up with High-rises, Consultant's Report Urges," *Chicago Sun-Times*, 1 August 1980.

3. Wille, *Forever Open*, 23.

4. Wille, *Forever Open*, 111–119.

5. *Chicago Daily News*, 26 September 1973.

6. Ibid.

7. Graham Grady, interview with the authors, 1999.

8. Gary Washburn, "Proposal Gives Townhouse Design, Development a Makeover," *Chicago Tribune*, 6 March 1998, Metro Section, 3; Jacquelyn Heard and Dionne Searcey, "Flimsy and Fuchsia Have City Seeing Red: Michigan Avenue's Taste of Garish has Natarus Wincing," *Chicago Tribune*, 23 February 1996, 1; Andrew Martin, "Strip Stake: Chicago Law Would Add More Flavor to Retail Center Design," *Chicago Tribune*, 22 May 1999, New Homes Section, 12.

9. John McCarron, "One Man's Grand Plan for Chicago," *Chicago Tribune*, 14 April 2002.

10. Graham Grady, interview with the authors, 1999.

11. City of Chicago, "Guide to the Chicago Landscape Ordinance," 1991 (Municipal Reference Collection, Harold Washington Library, Chicago), 9.

12. Gary Washburn, "Green Fees: City to Demand Money from Developers to Create More Open Space," *Chicago Tribune*, 4 April 1998; Martin E. Toth, *Voices from the Past, Visions for the Future: A Modern Assessment of Harry F. Chaddick's 18 Essential Planning Ideas for Chicago*, ed. Joseph P. Schwieterman (Chicago: Chaddick Institute for Metropolitan Development, 2000), 105–107.

13. The ordinance stipulates that the funds had to be spent in the same neighborhood where they were generated. This ordinance was an outgrowth of a large-scale initiative that culminated in Chicago's CitySpace Plan, a document released in 1995. A collaborative effort between the Chicago Community Trust, the Park District, the Cook County Forest Preserve, the city and other institutions, the plan provided a blueprint for the creation of new parkland to alleviate an apparent shortage of open space. See Toth, *Voices from the Past*, 105–108.

14. Washburn, "Green Fees," 4 April 1998.

15. City of Chicago, Title 17 of the Municipal Code of Chicago, Chicago Zoning Ordinance, Section 7–13.

16. Washburn, "Green Fees," 4 April 1988.

17. Martin, 22 May 1999, 12.

18. Title 17 of the Municipal Code of Chicago, Chicago Zoning Ordinance, Section 11.11A.

19. Ruth Eckdish Knack, "Troubadour Babcock," *Planning*, August 1987: 23.

Chapter 11

1. Miller, *City of the Century*, 452.
2. Einhorn, *Property Rules*, 90.
3. Richard Thale, "Aldermanic Courtesy," *Encyclopedia of Chicago*, (Chicago: University of Chicago Press, 2004), 14.
4. Bill and Lori Granger, *Lords of the Last Machine* (New York: Random House, 1987), 33.
5. Thale, *Encyclopedia of Chicago*, 14.
6. Ibid.
7. Chicago Home Rule Commission, *Chicago's Government*.
8. Ibid.
9. Leon Despres, interview with Jane Heron, 6 December 2004.
10. Ibid.
11. Wille, *Forever Open*, 113.
12. Joel Rast, *Remaking Chicago: The Political Origins of Urban Industrial Change* (DeKalb, Ill.: Northern Illinois University Press, 1999), 41.
13. Ibid.
14. Jay McMullen, "Zone Change in Gold Coast Assailed," *Chicago Daily News*, 1 December 1967.
15. Wille, *Forever Open*, 113.
16. "City Committee to Study High Rise Zoning Request," *Chicago Tribune*, 1 June 1971.
17. For a summary of the zoning issues associated with the Ritchie Court apartment tower debate, see *Chicago Daily News*, 2 April 1969; *Chicago Daily News*, 1 November 1969, 11; *Chicago Daily News*, 11 February, 1971; and *Chicago Tribune*, 4 June 1971.
18. Leon Despres, interview with Jane Heron, 6 December 2004.
19. Mike Royko, "There's Gold in Zoning Laws," *Chicago Daily News*, 14 January 1970.
20. Wexler noted that hearsay reports of the aldermen's views before the ZBA could prove fatal, since the alderman had not given testimony nor been cross-examined. See Richard L. Wexler, "'A Zoning Ordinance is Not Better Than Its Administration'—A Platitude Proved," *The John Marshall Journal of Practice and Procedure* 1 (Spring 1967): 74–91.
21. Ray Hanana and Harlan Draeger, "Zoning Clout Means Big Campaign Cash," *Chicago Sun-Times*, 19 July 1987.
22. Ibid.
23. From 1973, over a span of 20 years, at least 17 aldermen were convicted for these offenses.
24. "Family Ties Apparent in City Rezoning," *Chicago Sun-Times*, 19 July 1987.
25. Jonathan H. Marshall, "Aldermen Wield Real Zoning Power," *Lerner Newspapers* (Chicago), 2 October 1991.
26. "City Council Consider Local Zoning Control," *Austin News* (Chicago), 3 July 1974.
27. Greg Hinz, "Should Residents Have a Voice in Rezoning?" *Lincoln-Belmont Booster* (Chicago), 6 December 1975.
28. Ibid.
29. See Ronald Roenigk, "Mayor's Zoning Reform Show Hits the Road, Overhaul Debated as Alderman Seek to Retail Local Control," *Inside*, July 2002, http://www.insideonline.com/site/egpage/5880_162.htm; Gary Washburn, "City Seeks to Clean Up Out-of-date Zoning Code," *Chicago Tribune*, 4 June 2004.
30. Milton Rakove, "Chairman Dunne—A Little More Democratic Than Daley," *Illinois Issues* 13, July 1978.
31. This quote by Edward Bassett appears in Keith D. Revell, *Building Gotham: Civic Culture and Public Policy in New York City, 1898–1938* (Baltimore: Johns Hopkins University Press, 2002).

CHAPTER 12

1. "Revision of City Zoning is Begun by Chaddick," *Chicago Sun-Times,* 24 August 1967.
2. Ibid.
3. Chicago Zoning Ordinance Review Committee, "Items to be Considered for Revision of Chicago Zoning Ordinance," 15 August 1967. (Copy in Chaddick Archives, DePaul University, Chicago.)
4. Chicago Zoning Ordinance Review Committee, "Items to be Considered for Revision of Chicago Zoning Ordinance," First List of Priority Items, 15 August 1967. (Copy in Chaddick Archives, DePaul University, Chicago.)
5. Robert J. Boylan, interview with the authors, 1999.
6. Chaddick, *Success,* 84–85; Joy Darrow, "Zoning Dream Fades for Chaddick Backers," *Chicago Tribune,* 28 January 1968; Basil Tabbot, Jr., "A North Side Firm Hired as Experts on Zone Changes," *Chicago Sun-Times,* 24 January 1968.
7. Joy Darrow, "Zoning Dream Fades;" Jay McMullen, "Chaddick Quits Zoning Review Post," *Chicago Daily News,* 19 January 1968; Ruth Moore, "Zoning Unit Director Quits, Office Closed," *Chicago Sun-Times,* 23 January 1968.
8. McMullen, "Chaddick Quits," 1.
9. Chaddick, *Success,* 84–85.
10. Boylan, "History of Chicago Zoning," 6.
11. Ibid.
12. Ibid.
13. "Total Rezoning of City Slated," *Chicago Daily News,* 2 June 1976.
14. Jane Heron, interview with the authors, November 2004.
15. Boylan, "History of Chicago Zoning," 7–8.
16. Jack Guthman, "City Needs New Zoning Law," *Chicago Tribune,* 3 February 1984.
17. John McCarron, "Chicago Needs Zoning Reform to Help New Growth Complement the Old," *Chicago Tribune,* 20 December 1987.
18. "Recommended Zoning Ordinance Revision Program for City of Chicago," Prepared by Harry F. Chaddick Associates, December 1991. (Copy in Chaddick Archives, DePaul University, Chicago.)
19. Steven R. Strahler and Mark Hornung, "Politics, Economics, History Resist Zoning Code Revamp," *Crain's Chicago Business,* 4 September 1989, 15, 23.

CHAPTER 13

1. This housing information is derived from Jaeger, *Are Central Cities Coming Back?* (Chicago: Center for Urban Real Estate, University of Illinois at Chicago, 28 September 2001).
2. Jane Jacob's views on the choices offered by cities are described in Chapter 8 of *Death and Life of Great American Cities* (New York: Random House, 1961).
3. For a summary of the evolution of TIF in Illinois, see the Summer 2002 issue of *Pragmatics: The Journal of Community-Based Research,* a publication of the Policy Research Action Group.
4. Alderman Lorraine Dixon also served on the commission prior to her death in 2002.
5. John McCarron, "Danger Zone: Here Comes More Zoning Reform," Commentary, *Chicago Tribune,* 31 July 2000.
6. *Chicago Sun-Times,* 22 June 2001.
7. The commission formed six subcommittees to explore specific aspects of the zoning ordinance: the central business district; transportation and parking; residential; open space; neighborhood commercial, retail, and industrial; and administration and enforcement.
8. Under the old system, some affected property owners never received their notices; others had difficulty picking up the certified letter from the post office. The measure requiring that signs be posted was passed 7 February 2001.

Notes from Chapter 13, continued

9. The city also relied heavily on Clarion Associates, Dyett & Bhatia, and Lane Kendig for technical assistance, while turning to Camiros, Ltd., and Farr Associates for assistance in architecture and urban design, Applied Real Estate Analysis for market analysis, and Jacobs/Ryan Associates to evaluate landscaping issues.

10. See especially Peter Skosey and Christina Sellis, *Lay of the Land: A National Survey of Zoning Reform* (Chicago: Metropolitan Planning Council, 1999). MPC also distributed more than 1,000 CD-ROMs to inform the general public about the urgency and importance of the task at hand. See Chicago Metropolitan Planning Council, *Revise, Recreate, Rezone: A Neighborhood Guide to Zoning—What Is Zoning?* (2001).

11. Blair Kamin, "After 50 years of zoning out, the city's reforming the code," *Chicago Tribune*, 10 June 2002.

12. This study, "Socio-Economic Analysis of Chicago's Zoning Reform Proposals," by Gary Papke, principal at Clarion Associates, constituted one of the most significant research efforts focusing on zoning in Chicago in many years. Through the use of a geographic information system, the study compared the level of "excess capacity" in the existing (1957) and proposed (2004) zoning ordinances. (Excess capacity is a measure of the difference between the maximum allowable density of development and the actual density of development). After quantifying the current population and the "potential population" of various neighborhoods under different zoning scenarios, the study concluded that "the proposed changes in residential districts will reduce excess capacity only slightly" and that "the proposed changes ... should not limit the residential market on either a city-wide or neighborhood basis." The existing zoning ordinance was found to allow for a potential population of up to 8.12 million residents; the proposed ordinance would allow up to 7.57 million.

Another section within reviewed changes in the number of dwelling units built in various neighborhoods since the 1940s, the percentage distribution of rental versus owner-occupied housing, and

the amount of vacant land in residential areas. The report, commissioned by the city and presented to the Zoning Reform Commission in 2004, supported the city's view that the proposed changes would not be punitive toward development.

13. This quote appears in a letter from Robert A. Wislow, chairman, and Michael Tobin, chairman, Zoning Committee of the Chicago Development Council, to Mayor's Zoning Reform Commission, dated 10 August 2002. The CDC's zoning committee actively monitored the rezoning process and made known its concerns about many provisions of the new ordinance, including the new "triggers" for planned development. Wislow is chairman and CEO of U.S. Equities Realty; Tobin is a principal at the Northern Realty Group.

14. The new zoning ordinance, for example, was the focus of an article in a national magazine devoted to municipal governance. See Christopher Swope, "Unscrambling the City," *Governing* (June 2003).

15. Interview by the authors with Jack Guthman, November 2004.

16. Nichols, *Zoning in Chicago*, 3.

17. As quoted by Revell in *Building Gotham*, 226.

18. Richard F. Babcock and Charles L. Siemon, *The Zoning Game—Revisited* (Boston: Lincoln Institute of Land Policy Book, 1985), 259.

Appendix A

1. Quote from Charles B. Ball, "City Zoning: How to Provide Light and Air in Growing Cities," reprinted from *Health*, 1922 (Copy in Edward M. Bassett Archives, Cornell University).

2. Robert Lewis, "Planned Manufacturing Districts in Chicago: Firms, Networks and Boundaries," *Journal of Planning History* 3, no. 1 (February 2004): 29–49.

3. Rast, *Remaking Chicago*, 89.

4. Jack Swenson, former Deputy Commissioner of Planning and Development, notes that prior to the development of PMDs, the

city generally used targeted incentives, such as tax abatement and subsidies, to foster industrial retention. The creation of the first PMDs, initiated during the mayoral term of Harold Washington, constituted an important philosophical shift away from these financially oriented approaches towards a land-use based approach, which, in many parts of the city, provided benefits to a larger number of industries.

5. *Chicago Tribune,* 24 May 1997.
6. Richard F. Babcock and Wendy U. Larson, *Special Districts: The Ultimate in Neighborhood Zoning* (Cambridge, MA: Lincoln Institute of Land Policy, 1990).
7. Joel Rast, "Curbing Industrial Decline or Thwarting Redevelopment: An Evaluation of Chicago's Planned Manufacturing Districts" (Center for Economic Development, University of Wisconsin–Milwaukee, 2005).
8. Ibid.
9. Rast, *Remaking Chicago,* 155.

APPENDIX B

1. For a summary of some of the contributions of the Chicago School of Sociology to the zoning movement, see Bosselman, 559–583.
2. Ernest W. Burgess, "The Growth of the City: An Introduction to a Research Project," in Robert E. Park and Ernest Burgess, *The City* (Chicago, University of Chicago Press, 1925)
3. Harvey M. Zorbaugh, *The Gold Coast and the Slum* (Chicago: University of Chicago Press, 1929).
4. Freund, "Inadequately Discussed Problems," 43.
5. William Alonso, *Location and Land Use: Toward a General Theory of Land Rent* (Chicago: Harvard University Press, 1964); Edwin S. Mills, "An Aggregative Model of Resource Allocation in a Metropolitan Area," *American Economic Review* 57 (May 1967): 197–210; Richard Muth,

Cities and Housing: The Spatial Pattern of Urban Residential Land Use (Chicago: University of Chicago Press, 1969).
6. Ronald Coase, "The Problem of Social Cost," *Journal of Law and Economics* 3, no. 1 (1960), 1–44.
7. Robert C. Ellickson, *Order Without Law: How Neighbors Settle Disputes* (Cambridge, Mass.: Harvard University Press, 1991), 1–60.

APPENDIX C

1. Freund, "Inadequately Discussed Problems," 43.
2. Richard Babcock, "Illinois Supreme Court and Zoning: A Study in Uncertainty," *University of Chicago Law Review* 15 (1947): 87.
3. For a summary of Babcock's career, see especially Ruth Eckdish Knack, "Troubadour Babcock," 21–27.
4. Babcock and Siemon, *Zoning Game—Revisited*; Richard F. Babcock and Fred P. Bosselman's *Exclusionary Zoning: Land Use Regulation and Housing in the 1970s* (New York: Praeger, 1973).
5. Brian Blaesser, "Remembering Richard Babcock: A Compelling Man," *Journal of Land Use and Environmental Law* 3 (November 1993): 7–8.

APPENDIX D

1. Edward M. Bassett, *Autobiography of Edward M. Bassett* (New York, Harbor Press, 1939), 110–116.
2. Ibid.
3. Chicago Real Estate Board, "Final Report of the Library, City Planning and Zoning Committee of the Chicago Real Estate Board on Zoning in Chicago," 10.
4. Letter from Frederick Law Olmstead dated January 1, 1937 to Edward M. Bassett, collection of Cornell University, Edward M. Bassett collection.

APPENDIX E

1. For example, it could no longer issue a variation to "permit a non-conforming use which will materially interfere with the use of adjoining premises" or to "permit a specialty shop, business, commercial, manufacturing or industrial use" in a residential district. The amendment also imposed tighter limits on the enlargement and improvement of nonconformities. One new variation was introduced permitting "the remodeling or dividing of apartments in a nonconforming apartment house." While helping alleviate the severe housing shortages, this provision also opened the door to blight in some parts of the city.
2. Babcock, "New Chicago Zoning Ordinance," 194, 200.
3. Babcock, "New Chicago Zoning Ordinance," 194.
4. Wexler, "Zoning Ordinance Not Better Than Administration," 74–91.
5. For a summary of the change in caseloads between 1923 and 1995, see Douglas Ferguson, "A Historical Narrative of Chicago's Zoning Board of Appeals: 1923–2001," master's thesis, DePaul University, Chicago, 2002.
6. Milton Rakove. "Zoning Appeals: The Board That Holds the City Together," *Chicago Tribune*, 13 May 1976.
7. It should be noted that the effectiveness of this policy has not yet been fully tested.

APPENDIX F

1. Chaddick, *Success*, 71–75.

APPENDIX H

1. We were unable to determine the year Harry Manley replaced John Maloney as zoning administrator. The year we provide is only an estimate.

PHOTOGRAPHY CREDITS

1. We list below the image/negative numbers of photographs from the Chicago Historical Society Collection used in this book: cover photo: ICHi-20961; photo facing Chapter 1: ICHi-05818; p. 8; ICHi-03211; p. 14: ICHi-26026; p. 15: ICHi-04192; p. 19: DN-0004945; p. 23: ICHi-2300814; p. 24: ICHi-05790; p. 26: ICHi-05806; p. 29: ICHi-00814; p. 32: 4.5 ICHi-23493; p. 33: ICHi-05790; p. 42: ICHi-23500; p. 50; 18506x2; p. 69: HB-SN825-13; p. 82: ICHi-20261; p. 84: ICHi-24213; p. 85: Photo by Raymond Trowbridge; Ready Print, Box 200, #2; p. 90: HB-28520F; p. 91: ICHi-15788; p. 104: ICHi-22530; p. 105: ICHI-35556; p. 135: ICHi -05773.

Photo Credits and Permissions

We express our gratitude to the Chicago Historical Society (CHS) for its extensive photographic assistance. The image appearing on page 19 is from the CHS's *Chicago Daily News* collection; the images on pages 26, 32, and 33 as well as the cover photo are from the Chicago Aerial Survey Co. Collection. In the Notes section on page 176, you will find the image number for each CHS photograph.[1]

We thank Teresa Yoder, Archival Specialist for the Special Collections and Preservation Division, Harold Washington Library Center. All photographs from the Library Center's collection are credited to the Chicago Public Library. We also recognize Ruth Knack of the American Planning Association and Lawrence Okrent of Okrent Associates for the use of images from their extensive collections.

The contemporary photographs credited to the Chaddick collection in Chapters 8, 9, and 10 are by Joseph Schwieterman, except the images on pages 107 and 108, which are by Joseph Kearney. Photographs credited to DePaul Special Collections and Archives are taken from the Harry F. and Elaine M. Chaddick Archives; we thank Renee Bartley and Kathryn DeGraff for their support in reproducing these images. Both of these photographic collections are housed at DePaul University.

The headlines on pages 71 and 121 are courtesy of the *Chicago Sun-Times.* The photograph of Lewis Hill on page 114 is courtesy of Norman Elkin. We thank Metro Self Storage for providing access to take the photograph appearing on page 89.

Finally, we thank the Harry F. and Elaine M. Chaddick Foundation for authorization to reprint materials from *Chaddick: Success Against All Odds* on pages 151–152.

Bibliography

Babcock, Richard F. "The Chicago Zoning Ordinance." *Northwestern Law Review* 52, no. 2 (1957): 174–201.

Babcock, Richard F. *The Zoning Game.* Milwaukee: University of Wisconsin Press, 1966.

Babcock, Richard F., and Fred P. Bosselman. *Exclusionary Zoning: Land Use Regulation and Housing in the 1970s.* New York: Praeger, 1973.

Bassett, Edward M. *Autobiography of Edward M. Bassett.* New York: Harbor Press, 1939.

Bosselman, Fred P. "The Commodification of 'Nature's Metropolis': The Historical Context of Illinois' Unique Zoning Standards." *Northern Illinois University Law Review* 12 (summer 1992): 527–84.

Boylan, Robert J. "History of Chicago Zoning for Harry F. Chaddick Foundation." Special Collections, John T. Richardson Library, DePaul University, Chicago. Transparency Duplicator (photocopied), 1991.

Burchell, Robert W. *Planned Unit Development: New Communities American Style.* New Brunswick, N.J.: Rutgers University, 1972.

Chaddick, Harry F. *Chaddick! Success Against All Odds.* Chicago: Harry F. Chaddick Associates, 1990.

Chicago Home Rule Commission. *Chicago's Government: Its Structural Modernization and Home Rule Problems.* Chicago: University of Chicago Press, 1954.

Chicago Plan Commission. *Master Plan of Residential Land Use of Chicago.* Municipal Reference Collection, Harold Washington Library, Chicago, 1943.

Chicago Real Estate Board. *Final Report of the Library, City Planning and Zoning Committee of the Chicago Real Estate Board on Zoning in Chicago.* Municipal Reference Collection, Harold Washington Library, Chicago, 1923.

Chicago Zoning Commission. *Zoning Chicago.* Municipal Reference Collection, Harold Washington Library, Chicago, 1922.

Chicago Zoning Commission. *Final Report of the Chicago Zoning Commission Together with a Proposed Zoning Ordinance for the City of Chicago.* Municipal Reference Collection, Harold Washington Library, Chicago, 1923.

City Council of Chicago. *1998 Title 17, Municipal Code of Chicago: Chicago Zoning Ordinance, Including Off-Street Parking and Loading Provisions Passed by the City Council of the City of Chicago on May 29, 1957.* Chicago: Index Publishing Corp, 1998.

City Council of Chicago. Committee on Buildings and Zoning. *Rezoning Chicago.* Municipal Reference Collection, Harold Washington Library, Chicago, 1952.

City Council of Chicago. Committee on Buildings and Zoning. *An Amendment to the Chicago Zoning Ordinance for Off-Street Automobile Parking Facilities.* Municipal Reference Collection, Harold Washington Library, Chicago, 1952.

City Council of Chicago. Committee on Buildings and Zoning. *Zoning for Off-Street Parking and Off-Street Loading.* Municipal Reference Collection, Harold Washington Library, Chicago, 1953.

City Council of Chicago. Committee on Buildings and Zoning. *Proposed Comprehensive Amendment to the Chicago Zoning Ordinance.* Municipal Reference Collection, Harold Washington Library, Chicago, 1954.

City Council of Chicago. Committee on Buildings and Zoning. *Proposed Comprehensive Amendment to the Chicago Zoning Ordinance.* Municipal Reference Collection, Harold Washington Library, Chicago, 1955.

City of Chicago. *An Ordinance Amending the Chicago Zoning Ordinance.* Municipal Reference Collection, Harold Washington Library, Chicago, 1934.

Cronon, William. *Nature's Metropolis: Chicago and the Great West.* New York: W.W. Norton, 1991.

Davidson, Michael, and Fay Dolnick. *A Glossary of Zoning, Development, and Planning Terms* 188. Chicago: American Planning Association, 1999.

Department of City Planning. *Rules, Regulations, and Procedures in Relation to Planned Developments to the Chicago Zoning Ordinance as Amended.* Municipal Reference Collection, Harold Washington Library, Chicago, 1963.

Department of Planning. Department of Economic Development. *Clybourn Corridor Planned Manufacturing District.* Municipal Reference Collection, Harold Washington Library, Chicago, 1988.

Department of Planning and Development. *A New Zoning Bonus System for Chicago.* Draft report for public review and comment. Municipal Reference Collection, Harold Washington Library, Chicago, 1998.

Dubin, Jon C. "From Junkyards to Gentrification: Explicating a Right to Protective Zoning in Low-Income Communities of Color." *Minnesota Law Review* 77 (April 1983): 739–801.

Ellickson, Robert C. *Order Without Law: How Neighbors Settle Disputes.* Cambridge, Mass.: Harvard University Press, 1991.

Ferguson, Douglas. "A Historical Narrative of Chicago's Zoning Board of Appeals: 1923-2001." Master's thesis, DePaul University, Chicago, 2002.

Fischel, William A. *The Economics of Zoning Laws: A Property Rights Approach to American Land Use Controls.* Baltimore: John Hopkins University Press, 1985.

Flint, Barbara J. "Zoning and Residential Segregation: A Social and Physical History, 1910–40." Ph.D. diss., University of Chicago, 1977.

Green, Paul M., and Melvin G. Holli, eds. *The Mayors: The Chicago Political Tradition*, Carbondale, Ill.: Southern Illinois University Press, 2005.

Haar, C. M., and J. S. Kayden, eds. *Zoning and the American Dream: Promises Still to Keep*. Chicago: Planners Press, 1989.

Halpern, Kenneth. *Downtown USA: Urban Design in Nine American Cities*. New York: Whitney Library of Design, 1978.

Kamin, Blair. *Why Architecture Matters: Lessons from Chicago*. Chicago: University of Chicago Press, 2003.

Karlen, Harvey M. *The Governments of Chicago*. Chicago: Courier Publishing, 1958.

King, Andrew J. *Law and Land Use in Chicago: A Prehistory of Modern Zoning*. New York: Garland Publishing, 1976.

Krueckeberg, Donald A., ed. *Introduction to Planning History in the United States*. New Brunswick, N.J.: Center for Urban Policy Research, Rutgers University, 1983.

Mayer, Harold M., and Richard C. Wade. *Chicago: Growth of a Metropolis*. Chicago: University of Chicago Press, 1969.

McDonald, John F., and Daniel P. McMillen. Land Values, Land Use, and the First Chicago Zoning Ordinance. *Journal of Real Estate Finance and Economics* 16, no. 2 (1998): 135–50.

Miller, Donald L. *City of the Century: the Epic of Chicago and the Making of America*. New York: Simon & Schuster, 1996.

Nelson, Robert H. *Zoning and Property Rights: An Analysis of the American System of Land-Use Regulation*. Cambridge, Mass: MIT Press, 1977.

Nichols, Charles M. "Zoning in Chicago: Containing the 'Glackin' Enabling Act, and Recommendations of Law Department of the City of Chicago, as to how to Proceed Under this Act." 2 Chicago: Chicago Real Estate Board, 1919.

Philip Zeitlin Associates. "Chicago Zoning Ordinance Review." Municipal Reference Collection, Harold Washington Library, Chicago. Transparency Masters (photocopied), 1982.

Plotkin, Wendy. "Deeds of Mistrust: Race, Housing and Restrictive Covenants in Chicago, 1900–1953." Ph.D. diss., University of Illinois at Chicago, 1999.

Quail, Vanessa. "Use, Volume and Bulk in Chicago Zoning Reform: A Technical Study of the 1923, 1942 and 1957 Ordinances." Seminar paper, DePaul University, Chicago, 2004.

Rast, Joel. *Remaking Chicago: The Political Origins of Urban Industrial Change*. DeKalb, Ill.: Northern Illinois University Press, 1999.

Schwieterman, Joseph P., and Martin E. Toth. *Shaping Contemporary Suburbia: Perspectives on Development Control in Metropolitan Chicago*. Chicago: Law Bulletin Publishing, 2001.

Shlay, Anne B. "Zoning for Whom: The Impact of Zoning on Tract Housing and Population Changes from 1960 to 1970 Within the Chicago SMSA." Ph.D. diss., University of Massachusetts, 1981.

Simpson, Dick W. *Rogues, Rebels, and Rubberstamps: The Story of Chicago City Council from the Civil War to the Third Millennium.* Boulder, Colo.: Westview Press, 2001.

Spinney, Robert J. *City of Big Shoulders: A History of Chicago.* DeKalb, Ill.: Northern Illinois University Press, 2000.

Village of Euclid v. Ambler Realty Corp., 272 U.S. 365 (1926).

Wexler, Richard L. "'A Zoning Ordinance Is Not Better than Its Administration'—A Platitude Proved." *The John Marshall Journal of Practice and Procedure* 1 (spring 1967): 74–91.

Wille, Lois. *At Home in the Loop: How Clout and Community Built Chicago's Dearborn Park.* Carbondale, Ill.: Southern Illinois University Press, 1997.

Willis, Carol. *Form Follows Finance: Skyscrapers and Skylines in New York and Chicago,* Princeton, N.J.: Princeton Architectural Press, 1995.

Wrigley, Robert L. Jr., *Introduction to Planning History in the United States.* Edited by Donald A. Kruekeberg. New Brunswick, N.J.: Center for Urban Policy Research, Rutgers University, 1983.

Young, Hugh E. "Paper on Need for and Some Practical Method of Rezoning Urban Areas." Presented at the meeting of the City Planning Division, American Society of Civil Engineers. New York City, January 21, 1937.

Index

Pages with photographs shown in bold.

About the Authors and Editor

THE AUTHORS

Joseph P. Schwieterman, Ph.D., is professor of public service management and director of the Chaddick Institute for Metropolitan Development at DePaul University. He has published extensively on urban and transportation topics and hosted the Chaddick Institute's workshops on planning and zoning for the past 12 years. Schwieterman earned his M.S. in transportation from Northwestern University and his Ph.D. in public policy from the University of Chicago, and is a member of the American Planning Association and Lambda Alpha International. He is the author of several books on urban issues and works closely with DePaul's Real Estate Center.

Dana M. Caspall earned her B.A. in accounting from Michigan State University and her M.S. in Public Service Management from DePaul University, where she wrote a master's thesis entitled *Managing A Modern Metropolis: A Historical Sketch of Zoning in the City of Chicago*. An experienced auditor who works for the federal government, she has spent much of her professional life investigating business and governmental programs.

THE EDITOR

Jane Heron, a University of Chicago graduate, is an urban planner who has studied and observed development and zoning in Chicago for many years. She has written extensively on zoning, housing, and building-code matters, and chaired the inter-agency Zoning Coalition from 1984 to 1992. She lives in the Logan Square neighborhood.

About the Chaddick Institute

The Politics of Place: A History of Zoning in Chicago is the culmination of a research effort undertaken by the Chaddick Institute for Metropolitan Development at DePaul University. Located in downtown Chicago, the Institute offers planners, attorneys, and development specialists a forum to share expertise on difficult land-use issues through workshops, conferences, and policy studies. The Institute also offers a certificate in metropolitan planning in cooperation with the Public Services Graduate Program.

Research for this historical volume began as a special project sponsored by the Harry F. and Elaine M. Chaddick Foundation. Additional information about the Institute and a summary of the civic contributions of Mr. Chaddick are available at www.depaul.edu/~chaddick.

LAKE CLAREMONT PRESS

Founded in 1994, Lake Claremont Press specializes in books on the Chicago area and its history, focusing on preserving the city's past, exploring its present environment, and helping to cultivate a strong municipal identity and sense of place for the future. Visit us on the Web at www.lakeclaremont.com, and contact us for a catalog at 773/583-7800 or lcp@lakeclaremont.com.

BOOKLIST

Finding Your Chicago Ancestors:
A Beginner's Guide to Family History
in the City and Cook County

Wrigley Field's Last World Series:
The Wartime Chicago Cubs and The
Pennant of 1945

The Golden Age of Chicago Children's
Television

Chicago's Midway Airport: The First
Seventy-Five Years

The Hoofs & Guns of the Storm:
Chicago's Civil War Connections

Great Chicago Fires: Historic Blazes
That Shaped a City

The Firefighter's Best Friend: Lives and
Legends of Chicago Firehouse Dogs

Graveyards of Chicago: The People,
History, Art, and Lore of Cook
County Cemeteries

Literary Chicago: A Book Lover's Tour
of the Windy City

A Native's Guide to Chicago,
4th Edition

A Native's Guide to Northwest Indiana

A Cook's Guide to Chicago,
2nd Edition

AWARD-WINNERS

The Chicago River: A Natural and
Unnatural History

Near West Side Stories: Struggles for
Community in Chicago's Maxwell
Street Neighborhood

Hollywood on Lake Michigan: 100
Years of Chicago and the Movies

The Streets & San Man's Guide to
Chicago Eats

COMING IN 2006

A Field Guide to Gay and Lesbian
Chicago

Today's Chicago Blues

A Chicago Tavern: A Goat, A Curse,
and the American Dream

Chicago's Business and Social Clubs

From Lumber Hookers to the Hooligan
Fleet: A Treasury of Chicago Maritime
History

On the Job: Behind the Badges of the
Chicago Police Department